ABSENT WITHOUT LEAVE

ABSENT WITHOUT LEAVE

French Literature under the Threat of War

DENIS HOLLIER

Translated by Catherine Porter

HARVARD UNIVERSITY PRESS
Cambridge, Massachusetts
London, England
1997

Printed in the United States of America

First published as *Les Dépossédés (Bataille, Caillois, Leiris, Malraux, Sartre)*
copyright © 1993 by Les Editions de Minuit.

Library of Congress Cataloging-in-Publication Data

Hollier, Denis.
[Dépossédés. English]
Absent without leave : French literature under the threat of war /
Denis Hollier : translated by Catherine Porter.
p. cm.
Includes index.
ISBN 0-674-21270-3 (cloth : alk. paper). — ISBN 0-674-21271-1 (paper : alk. paper)
1. French literature—20th century—History and criticism.
I. Porter, Catherine. II. Title.
PQ305.H6513 1997
840.9'00912—dc21 97-16188
CIP

CONTENTS

ABSENT WITHOUT LEAVE

MUST LITERATURE BE POSSIBLE?

THIS IS A PIPE

This collection respects unity of place in its most minimal guise. The essays included here were all written at a respectable distance from Paris, in anglophone territories—first California, then New York.

At Berkeley, above the table where I worked, among the assorted pictures and notes tacked to the wall, there was a black-and-white postcard I had found in a general store in that computer-age paradise, the suburban Far West. It was a photograph of an object made by Native Americans. I've forgotten the name of the tribe. The card featured a ceremonial hatchet. The handle's grip was decorated with ribbons that hung down in a skein, like scalps. The association is not gratuitous. On the iron blade there was a crudely engraved scene: a vigorous redskin was brandishing his ax at arm's length, while with his other hand he was grasping the hair of a trapper on whom he was about to perform the horrific ritual. The scene provided instructions for using the object on which it was represented. America cultivates this sort of redundancy, in which mimicry functions as a strategy not so much for camouflage as for exhibition or even advertising. People here are fond of objects that display their own function. Hot dogs are sold in stands shaped like hot dogs.

On the back of the postcard, the caption turned the situation inside out.

I don't remember the exact words. But in its own way the text declared: this is not an ax. It was a pipe. The handle was hollow. As for the blade, which was also hollow, it became a bowl whose roundness was concealed by the viewing angle. Warring parties camouflage their military installations under peaceful exteriors. Here, to fool a friend, the peace pipe had been camouflaged as a tomahawk.

One can imagine the after-dinner stories, back when there were storytellers, to which pipes of this sort must have given rise time and again in Boston, Berlin, Oxford, Strasbourg, or St. Petersburg, as the pipe's owner, some anonymous Marlowe, would light up and answer the questions it provoked.

OF LITERATURE

The cluster of authors on which the following essays focus—Sartre, Bataille, Caillois, Leiris, Malraux—might lay claim to a rather supple form of temporal unity as well, that of a generation; their works are rooted in the 1930s and 1940s. But beyond the relative coincidence of dates, the fact that these authors belong to the same era is only the external aspect of what I shall call, so as not to abandon the criteria of classical dramaturgy, unity of subject or of action.

The hatchet-pipe orchestrates a happy ending. The object of peace manages to contain the scene of war for which it is the support structure; it is not overwhelmed by its subject. Like the dove announcing dry land, the pipe is a precursor of peace. The story hour is approaching; it is nearly time for the storytellers, those birds of Minerva whom Roquentin abhors ("you have to choose: live or tell")[1] and whom Sartre continues to mock in *What Is Literature?*: "We are first presented with the audience, a brilliant and worldly society which has assembled in a drawing-room after dinner. It is night-time, which dispels fatigue and passion. The oppressed are asleep, as are the rebellious; the world is enshrouded; the story unfolds . . . [The narrator] tells his story with detachment. If it has caused him suffering, he has made honey from this suffering."[2] Men with experience tell what they accomplished, once upon a time.

Walter Benjamin does not share Sartre's scorn for storytellers. In "The Storyteller," an essay written about the same time as *Nausea* (1936), Benjamin contrasts the narrative universe of tales with that of novels. The tale is the narrative form belonging to what he calls transmissible experience, a world in which individuals and generations share what has happened to them, a world in which each object, each personal or professional situation, is paired with matching stories that function somewhat like a user's manual transmitting practical experience along artisanal lines. Unlike a tale, a novel conveys an experience that is too solitary, too individual to enter into the narrative or pragmatic patrimony of its public. A novel is the story of an individual who is not integrated into collective experience. But the world of tales is drawing to a close. Truth is losing its epic, communitarian character. Narration is threatened by information. And experience is less and less communicable. Benjamin's first example of this modern degradation of experience and its consequences is war. One of his statements in particular is often quoted: "Was it not noticeable at the end of the war that men returned from the battlefield grown silent—not richer, but poorer in communicable experience?"[3] A great deal has been written about the aphasia of soldiers on leave. The war—Benjamin is referring to the war of 1914—did not transform its survivors into storytellers: war is one of the most powerful instances of the industrial degradation of experience that prevents it from being communicated or shared, from transforming itself into a story to be told.

Sartre pursues the same idea in "Departure and Return," his essay on Brice Parain's philosophy of language. Brice Parain offers another example of the silence of the soldier on home leave: for him war is above all an uprooting from collective experience, from the narrative community; thus the experience of war is not transmissible.[4] But Benjamin and Sartre valorize opposite ends of the spectrum. Benjamin misses the storytellers; Sartre cannot abide them. Sartre chooses the world of noncommunicable experience, from which no lesson, no rule, no good can come because this sort of experience allows no escape, it can never be left behind; it never recedes to the distance that would be necessary if some lesson, some wisdom were to be derived from it. For Sartre, too, the key date is that of a war (the war of 1940). But whereas for Benjamin the First World War was responsible for the impoverishment of contemporary fiction, Sartre celebrates the opportunities afforded the modern novel in the Second World War. This is the war that ends the reign of "narrators" once and for all. It destroys narrative distance, brings the narrator out of hiding. At the hour of the night fliers, the sky is crowded, too dangerous for Minerva's birds. Raymond Aron (in *Introduction to the Philosophy of History*) and André Malraux (in *Man's Hope*) diagnose the narrative implications of the crisis of the 1930s and 1940s in much the same way. Like the sorcerer's apprentice, writers respond to the appeal for stories without knowing where these stories will take them. Until recently, the scene of war was framed tightly enough to prevent the Indian pipe from becoming a battle-ax. Now words, as Sartre puts it, are turning into loaded guns.

Wartime memories? War leaves no time for memories. Rather than having stories to tell, we are left with the impossibility of telling stories. Like a moth attracted to a flame, literature turns toward war not because it sees war as its source, the condition of its own possibility, but on the contrary because it sees war as what threatens—or promises—to take away its conditions of possibility. War forces literature to take the risk—or gives it the hope—of being stricken at last with impossibility, of having nothing at all to fall back on. The *Odyssey* folds back into the *Iliad*, and the island of the Sirens becomes Troy in flames. Through its suffering, its chaos, its urgency, war defies description; like a reality that would refute the words used to name it, it sets a sort of objective limit to realism. But that is not all. Not satisfied with being an unnamable referent, war institutes a regime of total mobilization that takes away time for writing. Freedoms are suspended. War essentially holds suspect anyone who finds time to write. *The War* opens with the pages of a diary Marguerite Duras kept during the liberation of Paris. In one entry, she is seated at a table in the Orsay train station, taking notes, interviewing refugees. An officer appears. "You're allowed to work standing up, but I don't want to see this table any more."[5] The scene can be read as an allegory. War removes the support structures, the foundations, on which writing relies. Writers have nothing to fall back on. Nothing stable on which to write. Literature is no longer based on anything. This same note is struck forty years later in Duras's perplexity when she comes across the diary again. She recalls the scene, the events, but she cannot see herself writing in the midst of it all; she does not succeed in seeing the table on which the officer did not want to see her writing. It is a scene in which there is no place for her. "I can see the place, the Gare d'Orsay, and the various comings and goings. But I can't see myself writing the diary."[6] It is just as if the writing—stricken with what Lacan would have called *nullibiety*[7]—has not taken place, has not managed to find a place, to inscribe itself in space. Kassner, Malraux's protagonist in *Days of Wrath*, is in a similar situation. His Nazi jailers have put him in a situation the most salient feature of which, for him, is the impossibility of writing. He reiterates the motif again and again: "How could he write, here in the cell? . . . Oh, to be able to write, to write!"[8] The generation of writers considered in these essays was highly sensitive to narratives that begin once the world in which the means for writing exist has been left behind, once the threshold of possibility of writing has been crossed. How would literature be possible in a place where writing is impossible? The question has to be turned around: How would literature be possible if there were a way to write?

Modernity does not hold the exclusive title to this kind of short-circuit. Stendhal, for example, had a gift for putting himself in situations in which his hand did not follow his thought, in which a sort of paralysis prevented him from carrying out the gestures of writing. He let himself be overcome by some event that left him wordless. *The Life of Henry Brulard* ends in a flurry of happiness that immobilizes his pen: "My hand can no longer write, I shall put it off to tomorrow"; "the subject surpasses the teller."[9] Some thirty years before, he had already had the experience of being overwhelmed by the events he was recounting. On February 11, 1805, for example, he noted in his diary: "For the past quarter of an hour, I've been making an effort to write, my feelings are so strong that writing (the physical action) is hard work for me."[10] The process of writing remains forbidden. Unhorsed, glued to the spot by a sudden happiness, writing does not go on. There is a touch of modernity in that broken column, marking the passage of what Leiris would have called the bull's horn. Stendhal is brought up short by happiness. Our own bulls' horns are darker, more tragic. There is another difference, too: while the unrepresentable may leave us wordless, it does not deprive us of speech. This observation is even the point of departure for modern criticism. The unhappiness of some writers produces felicitous turns of phrase. Blanchot explores this motif at the outset of *Faux pas* (False Steps), his first collection of essays, when he describes the condition of the modern writer: "What accounts for the destruction of language in him also accounts for his need to use language. He is like a hemiplegic whose affliction simultaneously obliges him to walk and prohibits him from walking . . . The one who writes is driven to write by the silence and absence of language that reach him."[11] What interrupts the writer's voice is also what gives the interruption voice in him. The more words are lacking, in him, the more their lack speaks. Obligation and prohibition are two sides of the same coin. Impossibility is not an obstacle, it is a springboard. Artaud, who speaks with rare power of his "absence of voice for crying out," is an exemplary figure of this contradictory fate. And Kafka, the exact opposite of Stendhal, is astonished that there is no misfortune so profound that it would keep him from writing. "I could never understand," he notes in his journal, "that it was possible for almost anyone who could write to objectivise pain in pain. For example, in my misery, with my head still burning with misery, I can sit down and write to somebody: I am miserable. I can go still further and, in various flourishes, according to my capacities, which seem to have nothing in common with my misery, I can improvise on this theme, simply, or antithetically, or even with entire orchestras of associations."[12] Elsewhere he writes: "There is undeniably a certain happiness in being able calmly to write down: *suffocation is inconceivably horrible.*"[13] When she opens up the manuscript of *The War*, Marguerite Duras is similarly astonished by the assurance, the impassiveness of her own writing; she is amazed to see that her own hand wrote out those appalling words without flinching, that she could describe what she saw with an untrembling hand: "I found myself looking at pages regularly filled with small, calm, extraordinarily even handwriting."[14]

THE IMPOSSIBILITY OF CROWS

The essays brought together in this volume deal with a paradoxical form of *littérature engagée*, a paradoxical form of the literature of commitment: literature committed to its own exclusion. The aesthetic imperative this literature obeys is the ethical imperative turned upside down. Kant's "You must, therefore you can" is inverted, replaced by the conjunction of impossibility and necessity, the affirmation of impossibility as necessity: "You cannot, therefore you must." These pages deal with writers who, carried away by the excesses of that paradoxical heroism, saw war as the context that assured them of absolute decontextualization: in war, literature will never be in its place.

Debates over the literature of commitment reached a peak around the time of the Liberation, when Sartre's *What Is Literature?* appeared. Sartre does not ask writers to commit themselves, as we know; he shows that they have already done so. He does not ask them to choose between a literature that is committed and one that is not. He shows that, whether they like it or not, whether they know it or not, commitment is a constitutive dimension of literature. Thus commitment in literature is not a matter of altruism on the part of aesthetes who consent to forget themselves in order to connect with humanity: the more committed it is, the better literature fulfills its own definition, its vocation, the less it forgets itself. To want literature to exist is first of all to want a world in which literature is possible, a world that acknowledges its right to exist. The writer must work toward the existence of a world that can give him the means to write and to be read. Committed literature is thus simply literature taking responsibility for its own conditions of possibility. But this analysis implies that literature insists on being possible.

What Is Literature? provoked a host of defensive reactions. On the side of the uncommitted, literature was said to have better things to do than shoulder the weight of the world; it should be making its readers forget that burden. A second critical thrust (coming especially from Bataille and Blanchot) countered Sartre's notion of commitment with the opposite stance. It was not a question of sheltering literature from politics, restoring the autonomy of art, carving out safe places where art would be protected from propaganda. Nor was it a question of protecting art against the world. Quite the contrary: it was a question of exposing art to a world in which it would no longer have any protectors.

The historical references invoked by Blanchot and Bataille are very different from Sartre's. Sartre has democratic socialism in mind ("[Literature's] chance today, its only chance, is the chance of Europe, of socialism"),[15] while Blanchot and Bataille refer back to the Terror, and for the opposite reasons: there, the fortunes of literature are reduced to zero. Bataille begins his chapter on Sade in *Literature and Evil* by asking: "Why should a period of revolution lend a lustre to the arts and the world of letters? Armed violence is ill matched with the enrichment of a domain which can only be enjoyed in peacetime."[16] And in "Literature and the Right to Death," the anti-Sartrean manifesto published in *Critique*, Blanchot refers to the Terror as a wholesale mobilization, the institution of a society without secrets, an exceptional situation with no holds barred: "No one has a right to a private life any longer, everything is public, and the most guilty person is the suspect—the person who has a secret, who keeps a thought, an intimacy, to himself. And in the end no one has a right to his life any longer, to his actually separate and physically distinct existence. That is the meaning of the Reign of Terror. Every citizen has a right to death, so to speak; death is not a sentence passed on him, it is his most essential right; he is not suppressed as a guilty person." And Blanchot continues: "The writer sees himself in the Revolution."[17] In other words, the writer sees himself in the Reign of Terror as in the most unliterary space there is, a totalitarian space in which, by imposing the law of the whole, action allows literature to go beyond the work of negation, beyond the negation of negation, in order to carry out its task of global negation; it allows literature to deny everything, to deny the whole, in order (as Blanchot says) to be merely—at a vast remove from particular cases, from determined things and defined work—master of everything. "Unreality begins with the whole,"[18] but the whole begins with Terror. Thus the writer recognizes himself in the dry spells of literary history, periods in which historical urgency reduces literature to nothing (Sade in prison). This view puts us at the opposite pole from Sartre. Sartre showed writers that they had an interest in constructing a world in which the existence of a right to literature would be recognized. For Blanchot, literature, which has an interest in transforming the world, places its bets on the appearance of a totalitarian world—a world of terror, a world at war—that would deprive literature of all rights but one: the right to death.

This anti-aesthetics of Terror serves as a matrix for the literary Communism that Bataille and Blanchot developed at the start of the Cold War. Victor Kravchenko had left the Soviet Union and published *I Chose Freedom.* The title alone sufficed to show that Kravchenko was not a writer: literature needs Communism, for Communism, by prohibiting literature, allows literature to be faithful to its own definition of itself. Literature does not expect to be made possible by a transformation of the world; rather, in a transformed world literature will be able to realize its own essence by ceasing to be possible. Impossibility is literature's essential attribute, its condition of possibility. One of the most compelling illustrations of this paradoxical movement appears in the chapter on Kafka in *Literature and Evil.* Bataille's line of reasoning here is powerful and perverse. Everything Kafka wrote, he says, can be viewed as a demand addressed to a father who could not bear the fact of his son's writing; everything Kafka wrote stemmed from his desire to be acknowledged as a writer by the one person who was absolutely certain never to acknowledge him. Bataille goes on to say that Communism is the equivalent for literature of the paternal sphere for Kafka. If a writer militates in favor of Communism, it is not because he expects it to give him the freedom to write, or because he expects to be a prophet in his own country, because he expects his talent to be recognized and rewarded with the medal of the Legion of Honor, a nice flat, a salary, a comfortable pension and a dacha. On the contrary, writers militate in favor of Communism because under Communist regimes no one writes innocently. Only Communist regimes actually place high value on literary impropriety: under Communism, literature can finally, in Blanchot's words, "plead guilty." Kafka's work calls the world communistic, but that is because such work "has no place in Communist society."[19] Even if he could flee, Kafka would not choose freedom. In *The Infinite Conversation* Blanchot quotes one of Kafka's apologues: "Crows claim that a single crow could destroy the sky. This is no doubt so, but it proves nothing about the sky for the sky signifies precisely: the impossibility of crows."[20]

Sartre defended commitment because "the art of prose is bound up with the only regime in which prose has meaning, democracy."[21] Bataille—who had acted on behalf of an anti-Communist front to withdraw an article from *Les temps modernes*—"defended" Communism for the opposite reason: it is the only regime under which literature will escape the work of meaning, where it will not allow itself to be appropriated, pardoned, redeemed. It is the only regime where the negativity of literature is not needed, the only one where a writer will not run the risk of being offered a job, where he will be consigned, as Francis Ponge put it, to the bottom of the heap where he belongs.

How to write after Auschwitz? After Auschwitz, literature should no longer be possible. Auschwitz ought to have done away with the world's right to literature. Not only is literature "illegitimate," according to Blanchot; perhaps it "has no right to consider itself illegitimate."[22] It does not even have the right not to have any rights; it can invoke no higher legitimacy to justify its improprieties. But as there is no such thing as an innocent sovereign, this is how literature achieves a sovereign gratuitousness. Moreover, if it were permitted, it would not be literature. Philippe Sollers recently said the same thing with reference to Hemingway: a writer is first of all someone whom everybody forbids to write, someone who writes in spite of everything and everyone. The modern Sirens say: Poet, leave your harp alone. Literature, for this generation, has been an art of despiteness.

A way out may seem to beckon. It is possible, for example, to see the sign of a generational shift when a writer like Pascal Quignard couples his views of the contemporary world with a discouraged sigh: "For the first time, the existence of a society is opposed to the existence of a literature."[23] Would it not be rather the first time in a long time that a literature has dreamed of being accepted? that it has consented to exist? And, if things go on as they are, we may be reduced, like Stendhal's Signora, to regretting that such a thing is allowed, that it is no longer a sin.

POWERS OF THE NOVEL

What is called existentialism started out, on the aesthetic level, as a radical antinaturalism. Existentialism opposes efforts like Hippolyte Taine's to deduce works of art, to ensconce them in a given landscape, a valley, a genealogy. The works to which the essays in this book refer are all engaged in the consolidation of a context from which it would be impossible to deduce them, one in which they would be either impossible or forbidden—a context that, at best, would make them improbable. This is true of Leiris's conjugal space, of Malraux's revolutionary apocalypse, of Blanchot's Terror, of Bataille's Stalinism.

The same schema underlies *Puissances du roman* (Powers of the Novel). In this essay written in 1940, Caillois accuses the novel of complicity with liberalism: in order to triumph, the genre needs a society that permits individuals to have reservations about that society. The schema is a classic one, similar to the one Benjamin adopts in "The Storyteller." But whereas Benjamin contrasts the storyteller's world with that of the novelist, Caillois contrasts societies that favor novels with societies that favor architecture. With their massive construction projects, architecture-societies function according to principles of total mobilization that leave no place (no void, no vacancy, no availability) for the slightest distance. Caillois's position becomes original, however, when he moves beyond this sociological condemnation of the novel. In the crop of novels produced in the 1930s, Caillois in fact diagnoses a promising but also suicidal evolution owing to which the opposition between novels and architecture has become blurred.

An increasing number of recent novels, he reports, present heroes who are hostile to novelistic reserve: "We have once again entered an era of architecture, of pyramid-building and cathedral-building." Novels of the 1930s (he cites Henry de Montherlant, Malraux, Ernst von Salomon), lacking critical distance, are catalysts for a society in which "there is no longer a place for novels."[24] The novelist, rejoining the freewheeling body of sorcerers' apprentices, sets about to saw off the branch on which his predecessors perched; he is working toward the accomplishment of his own conditions of impossibility. In 1974, introducing a new edition of *Puissances du roman*, Caillois acknowledges that he allowed himself to go a little too far: "I deduced that in the full society imagined by the College of Sociology, there would no longer be any place for novels. I did not suspect that that wholly imaginary city was itself nothing but a lure of the moment, a product of the eternal and always complementary solicitation operated by novels."[25]

To illustrate the novel's hold on the mind of its reader, Caillois mentions the letter that one reader, dragging herself reluctantly away from *The Life of Jesus*, was said to have written to thank Renan for sending her his book. "She had almost finished reading it," she wrote, and it was hard to pull herself away from her reading to send him a note "so eager was she to finish the book 'to see how it comes out.'"[26] More than twenty years later, *Pontius Pilate* reintroduces the same sort of novelistic suspense in its account of one of Christianity's most crucial moments: Caillois's historical fiction depicts a Pilate who refuses to condemn Jesus.

After a day of consultations during which everyone presses him to give in to Caiaphas and have the religious agitator executed, the procurator decides to do just the opposite. He frees Jesus. The decisive moment comes during Pilate's consultation with Mardouk. The Chaldean magus, a kind of Renan-as-futurologist, sketches in the events that are supposed to follow the sacrifice of the Messiah. He puts the future on display: two thousand years of Christian history. But to come into being, this future requires Pilate's signature. Mardouk works on him by appealing to his vanity as a state official: the execution, Mardouk says, will make you a *cause célèbre;* the doctors of the new religions will argue endlessly over your free will. He invokes the bibliography of works that will be devoted to him by casuists, theologians and historians. He even mentions "the French writer who, a little less than two thousand years later, would reconstruct his discourse for publication by Gallimard and Macmillan—and no doubt he flattered himself that he had imagined that name."[27]

Nothing is easier for a modern writer than to invent a character who predicts the present from his vantage point in the past. But the present, here, is the book the reader has in his hands. And this is where things get more complicated. If you want history to remember your name, Mardouk tells Pilate, have Jesus crucified. It's up to you whether or not Caillois will write a book that will tell the story of your choice. But Pilate is not a Pascalian; he prefers to play to lose, and he makes the opposite choice. And the story ends with these lines: "Because of a man who despite every hindrance succeeded in being brave, there was no Christianity. Except for Pilate's exile and suicide, none of the events predicted by Mardouk came to pass and history, save on this one point, took another course."[28] The end. Mardouk had in fact predicted to the procurator of Judea the future that seems to have been in store for Pilate. The procurator's exile and suicide are not the only events prophesied by Mardouk that actually took place. The concluding remark "save on this one point" is undermined by the book in which it appears: despite Mardouk's blackmail, and even though the book in question does not relate—as Mardouk had predicted it would—the crucifixion of the Messiah, the *Nouvelle revue française* nevertheless did publish, in 1961, the *Pontius Pilate* that Mardouk had announced.

Caillois's fable is built around two competing visions of the future. A first series of events, inaugurated by the death of Christ, leads one thousand nine hundred sixty-one years after the birth of the future Crucified One to the publication of the narrative. We are not privy to any specific information about the second series. The story's conclusion nevertheless informs us that (with two exceptions) it includes none of the events of the first. The two series are mutually exclusive. Yet it is in the first series that we find the book in which we learn that Pilate has chosen the second. The book we are reading is, as it were, ruled out by the events it chronicles. Pilate's choice makes the narrative account of that choice impossible. In *Approches de l'imaginaire* (Approaches to the Imaginary), Caillois used the expression "novelistic temptation" for the dream of a world in which novels would be impossible. In *Pontius Pilate*, this temptation is embedded within a novel.

But that does not prevent it from existing.

In its own way, and without allowing us to decide whether Caillois is doing this on purpose or not, *Pontius Pilate* follows the scenario described in *Puissances du roman.* It is a novel that portrays the genesis of a universe in which there will be no place, if not for the novelistic genre as a whole, at least for the particular novel at hand. However, certain differences throw this parallelism out of kilter. The first difference has to do with the fact that *Pontius Pilate* is a novel, while *Puissances du roman* is an essay on the novel. The second has to do with the fact that nothing in the character of Pontius Pilate evokes the Luciferian conquerors who dominated novels in the 1930s, fanatics of oversocialization who drove the novel as a genre into an impasse.

The resistance Pilate offers his interlocutors brings that difference into full relief. His opponents' arguments can be reduced to variations on the founding theorem of sacrificial logic: "It is not undesirable that one man die for the salvation of a people"; "the welfare of all justifies the sacrifice of one."[29] These arguments—a mix of Frazer and Girard before the fact, accounting for Christ's destiny in the light of rituals like those of the scapegoat or the carnival kings—could have been developed before there was a College of Sociology—and indeed they were, by Caillois himself, in the talks he published in *Man and the Sacred*, especially "Theory of the Festival."

But Pilate is not willing to be convinced. He has no sympathy for "a religion that relied on injustice or a man's cowardice to lay its foundation."[30] It may be a perfectly normal way for a religion to behave; but that is exactly why Pilate holds religions in contempt. Here, however, things go further still, well beyond this level of generality. Pilate is not simply resisting the form of the sacrificial argument; his resistance takes into account the individual to whom the argument is being applied in this particular case. Pilate does not know very much about Christ, but through what is said by those who are determined to have him put to death he guesses that the rules for behavior he taught were "exactly opposite principles."[31] Mardouk confirms this impression. The Jews are asking Pilate to crucify Christ because Christ poses a threat to the logic of sacrifice: nothing could be more coherent. This is not the case with Judas and Mardouk: they are pushing for crucifixion in order to escape from that logic. You do not exorcise sacrifice by means of a sacrifice.

Caillois's philosophical fable hinges in fact on the possibility of interrupting the cycle of religious violence. The novel's two most important characters, Pilate and Christ, attempt to break out of this cycle. How can they escape from the roles assigned them by the meaning of history? How can they avoid playing the game? Tonight we improvise. These questions strike a new note in Caillois's work. To my knowledge, this is the first time he gives voice, even if he does so through Pontius Pilate, to the desire to escape from the logic of the sacred, a logic whose exploration had dominated his work from the time the College of Sociology was founded. But this novelty goes hand in hand with another one.

Here we need to look again beneath the surface parallelism of *Puissances du roman* and *Pontius Pilate* to see the basic differences. *Pontius Pilate* is a novel, Caillois's first. For the first time, the author of countless meditations on the sacred has abandoned sociology in favor of fiction; he has dropped the essay form and turned to a literary genre that he had once denounced (in *Puissances du roman*) as symptomatic of a society that had succumbed to the law of the profane. Whereas the 1940 essay had condemned the novel in the name of the sacred, *Pontius Pilate* escapes the sacred by way of the novel. *Pontius Pilate* thus represents a double rupture: on the level of expression, Caillois has changed genres; on the level of content, he has shifted position and taken a stand against the sacred. *Pontius Pilate* is not a great novel. But what is arguably most interesting about it is that, in order to escape from his fascination with the sacred, its author had to give up the essay form. Just as he is about to make his decision, Pilate recalls the title of his favorite among Cicero's works: *De finibus potentiae deorum.* This text could serve as the definition of the novel itself. One enters the space of what did not take place: a world without Christianity.

Caillois and Benjamin share the same (poor) opinion of the shift from myth to literature, from tales to novels, that is, the institution of a regime of mechanical reproduction and dispersive serialization: they view this shift as degradation and loss, in terms of content (the experience transmitted) and form (the way in which the experience is transmitted) alike. For both writers, this loss is associated with gains on the part of the profane.

Perhaps such a view needs to be turned inside out. Perhaps the novel is, on the contrary, the last refuge of the profane, one of the last pockets of unreality spared by the secularization of the sacred. Deplorations of the death of the sacred are not in short supply, but the want of gods brings a full house. What unites men? Goethe asks. The answer is the sacred—or its absence, which is sacred as well. The sacred may no longer have the Dionysian or carnivalesque exuberance it once did, but it gains in extension what it has lost in intensity. Thus in the frantic secularization of vacations, what is regrettable is less the ebbing of the sacred than the defeat of the profane. The term "secular," after all, can have religious overtones, as in "secular humanist." A watered-down cocktail of the worst aspects of both regimes, at once sacred and labored. But the profane has a musical quality that does not evoke anything like a political assignment for those who refuse to attend church. And this is why no one talks about secular music. The distinction must be maintained, but in such a way that we can exit surreptitiously, subtly, secretly, *extemplo*, from the temple. The distinction must be maintained, but in order to save the profane, a profane in itself, as one speaks of an end in itself; a profane without profanation, for pleasure: the profane for the profane.

What will become of literature if it can no longer plead guilty? For want of being forbidden, it will be condemned to plead guilty in the second degree. Would to heaven that that were a fault. That my hands were dirty. After the fashion of those pleasures about which, like Stendhal's heroine, there is only one thing to say: too bad it's not a sin. *Peccato che non sia un peccato.*

2

DEEDS WITHOUT WORDS

> "Why, yes," went on the Duchess, adding more and more to her words . . . , thanks to her way of pronouncing them, the equivalent of what on the printed page are called italics.
>
> Marcel Proust, *The Guermantes Way*

The printed text of a play requires three different typographic elements.[1] Standing apart in the middle of a page, capital letters indicate the names of characters with lines to speak. Those lines follow, in roman type. Finally, in italics, sometimes set off between two utterances and sometimes inserted parenthetically within a character's lines, stage directions describe aspects of the stage business that are not self-evident in what the characters are saying. The staging of a play filters out everything that appears in capital letters and italics in the printed version; during a performance, the audience hears only the passages in roman type. The italicized instructions are intended for the director and the actors, as well as for anyone who might read the play without having seen it.

Sartre's theater challenges these more or less standard conventions with a persistent infraction. The audience should not be aware of the anomaly; it occurs so frequently, however, that it can scarcely be missed by the reader. Sartre repeatedly italicizes words spoken by his characters themselves. According to Sartre, when the director Charles Dullin was preparing to stage *The Flies*, he asked Sartre to strengthen the dramatic character of the dialogues; Dullin had found them overly discursive. Dullin was apparently not bothered by the frequent use of italics; these survived his censorship. Still, it would be interesting to know whether—and, if so, how—Dullin attempted to make them audible in the actors' performance, how he managed to give audible form to the strictly typographic artifice that consists in setting a word apart from its context by using a different typeface.

The italics sprinkled throughout texts that cannot give them voice are striking not only because they appear so frequently, but also because the lexical field to which they belong is so restricted: most of the italicized terms are pronouns or possessive adjectives, and of these the vast majority are in the first person singular. Orestes, returning to Argos for the first time since childhood, studies his native city closely. But the urban skyline leaves him cold. "This is not *my* palace, nor *my* door."[2] That is what Orestes says. But the printed text does not say how the actor playing Orestes is supposed to say it. No stage directions indicate how to make the italics of the actor's possessive form audible to the audience.[3] Italics proliferate with a persistence that could justify a new interpretation of the title. But there is nothing exceptional about *The Flies* in this respect. There is no play by Sartre in which the reader does not come across at least one first-person possessive form that the author, forgetting he is no longer a philosopher, has italicized right in the middle of some character's lines. Whenever Sartre is free from theatrical constraints, needless to say, he can let himself go with impunity; italics are common currency in his philosophical work. And in *Being and Nothingness*, especially in the analyses—which are all carried out in the first person—of the phenomenon of possession, property, or ownership, he resorts to this typographic device without the slightest restraint: "It is *my* field of snow," Sartre writes, "*my* environment," "*my* lamp"; they have "the quality of being *mine*."[4]

These italicized first-person possessives have yet another distinguishing characteristic. As we can see in the terms Orestes uses when he discovers an Argos that is not yet his, the italicized forms are almost all introduced, at least in the first part of *The Flies*, by negatives: "This is not *my* palace, nor *my* door." And the occasional affirmative use of italicized third-person forms does not constitute a variant of this structure. When Orestes refers a little later to "the Right Thing, *Their* Right Thing," Sartre emphasizes the possessive "their" so readers will understand that Orestes means "it is not *mine*." The same observation holds true for the deed that awaits every individual in the course of a lifetime, in Orestes' view. He himself complains that he is an exception to this law: they all have *their* deeds, "something they *must* do, a deed allotted," he says, but precisely because the possessive element is in italics, the affirmative third-person form he uses has to be interpreted as a first-person negative: *I* don't have one; there is no deed that belongs to *me*, that is *mine*.[5]

And indeed, when Orestes appears onstage at the beginning of *The Flies*, he can be defined grammatically and existentially as a subject without attributes. He has nothing of his own. He has been marked by nothing; he has left his own mark on nothing. He belongs to nothing, and nothing belongs to him. Other men, men of Argos in particular, possess all sorts of things—misfortunes, remorse, memories; they have property, even masters, a place of their own, accessible by a path that no one else can take. But Orestes' own relation to the realm of possession is one of pure deprivation. "But what can I call mine?"[6] he asks, and the question goes unanswered through the first half of the play.

Orestes is a contemporary of Meursault (*The Flies* was written the year *The Stranger* was published, 1942), and, like Meursault, he is a stranger, a foreigner, an outsider. He has no country, no homeland, no situation. He has no commitments anywhere. And yet, unlike Camus's character, and in keeping with Sartre's critique of the philosophical presuppositions behind Camus's novelistic technique, Orestes decides to bring his rootlessness to an end. He suffers from his estrangement; his lightness weighs him down. "My mind's my own, gloriously aloof," he explains. "I'm a mere shadow of a man . . . I wander from city to city, a stranger to all others and to myself, and the cities close again behind me like the waters of a pool." It is at this point that he decides to take root: "I want to be a man who belongs to someplace, a man among comrades."[7]

The true subject of *The Flies* may be identified quite precisely as Orestes' coming into property. The protagonist undergoes the apprenticeship of the possessive, transforms himself into a subject available to predication, a subject who appropriates his own attributes. He decides to take. And first of all to take in the sense a transplant is said to "take," that is, to make himself a place, to make himself fit his place, to make his own the place where he happens to be. He consents to taking on a situation. But in order to take (his) place, he must first take the place: and since he has decided to take Argos, Orestes has to begin by taking possession of the city. He has to conquer it, make it his own, attribute it to himself; all sorts of other complements will follow. The critical moment in this process of attribution is the murder he claims as his own deed. Once Orestes comes up against the decision—an irrevocable one—to kill his mother, Clytemnestra, along with her second husband, Aegistheus, his possessives change sign: from then on they are associated with affirmatives. The outsider who has said in effect, at the outset, that "nothing belongs to me, I possess nothing, this city is not mine, nor is that door my door," now declares peremptorily to Electra, now that he has *taken:* "You are *my* sister, Electra, and that city is *my* city." And as Orestes speaks, Sartre, whom I am quoting, emphasizes his possessives. The metamorphosis is complete. Owing to a double murder, the stranger we saw at the beginning of the play comes into his own at last, a man among men, like a fish in water in an Argos purified of all *Unheimlichkeit:* "Tomorrow I shall speak to my people," he announces; he does not ask the people to decide for themselves what they think of this possessive. Let us recall that the inhabitants of Argos were overwhelmed by remorse: their dead came back to torment them every night. Orestes exonerates them royally, and takes everything upon himself: "Fear your dead no longer; they are *my* dead."[8] Unsurprisingly, Sartre adds emphasis—but only to the second of the two possessives, the one that is in the first person.

Describing the lexical and syntactic profile of Sartre's italicized forms does not help resolve the problem of how to represent them onstage. It does allow us, however, to localize the central core of *The Flies.* The play's center of gravity is a desire for gravity. Orestes commits himself in order to escape dispersion and weightlessness, in order to recenter himself. The italics with which Sartre ballasts his characters' possessives thus serve, in this sense, only to confirm the numerous declarations through which Orestes himself signifies, to his teacher or to Electra, the desire for gravity that has been his impetus ever since he approached what Aristotelian physics would have designated as his natural site, his native land. Between Orestes' initial propositions (of the type "this door is not *my* door") and those that follow his conversion (of the type "this city is *my* city"), an about-face has occurred, the at once grammatical and existential transformation of a subject who is henceforth connected, a subject who makes his weight felt, who measures up, a grave subject who has endowed himself with substantial mass, a subject who has succeeded in taking on attributes, properties, and predicates. A subject capable of attributing to himself what he perceives, capable of saying: This world is mine.

The catalyst for this positive metamorphosis warrants some notice. "I'm still too—too light," Orestes complains. "I must take a burden on my shoulders, a load of guilt so heavy as to drag me down, right down into the abyss of Argos."[9] Like many other Sartrean characters, Orestes dreams of taking on an anthropological weight that cannot be acquired, as I have shown elsewhere, by eating;[10] it requires accomplishing a deed, committing an act. Only an act—and an act that can be described, without too much punning, as not lacking in gravity (what is at stake, after all, is a matricide coupled with a regicide)—can function as the *clinamen* that will allow an alien to escape the viewpoint of outer space and plug himself into the earth's gravitational system; only an act can allow him to escape the condition of nomadic nonexistence, to free himself from the dissemination implied by weightlessness. This act, which Orestes calls "*my* act," thus constitutes the first thing the protagonist recognizes as his own, his first objectivization; at the same time, it is the starting point and fulcrum for a process of rampant appropriation that quickly takes on rather imperialistic dimensions. This process allows Orestes to make Electra "his" sister, Argos "his" city, the people of Argos "his" people and their dead "his own." Thus, speaking to his erstwhile accomplice, Electra, who is already overcome by remorse, he can boast: "I have done *my* deed, Electra, and that deed was good . . . The heavier it is to carry, the better pleased I shall be; for that burden is my freedom. Only yesterday I walked the earth haphazard; thousands of roads I tramped that brought me nowhere, for they were other men's roads. Yes, I tried them all . . . but none of these was mine. Today I have one path only, and heaven knows where it leads. But it is *my* path."[11] The paths of liberty are never "borrowed"; they must be owned, and once they are one's own they must be kept. Orestes' deed gives him access to a directional, hierarchically organized space that Sartre's *Sketch for a Theory of the Emotions* terms "hodological." Earlier he was an outsider positioned at an equal (and indifferent) distance from every existing point, everywhere a stranger lacking fixed coordinates of his own. Orestes now discovers one-way lines, vectors, traces on which lie irreversible acts, points of no return. His own deed, by this token, constitutes an "absolute" event. Moments earlier it was up to him and him alone whether to commit the act or not. But now his commitment is out of his hands. The choice of act is no longer up to him. His act belongs to him to the precise extent that it is no longer up to him whether it belongs to him or not. This act marks Orestes' accession to property, and at the same time it escapes him completely; it is wholly beyond his grasp.[12] Its status prefigures the status Sartre attributed shortly afterward (in *What Is Literature?*) to works of art. A work of art, too, is an emanation of subjectivity that has managed to take on objective transcendence. "Gently, mortals, be discreet."[13] Orestes for his part wants to press down. At the beginning of the play, he lamented the ephemeral nature of the traces left behind by his own passage: "I wander from city to city . . . and the cities close again behind me like the waters of a pool." At the end, things have changed. With his double murder, Orestes has produced a finally ineradicable, indelible impression. Irrecoverable.[14]

Written in 1942 under the German occupation and intended, through its depiction of the remorse in which the inhabitants of Argos indulged, to denounce the passivity with which the French accepted the Vichy regime, *The Flies* is considered the first of Sartre's "committed" works.

The literature of commitment, according to the definition Sartre himself proposed after the war, relies on an activist theory of writing. According to this theory, literature is subject to a twofold requirement: it must valorize nonverbal action even as it transforms itself into verbal action. From this standpoint, the theory owes a great deal to the mystique of deeds to which Orestes is converted in *The Flies.* "The word is a certain particular moment of action and has no meaning outside of it," we read in *What Is Literature?* "To speak is to act." "The 'engaged' writer knows that words are action."[15] A work of literature must be a speech act that does not leave the world within which it is produced intact. Every page of a literary text must have the force of *actualité,* of active currency: it must weigh upon its era, engrave itself upon its time, leave an indelible trace. Literature is thus essentially an exercise of gravity. It separates "before" from "after."

And yet, notwithstanding the fact that both the texts we are considering valorize activism, there is a clear difference between Orestes' pronouncements and the theses of *What Is Literature?* For if Sartre's manifesto of committed literature subjects aesthetic considerations to the primacy of action and to the requirements of efficiency, it does so by transcending the opposition between these two levels. Thus it would be wrong to say that, by committing itself, literature subjects itself to action. Instead, literature can be said to accomplish itself, to carry out its own vocation by proceeding to act, by becoming action. By substituting performative realism for descriptive realism in this way, the literature of commitment puts an end to the cleavage between words and things, between language and action. Writing is not opposed to praxis; it is a form of praxis.

But the reconciliation of language and action implied by the literature of commitment does not apply to *The Flies*. In the first place, this is because Orestes' action is in no sense a speech act. On the contrary, his deed is done without speech; it is an act that requires silence for its execution. There is nothing linguistic about its medium: Orestes does not kill Aegistheus with words. This is by no means an irrelevant detail. It is implied in the logic that governs the passage to action, a logic that Orestes develops in the course of the discussions that pit him against his teacher. If Orestes ends up becoming active, it is not so that the bookish culture transmitted to him by his mentor may be brought to fruition, may find an application to reality; it is not so that Orestes can put into practice what would lose all its value if it remained theoretical. It is, much more radically, because Orestes wants to exit from a world in which—because it is prey to words—nothing indelible is produced. His act is an act to the precise extent that it is wordless. Whereas *What Is Literature?* seeks to transcend the opposition between acts and signs, *The Flies* goes in the other direction: it extends the opposition. The divergence between the two texts cannot be attributed to chronology alone. For although *The Flies* was written prior to the position-taking of *What Is Literature?*, *Dirty Hands* came afterward; Hugo, the protagonist of the later play, adopts an attitude on this issue that rigorously parallels Orestes'. Hugo reserves the term "action" for deeds done without recourse to language. Shortly before publishing *Dirty Hands*, Sartre had proposed journalistic "bulletins from the front" as the unsurpassable model of up-to-date literature, literature that is active because it is current. This does not prevent Hugo, a professional journalist who has put his writing at the service of the local revolution, from continually bemoaning the fact that the articles he has to write for the party keep him at arm's length from more tangible interventions; he dreams of exchanging his typewriter for a revolver, and he stirs things up in the hope of getting thrust into direct action.

The committed writer knows that language is action—but it is as if Sartre had jealously kept this knowledge to himself. As if he had not wanted to share it with his characters, or perhaps had not succeeded in convincing them of its truth. Contrary to their author's convictions, Sartre's protagonists go on believing that action starts where speech ends. Whereas Sartre seeks to enter into action via language, his characters want to exit from language via action.

More specifically, all the protagonists of his theater share the same basic aim: they want to stop being actors, to get away from the theater. They are all obsessed by the fear that their deeds, because they are produced on a stage, may be reduced to gestures, may become the opposite of deeds—unrealized, deactivated, defused acts. Nothing is more in keeping with Orestes' wishes than the English translator's rendering of his pronouncement "J'ai fait *mon* acte" as *"I have done my deed."* Unlike *"I have done—*or *performed—my act,"* "I have done my deed" cuts through the ambiguity of a verb that would refer simultaneously to what Orestes is doing and what the actor playing Orestes is doing. The translation of this expression constitutes the essential stake of Sartre's theater; his plays all hinge on the duel between two incompatible rivals, the actor and the hero, a contest to determine which of the two will impose his translation: will it be *"deed"* or *"act"?* Sartre entrusts his heroes with the job of putting an end to this ambiguity; he commits them to the elimination of all theatrical connotations in the verb *to act* and related terms. The Sartrean protagonist can be recognized by his impatience with respect to the actor whose voice he must borrow and whose silhouette he must adopt.

The italicizing of Orestes' first-person pronouncements is thus the paradoxical indicator of an escape from the linguistic dead end, from the secondarity and the iterability that define the world of signs. The act is unique. It does not tolerate repetition. To repeat it would be to deny it, to behave as though it did not suffice, as though it needed to be reinforced, consolidated, repaired, corrected, confirmed, commented upon, reworked. This singularity is also the guarantee of the absolute and exclusive appropriateness of the act and its author. It is "my" act only because no one other than myself can perform it: no one can do it for me, no one can replace me or help me while I do it. Now, in the theater or the movies, actors are replaced by stuntmen at such critical moments: actors are not heroes who expose themselves to real danger. For his part, Orestes rejects the cinema and the theater: if his life is to be played out, there will be no doubles.

A question arises here. We can see how Orestes, a neophyte activist, may be blinded by his own enthusiasm and may forget the real conditions under which he speaks. But what about the spectators? Can the hero's exaltation be so contagious that they too forget that they are in a theater? And that it is not Orestes himself, Orestes in person, but an actor who is certainly not irreplaceable, an actor who reiterates night after night the by no means unrepeatable words through which the character he embodies celebrates his very recent implantation in the zone of irreversible and nonrepeatable acts? Orestes would like to purge his performance of all theatricality. But how, behind the tragic mask of the character, can the actor's hypocritical smile be hidden? Behind the translator's back, the actor gloats at bringing it off: "*I've played* his *act.*"

This double game defines the deep structure underlying the Sartrean version of the actor's paradox, a paradox that constitutes the center of gravity, or rather the center of lightness, as it were, of Sartre's work as a whole. It is this paradox that makes it so difficult for Sartre's fictional heroes as well as his dramatic ones to live out what happens to them in the first person. But the same paradox governs whole sections of his philosophical works as well, and important ones at that, including his inaugural essay on the transcendence of the ego, the analyses of bad faith in *Being and Nothingness*, and the twists and turns of *Saint Genet, Actor and Martyr*. Hamlet's monologue is one of Sartre's favorite examples. Yet Sartre's version of the actor's paradox is formulated not so much in the terms used by the psychasthenic prince, *to be or not to be*, but rather in terms appropriate to the actor playing the prince's role: *to be and not to be.* The phrase is no longer "the question," but the Sartrean reply par excellence: for, in the vocabulary of phenomenological ontology, to play a theatrical role is very precisely to-be-in-the-mode-of-not-being. Thus one must reject Diderot's view that because the actor pretends to experience the feelings he expresses, he does not experience them. Doubtless he does not really feel them. But that is because he feels them unreally. "It is not the character who becomes real in the actor," Sartre writes in *The Psychology of Imagination;* "it is the actor who *becomes unreal* in his character."[16] So the specificity of the Sartrean theatrical event has to be defined by the crisscrossing of two symmetrical movements: in one case, an actor derealizes himself in playing a character—Orestes or Hamlet—other than himself; in the other case, a character attempts to realize himself in spite of the actor who is lending him life. The Sartrean character always dreams of making the audience forget the actor who is speaking in his name; the character is virtually defined, as we saw with Orestes and his deed, by his hope that he will one day succeed in speaking without a double, that he will be able to speak in his own name, with his own voice, will be able to behave in such a way that his own first person will not be constantly overtaken by the hypocritical and parasitical ventriloquist who is playing his role.

In this sense, Orestes' act effects a rupture not only with his own past but also with the eradicable (because repeatable) gestures that made that past resemble an actor's life. At the beginning of the play, he speaks in unison with the actor who is playing his role. Which of the two is speaking when he deplores the fact that his life is only a comedy (lacking, alas, in gravity)? Both character and actor lend themselves to what the other is expressing. The one goes from place to place as the other goes from play to play, without ever meeting the slightest egological anchoring in reality. And both can subscribe in identical terms to the words Sartre has prepared for them: the actor, like his character, can say: "I'm a mere shadow of a man." "I let sounds and scents, the patter of rain on housetops, the golden play of sunbeams, slip past my body and fall round me—and I knew these were for others, I could never make them *my* memories."[17] But this unison is precisely what Orestes' deed brings to an end. By his deed, Orestes claims the exclusive possession of the first person, with no sharing or doubling.

However, in this respect Orestes constitutes a first and last exception in Sartre's theater. If, as we have seen, he leaves the stage reveling in the deed he has accomplished once and for all, a deed that will remain his own forever, he alone among all Sartre's characters benefits from such a windfall.[18] The fate of Orestes' successors is much more closely modeled on that of his victim, Aegistheus. Like Orestes, Aegistheus was in fact a criminal in his day (he too had done his deed: he had killed Agamemnon); but unlike Orestes, who reproaches him for this in his final monologue, he has not lived up to his own deed. He committed an act that he was unable to make his own, that he was unable to appropriate for himself. He committed it without having commensurate courage and pride; he never managed to assume, in solitude, the crime of which he had been the author. "A crime that its doer disowns becomes ownerless—no man's crime," says Orestes, who for his part has no intention of letting his own crime elude his grasp. And in this context Orestes uses an image that has a promising future in Sartre's theater. Orestes points out scornfully that after Agamemnon's murder, Aegistheus paraded about the city with "his arms red to the elbows, gloved in blood."[19] It is because the elegant Aegistheus had put on gloves that his crime was detached from him. Rather than entering into the skin of his character, he had put on the costume of a criminal. In order to have dirty hands, you have to kill barehanded.

Aegistheus' gloves are in effect the point of departure for *Dirty Hands*, the unquestionable masterpiece (along with *Kean*) of Sartre's theater. Indeed, in its broad outlines the plot of *Dirty Hands* repeats that of *The Flies.* Like Orestes, young Hugo in *Dirty Hands* decides to take on anthropological weight by accomplishing a deed that consists in killing a mature man who holds a position of power. Thus, just as Hugo is Orestes' heir, Hoederer inherits Aegistheus' mantle. But the parallelism between the two plays ends here, or rather from this point on it is turned inside out. For if youth and murder are attributes shared by Orestes and Hugo, at the level of behavior Hugo resembles the old Aegistheus as clearly as the old Hoederer resembles Orestes. Orestes found Aegistheus guilty of wearing a pair of red gloves after Agamemnon's murder. In the later play, Hoederer, the exclusive holder of the privilege of dirty hands, accuses Hugo of the same bloody dandyism. "Red gloves," he retorts; "that's elegant." And Hugo himself, after Hoederer's murder, says more or less the same thing. In the play's final tableau, Hugo returns to the scene of a murder he committed two years earlier; he is no longer able to say, as Orestes does after committing his murder, "I have done *my* deed, and that deed was good." Hugo too has found himself lacking in gravity, he too has dreamt of ballast: "I wanted to hang a crime around my neck, like a stone." But Hugo's hell stems from the fact that good intentions alone are not enough to transform Hoederer's blood into a millstone, so that blood can become for him the precious "burden" that Aegistheus' blood is for Orestes. On the contrary: Hugo despairs of the lack of gravity entailed by his murder; he finds his crime "light, horribly light." "It has no weight," he complains. "It's not mine." Orestes accuses Aegistheus of letting his crime be depersonalized, of letting it get away from him and become no one's crime.

Now it is Hugo's turn; he is astonished to find that he has been the instrument of "an assassination without an assassin."[20]

"I wonder whether I really killed him at all," Hugo says to Olga. "What if it were all a comedy? . . . I really drew my finger back. Actors do that too, on the stage. Look here: I cock my forefinger. I aim at you. It's the same gesture. Perhaps I wasn't real."[21] Stage directions, printed in italics and in parentheses, are inserted in the middle of Hugo's speech. The words he utters ("I cock my forefinger. I aim at you") are followed by their silent echo specifying in the third person, for the director's benefit, that the character does what he is saying precisely as the actor says what he is doing: "*(He aims at her with the right hand, his forefinger coiled back.)*"

In this seventh and final tableau of *Dirty Hands*, the character himself, Hugo, is the one who replays the preceding scene for Olga, the fourth scene of the sixth tableau, the scene of Hoederer's murder. But what he produces, in his derealizing staging of reality, is the actor who has already interposed himself between the character and his victim, who (as he says) has prevented his murder from being real, from being anything but a stick-figure murder. It is thus Hugo himself, the play's hero, who is responsible for inserting, within the representation, the device that makes it less real; it is he who unmasks the actor playing his role, the actor whom the protagonist has not succeeded in jettisoning.

Sartre, a propagandist for the literature of commitment, reminded writers that words are loaded guns. But his own plays, *Dirty Hands* and the rest, show, on the contrary, that in the theater a gun does no more harm than words. At the end of *No Exit*, Estelle rushes up to Inez, a paring knife in hand. Inez does not budge. "What do you think you're doing?" she asks. "It has happened *already*."[22] These creatures who dream of putting their lives on the line forget that for a long time now they have had nothing left to risk. We might have wondered whether Orestes' enthusiasm could ever be powerful enough to make spectators forget the actor who plays his role. But for Orestes' successors, for Hugo and the other protagonists of Sartre's dramas, that difficulty does not involve the spectator; it is what constitutes the protagonists themselves as such. Hugo, Inez, Goetz: it is they who cannot forget the actors who lend them their shadowy existence. They cannot forget the actors who, by becoming less real, undo their own striving toward reality. The protagonists themselves are reduced to verbal denunciations of the theatrical structures of their own utterances. They cast off their masks to such an extent that finally the actors who have been speaking in their place now speak for themselves. "Look here: I cock my forefinger. I aim at you." To whom should these words, excerpted from Hugo's role, be attributed? To Hugo himself, or to the actor who is playing his part? Even without counting Sartre and myself, at least two other enunciators may take credit for this first-person pronouncement.

Let us recall the scene between Hugo and his wife, Jessica, at the point when she has just discovered a revolver in her husband's luggage. She asks him what he intends to do with that dangerous object. "It's to kill Hoederer," he replies.

Jessica: Don't tease me, Hugo. I tell you I'm not playing now. . . .
Jessica: . . . I love you.
Hugo: Tell it to me now.
Jessica: What?
Hugo: That you love me.
Hugo: But mean it.
Jessica: I love you.
Hugo: But you don't really mean it.
Jessica: What's got into you? Are you playing?
Hugo: No, I'm not playing . . . Come on, say it. Say it as if you meant it [Dis-le *bien*].

Sartre, in passing, underlines Hugo's pathetic plea. And from these italics Jessica concludes that she has to make an extra effort. "I love you. I love you. No: I love you. Oh, go to the devil."[23] Hugo's drama, in this scene of Marxist-Leninist badinage, stems from the fact that, as speech-act theory affirms, there is no textual property, no syntactic or semantic feature, that would allow us to identify a text with certainty as a work of fiction. Hugo wants his wife to take him seriously, and so he asks her to stop playing. But what is serious, she responds, does not amuse her. "We'll work it out. I'll pretend to be serious." Hence Hugo's dismay—for he continues to believe that if she really believed it, if it weren't theater, the italics would be heard.

This might explain why Sartre's Saint Genet is diametrically opposed to the one canonized by the Catholic church. The latter may well have been both actor and martyr, but only by turns; one thing at a time. He would never have been martyred if he had not stopped acting. The scenario is well known: on a Roman stage, while the hero of the hagiographic tradition is acting out the comic role of a recently converted Christian to entertain the emperor Diocletian, the actor is suddenly overcome by faith. He stops acting and starts believing every word he utters. The entire play is put into Sartrean italics. The theater is turned into a church. The emperor is bored, then exasperated. Genest's martyrdom begins at this moment, after he has abandoned the actor's code of ethics: instead of dissolving his own reality into that of the character (instead of being a Christian in the mode of not being one), the actor makes the character a reality within himself. It is because he becomes "veritable" that Rotrou's Saint Genest becomes a martyr. And here Sartre's Saint Genet stands in contrast to his namesake: his own (self-inflicted) martyrdom depends on his inability to leave the theater, to stop acting, to be anything other than in-the-mode-of-not-being. Sartre's Genet is onstage everywhere, and he does not manage to espouse any of the thoughts he expresses. He is not affected by anything that happens to him; every time he opens a door, a NO EXIT sign lights up. His martyrdom consists in an intractable, transcendental anesthesia, one that—despite heroic skirmishes in favor of commitment, despite virtuous campaigns against depersonalization and psychasthenia—was in all probability the fundamental inspiration behind Sartre's work from the outset.

This transcendental anesthesia in fact constitutes the obligatory corollary to *The Transcendence of the Ego.* That inaugural essay proposed to amputate Husserl's transcendental ego from phenomenological doctrine, presenting that purified form of the first person as "superfluous" and "a hindrance."[24] Sartre puts forward the transcendence of the ego in opposition to its transcendentality. The ego is confined to transcendence in such a way as to prevent subjectivity from having access to the realm of pure consciousness. Provided it is carried out without bad faith, a well-conducted *epoch*—a methodical bracketing off of everything pertaining to the world—means that consciousness—which is henceforth pure—can no longer be vested in a first person: consciousness must be situated if it is to be able to say *I.* Sartre's entry onto the philosophical stage thus took the form of a campaign in favor of a depersonalization, a desubjectivization of consciousness. To use his own example, an up-to-date phenomenologist will no longer say: "I *have* consciousness of this chair," but "There is consciousness of this chair."[25] This is the same grammatical transformation that Roquentin will carry out, in *Nausea*, when he finds that, after Anny (the woman he loves) has left, every time he says "I" it sounds hollow. He then proceeds to write three or four pages of diary entries in the third person, the impersonal person, the person of the nonperson. "There is consciousness of suffering," he notes, for example, "but no one is there to suffer."[26]

Exactly as Aegistheus' and Hugo's crimes are no one's crimes, murders without murderers, a pathological stoicism prevents Sartre's characters from suffering their own suffering, keeps them from owning it by appropriating it. At the very most, they may succeed in becoming, in their own person, the theater of a suffering with respect to which they note, in lucid moments, that there is no one to suffer. Nowhere does this appear more powerfully than in *Kean*, who is, as it were, Sartre's true Saint Genet. "Why would you boo?" is the question put to his public by the sacred monster of the English stage, who has just flubbed his "acting out." "There is no one. No one. Or maybe an actor playing Kean in the role of Othello."[27] Once again, pushed into a corner, the Sartrean character says what he is doing, does what he is saying, describes with impassive lucidity the conditions of his own utterance: for across the footlights from the real spectators there is in fact, as the Kean character says, not Othello and not even Kean playing Othello, but some unspecified actor, an actor without a proper name, or perhaps even his understudy, who plays—and in every revival will continue to play—Sartre's Kean playing Othello. And it is that interchangeable actor, infinitely more than the person Kean or the character Othello, who fascinated Sartre in both Kean and Othello. That somehow transcendent actor who, by lending them his voice, gives the first person to all those persons he is not, to Kean, to Othello, but who must by the same token give up any possibility of saying "I" on his own behalf. Othello's transcendence and Kean's come in a direct line from that of the ego. Kean's "There is an actor who . . ." is the theatrical equivalent of "There is a consciousness that . . ." in *Nausea* and *The Transcendence of the Ego.* That is what gives the theater its privileged status in Sartre's work. The actor is in fact the only human being who can assume the status of a work of art, who can allow himself to be possessed by nonexistence, in whom can be embodied what Lacoue-Labarthe would call the "transcendental impropriety" of pure consciousness. This common transcendence precludes both actors and pure consciousness from ever speaking in their own name. So that, despite all Sartre's efforts to make the theater a mechanism for inducing commitment, in his work as a whole the stage constitutes the most effective mechanism for carrying out the Sartrean version of phenomenological reduction, that is, the desubjectivization of consciousness, the transposition of "I" into "there is."

3

MIMESIS AND CASTRATION 1937

"I think it will interest American readers to acquaint themselves with the latest and most peculiar phase in French literary reaction, which appears also as a bold manifestation of avant-garde thought."[1]

This statement figures among the very small number of contemporary references made in America to the College of Sociology.[2] It appears at the beginning of Meyer Schapiro's review of Roger Caillois's *La communion des forts* (Communion of the Strong) published in the winter 1945 issue of the *Kenyon Review* under the title "French Reaction in Exile."[3] Although all the articles reprinted in *La communion des forts* are from the prewar period (written before Caillois left France for Argentina), Schapiro reads the moral and political views developed in this book as a disquieting prefiguration of the regime the Allied victory and de Gaulle's subsequent return have in store for postwar France. If Caillois is to be its moralist, the Liberation does not promise to be heartening. Schapiro compares Caillois to Auguste Comte, who was similarly a partisan of a spiritual power that would restore the social hierarchy. Caillois, Schapiro points out, "lays great weight on the cohesion of society through sacraments, and I am told he has attempted, together with certain surrealists, to create modern rites and idols."[4] These rumors very probably had their origin in the circles of French avant-garde intellectuals exiled in New York, among them Denis de Rougemont, Georges Duthuit, André Masson, Jean Wahl, René Etiemble, and even Claude Lévi-Strauss, not to mention Patrick Waldberg, an American temporarily away from Paris.

The accusation of reactionary avant-gardism leveled against Caillois was not new. Before the war, virtually all the College's public manifestations were tarred with the same brush.[5] Caillois's declared opposition to Marxist problematics, his insistence on viewing social issues in emotional and religious rather than economic terms, his persistence in privileging elective affinities at the expense of class affiliations, his attention to myths rather than to relations of production, his indifference to the class struggle, all these choices subjected him—and he was, moreover, a compliant target—to a whole array of accusations pointing to reactionary tendencies. At the time, anything short of a phobic rejection of fascism tended to be taken for complicity. The desire to know became a form of sympathy. Anyone who looked into fascism or speculated about the mechanisms of its success was suspected of an interest in the phenomenon that went beyond epistemology. In any event, the accusation of ambiguity was certainly not unjustified: Caillois, for one, cultivated it carefully as long as he could.[6] He sought to maintain a provocative political undecidability as long as possible, putting off the choice that he was being hard pressed to make by everything around him. But is it legitimate to apply the label "reactionary" to a refusal to prove that one is not reactionary? By settling the question too hastily, it is the impatient questioner who assumes responsibility for a decision that he cannot bear to see another evade.

Reactionary or not, this ambiguity as such is part of the program of the College of Sociology. "The Winter Wind," one of the militant pieces Caillois wrote as a manifesto for the College, campaigns for a resacralization of social issues and enjoins the nucleus of refractory contemporaries to "most utterly oppose a society that has profaned itself to an extreme degree."[7] The sacred dimension to whose restoration Caillois dedicates the College is principally characterized by ambiguity. It is at once *tremendum* and *fascinans;* an object of respect and disgust, it attracts and repels simultaneously. The fact that the College of Sociology cultivated an active, virulent ambiguity in the face of the most burning problems of the day, that it refused to allow itself to be framed within the consensual axes of modern political life, is a fact that cannot be entirely dissociated from its project of reinjecting ambiguity, an attribute of the sacred, into contemporary social space.

On one point, however, Caillois took an unambiguous stand. And on this specific point Meyer Schapiro is right: Caillois's position was reactionary. The sacralization of social life, which was the aim of the College's sociological activity, implies the restoration of hierarchical differences. In the 1930s and 1940s Caillois regularly denounced the generalized egalitarianism of democracies, advocating in its place a hierarchical division of humankind, the classification of individuals as masters and slaves or, to use his own Saint-Simonian lexicon, as producers and consumers.[8]

Like one-way mirrors, real differences are not reversible. The distinctions are oriented. The one at the top is always alone in distinguishing himself from the others: a master is distinguished from slaves, but the converse is not true. The master distinguishes himself from the slaves; but that is also how he is distinguished from slaves. A slave is in the first place someone who is not distinguished, someone who is incapable of distinguishing himself from anything or anyone at all. On this point, this way of thinking about ambiguity has nothing ambiguous about it. Masters and slaves are no longer in opposition by virtue of symmetrical and antithetical attributes (some are wealthy, others are poor). Furthermore, they do not need to be in opposition. And their opposition, if it exists, need not be reciprocal. Slaves do not need to be opposed to masters; on the other hand, masters need to be opposed to slaves, or at least to be distinguished from them. The leaders in question are not demanding, or, if they are, they make demands on themselves alone. The only privilege on which they insist is the privilege of a distinction that is an end in itself, that has no content except distinction itself. Mastery is a formalism of difference. Distinction, in this sense, is what producers produce. It is less an attribute than an activity, the act of beings who, since they have the will and the power to distinguish themselves, *make* the difference. Those who have it do nothing but distinguish themselves, distinguishing themselves from the others in the process. Distinction thus culminates in the sense of etiquette: people either know how to behave or they do not. And those who threaten to behave badly have to be led by someone else. Meyer Schapiro evokes the rites that the College of Sociology had considered initiating. On several occasions, Caillois makes courtesy the cornerstone of a morality of masters.[9]

The master-slave hierarchy is ontological (existential) rather than social; it is moral rather than economic. In Caillois's tableau, there is no reason to pity the slave. Nothing prevents us from imagining a situation in which the slave, while remaining a slave, has lost all reason to feel sorry for himself: nothing prevents us from conceiving of a happy slave. A satisfied slave remains a slave. For the slave is no longer defined by his economic servitude and the subsequent alienation of his capacity for work; he is no longer defined by the sufferings that the reality principle would impose on him; rather, he is defined by his subjection to the pleasure principle. And that is why, in terms that owe more to Plato and Nietzsche than to Marx, Caillois identifies slaves with consumers rather than with producers. For in the last analysis a slave is always a slave to pleasure. Hence the fact that the hierarchy of beings hinges on the distinction between the pleasure principle and its "beyond," a distinction that is as decisive and as vital as the one between the real and the imaginary—a distinction with which the first one intersects. On the hither side of the pleasure principle, slaves imagine that pleasure is "the supreme goal of freedom"; on the nether side, masters know that pleasure is "the principal gateway to slavery."[10]

The sublimation of sexuality, then, is what gives rise to the hierarchy of beings. But this transcending of sexuality reinscribes sexual difference in its own way. Like the anatomical difference between the sexes, the difference between the sexual and the nonsexual is defined by the presence or absence of a congenital attribute, a contingent but unsurpassable given, a differential feature that divides humanity into two groups. Some have it, others do not. This crucial attribute is power. "Here," Caillois wrote, "one encounters a notion no less immediate, primary, and unbreakable than the opposition of the sexes."[11]

In what does this power consist? In the first place, it is the power not to experience pleasure. And not to experience it precisely because one is giving it: the power to give rather than take pleasure, to give it so as not to take it. Power is the capacity to escape from the pleasure one is imposing, to give a pleasure that will not be returned. The distinction between producers and consumers comes in again here: the person who produces pleasure must not consume it. This sums up Caillois's principle of exogamy: to taste the pleasure one is giving would be to violate as grave a taboo as that of incest. What is at stake here is no longer mere politeness; it is not simply a matter of self-effacement in front of others. The caveat "if it should please you" has been transcended. It is obligatory to give pleasure—even if this means imposing it on another—in such a way as to avoid experiencing it oneself.

In 1937 an elaboration of this theme ("domination is preferable to pleasure") led Caillois to develop a somewhat sinister fantasy. Domination and pleasure are mutually exclusive, but not as two separate, alien worlds that would condemn each other from afar without being acquainted. The worlds of domination and pleasure are contiguous. Each excludes the other, yet each is implicated in the other. All domination has simultaneous pleasure as its lining. Domination, indeed, is nothing other than the production of pleasure—production, that is to say, not consumption: the production of a pleasure that is not mine. Domination is thus exercised in the realm of pleasure alone; it relies on the pleasure that it expels, that it projects, that it rejects. Domination is therefore literally a pleasure that I do not experience. It is born of my resistance to the pleasure that I am imposing on the other. "One can imagine," Caillois writes, "that there are creatures who, in love, find enjoyment less in the pleasure they experience than in the pleasure they arouse, for the former does not leave them in possession of themselves, whereas the latter gives them possession of another . . . In the extreme case," he continues, "if such creatures commit rape, they do so not owing to the pressures of instinct or in order to achieve pleasure for themselves, but in order to make the victim feel pleasure in spite of herself, for rapists have been seduced by the strange cruelty of imposing sensual excitement for its own sake."[12]

This scenario is not limited to defending the right—some might even call it a natural right—to use others for one's own pleasure. Nor does it attempt to justify or excuse rape by arguing that both parties get something out of it, that, whatever her claims to the contrary, a rape victim takes pleasure in the experience. Nor is it a question of finding one's own pleasure in someone else's pain, according to Freud's classical definition of sadism. Rather, Caillois's scenario entails losing one's own pleasure in another's. Making the other experience pleasure, but a pleasure to which he does not consent. Making him undergo—suffer—a pleasure to which he does not give his assent, a pleasure that is not agreeable to him, one to which he would not have agreed. A pleasure that is not pleasing to him, *son bon plaisir*. Writing later on with reference to Sade, Pierre Klossowski alluded to a similar "right to compel pleasure."[13] It would be more accurate to speak of "inflicting pleasure," borrowing an oxymoron found in Pierre Drieu La Rochelle.[14]

The temporal sequence of pleasure and pain, guilt and punishment, is subject to a strange perversion here. For it is logical to think that guilty pleasure must be followed by punishment; one may even suppose that since pleasure is guilty by definition, all pleasure must be followed by punishment. It is this type of negotiation that allows moral algebrists to tot up their balance sheets. But in Caillois's scenario the pleasure and the pain are both incalculable: receipts and expenses are noted on the same side of the ledger. In this disquieting rose-tinted sadism, the pleasure itself has become the punishment.

This scenario depends on a grammar that does not allow pleasure to be conjugated in the first person. What is enunciated here in the form of an active distinction between power and pleasure only transforms into an imperative what a description would have handled in the indicative. Power transforms a structure into a requirement. It adds interdiction to impossibility. When it issues the order to enjoy, it merely transcribes into the imperative (its own verbal mode) the impossibility of first-person pleasure. It can enunciate pleasure only in the second person. For pleasure by definition is excluded from first-person utterances. And far from being in contradiction on this point, power and pleasure are in perfect agreement, each in its own characteristic mode. Each expresses the self-abnegation of pleasure, the subjective evacuation in which pleasure consists. The same anaesthesia is found, in a less aggressive form, in the remarks of the schizophrenic that Caillois cites as an epigraph to his "Procès intellectuel de l'art": "See these roses?" he might say. "My wife would find them beautiful; for me, they are just a bunch of leaves, petals, thorns and stems."[15] In keeping with the classic hierarchy of beings and their roles, it is the schizophrenic's wife, of course, who would take pleasure in what leaves him, a man, cold. The pleasure is all hers.

Beyond its sadism, the real driving force underlying Caillois's scenario is the refusal to take pleasure upon oneself. But it is impossible to take it upon oneself. Indeed, sexuality functions as a modality of *epoch*, as a way of bracketing off the self and subjectivity. A way of evacuating oneself, expelling oneself. The best of all possible worlds is thus a world in which what is forbidden also turns out to be impossible. Pleasure has to be the other's. In fact there is no pleasure but the other's. One never enjoys in the first person. If I were to give myself over to pleasure, I would lose myself; it would not leave me, Caillois says, "in possession of myself." Thus pleasure can never be mine. And it is precisely in order to avoid the expropriation of self through pleasure that Caillois's strong men want only a pleasure that would clearly not be their own. It is in order to avoid losing myself in an unappropriable pleasure that I must enjoy only through the pleasure of another. The opposition between pleasure and domination (or pleasure and power) is surreptitiously replaced by a hierarchy of pleasures: the (reprehensible) pleasure that one takes in one's own pleasure and the (praiseworthy) pleasure that one takes in that of another—that is, the pleasure that one takes in giving pleasure to another without taking pleasure oneself.

What remains, at this point, of the opposition between pleasure and power? In the place that should belong to the opposite of pleasure, that is, to power, a redundancy brings pleasure back in, beyond the pleasure principle. And this pleasure is once again defined as the impossibility of first-person enjoyment, as depersonalized pleasure. I have avoided losing myself in my own pleasure only to find myself experiencing a pleasure that is not my own. The remedy for alienation is no different from alienation itself.

It could be demonstrated that the Sartrean theory of commitment—although this theory too is presented as an apparatus of resistance to subjective renunciations and to depersonalization—is in fact nothing but the detour required for the production of an impersonal, nonsubjective, transcendent consciousness that is exempted from constituting itself as a center of action, and thus exempted from the obligation of expressing itself in the first person. Commitment is only the obverse of withdrawal.[16] For if Sartre demonstrates that the ego is wholly committed, that a subject is entirely in the world, belongs to it without reservation, without exception, this worldly commitment goes hand in hand with the distance and detachment implied in the concept of transcendence. In other words, transcendence is only a means for assuring the worldly evacuation of the ego. If the ego's transcendence engages the ego wholly in the world, this engagement is at the same time the occasion and even the condition of possibility for the absolute disengagement (what Sartre calls the transcendentality) of consciousness. Behind the militant screen of the ego's transcendence, consciousness accedes to weightlessness and transcendental impersonality. And for Caillois as for the young Sartre, the institution of the clergy remains the most reliable apparatus for achieving such an egological *epoch*.[17]

The last text included in Caillois's *Cases d'un échiquier* (Squares on a Chessboard), "Récit du délogé" (The Evicted Man's Story), is a fictional case history whose most peculiar aspect is undoubtedly the fact that, despite its subject, it is a first-person text from beginning to end. Is there a limit beyond which the narrative of an experience of depersonalization ought to abandon the use of "I"? Up to what point can a depersonalized consciousness continue to use first-person pronouns? Roquentin and Meursault would have something to say about that problem of narratology. Caillois's opening sentence takes us straight to the heart of the narrative paradox: "I had never really imagined that one could find oneself depersonalized."[18]

In one episode in the story, where the narrator evokes his earliest sexual experience, his stream of consciousness curiously develops the scenario imagined by Caillois in 1937 in "The Winter Wind." "I was obviously not impotent," the narrator remarks. "But I remained convinced for some time that I was frigid." The crisis of orgasm had in fact left him "lucid, if not critical, more attentive to the pleasure of my partner than swept away by my own."[19] Male frigidity has nothing in common with impotence; it does not entail falling short of a pleasure that is out of reach, but rather going beyond a disaffected, anesthetized pleasure. Pleasure does not cause a man to lose possession of himself; rather, it procures for him the possession of another. But is this not because, in pleasure, the "I" is another?

Thus, whether I give up pleasure or give in to it, the end result is the same: pleasure is never mine. Still, can one say that in giving up pleasure, one is sure to gain self-possession? Here is where the figure of the cleric comes in, as well as the projects of the College of Sociology. The cleric is not a consumer. He leaves to others the pleasures in which they lose themselves. But he lets them have those pleasures in exchange for a power in which he too loses himself. The Church, in fact, does not require of the cleric solely that he renounce worldly pleasures and attachments; the first and strongest of these attachments, the one he most urgently needs to abandon, is the attachment to himself. The sacrament of ordination serves to institute an agency of impersonal consciousness, detached from the first person, which it relegates to a position of subjective prosthesis; it is a psychologizing parasite, an impostor. Thus, referring to the cleric, Caillois writes: "His strength is not that of a man, but that of an organism in which his person disappears . . . By eliminating himself, the cleric makes room in himself for the Church."[20] The cleric, a soluble fish, disappears within the order that welcomes him; he vanishes in his adoptive milieu.

"Sociologie du clerc" (Sociology of the Cleric), the text in which these reflections are presented, was Caillois's contribution to the discussions about intellectuals and commitment that had been stirred up by the conflicts within the Popular Front and by the threat—and temptation—of fascism. By definition, according to Caillois, an individual who speaks in his own name cannot be called a cleric, no matter whether his intention is to intervene in worldly affairs or to distance himself from them. The cleric, because he is first of all a member of a Church, has given up speaking and even thinking in his own name, has given up saying what he thinks. His adherence to a given Church or College has forever deprived him of "the capacity to enjoy himself and even the capacity to be himself."

This brings us full circle, back to the situation from which the status of cleric was supposed to make it possible to escape. Being oneself and taking pleasure are no longer in opposition; they are now two variants of anticlericalism. Conversely, being ordained as a cleric deprives the subject of both self-possession and the pleasure in which he loses that self-possession. By giving up worldly pleasures, the cleric is no more master of himself than he would have been in giving himself over to those pleasures. What is the point of what Caillois used to promote as "austere virtues," if giving up pleasure produces the same result as pleasure? At the heart of the clerical vocation we find a raging temptation toward vertigo that that vocation was supposed to counter, the human tendency "to be lacking to oneself and, as it were, to desert oneself."[21] The cleric is always on the verge of giving in to the pleasure of playing dead. Which leads us to the seduction of mimesis, and thereby to the College of Sociology.

Mimesis and castration. Several years before the foundation of the College of Sociology, the topic of mimesis inspired Caillois to write his two most memorable articles (both of which are included in *Le mythe et l'homme*).[22] The first has its point of departure in the sexual habits of the praying mantis, a species in which the female is known to devour her mate during intercourse; the second compares certain forms of animal mimesis, notably among insects, to what Caillois, after Pierre Janet, calls legendary psychasthenia.

In the vocabulary of French psychiatry in use at the time, psychasthenia was a pathological lowering of the level of psychic energy, a sort of subjective detumescence, a loss of egoistic substance, a depressive exhaustion resembling what the monastic lexicon termed *acedia.* Caillois elevates psychasthenia into a cosmic, virtually metaphysical principle and makes it the heart of his study of "noontide demons" and his subsequent work on mimesis: the notion allows him to describe and interpret mimesis according to a thermodynamic model.[23] According to Carnot's first principle, every productive process presupposes an initial hierarchy, a primary distinction, an originary inequality, a difference between high and low or between a cold source and a hot one. But Carnot's second principle is the one that Caillois puts to work in his articles on the praying mantis and on mimesis. The entropy of a given system cannot decline. Psychasthenia is a lowering of energy: the initial gap diminishes, the power source heats up, production diminishes. The vital distinctions wither. Both the praying mantis, by assimilating her mate, and mimetic insects, by ceasing to distinguish themselves from their surroundings, illustrate this moment in which beings no longer have the energy to establish difference.

In reaction against this fatalism, Caillois projects the College as a condenser of energies. The temptation of the abyss may be universal, experienced by everyone; nevertheless, not everyone need succumb. Having made one's way up to the heights, one may well aspire to climb back down; but this is not sufficient reason to do so. The virtue of vertigo is first of all that it gives strong men an opportunity to overcome it. The description of mimetic behaviors is not a pretext for singing the praises of psychasthenia. On the contrary, Caillois begins with a plea for distinction: "From whatever side one approaches things, the ultimate problem turns out in the final analysis to be that of *distinction:* distinctions between the real and the imaginary, between waking and sleeping, between ignorance and knowledge, etc.—all of them, in short, distinctions in which valid consideration must demonstrate a keen awareness and the demand for resolution. Among distinctions, there is assuredly none more clear-cut than that between the organism and its surroundings."[24]

The biological strangeness of a phenomenon like mimesis stems precisely from the fact that, by submitting to it, an organism renounces that distinction; it abdicates the difference, the vital difference, between life and matter, between the organic and the inorganic. Marie François Xavier Bichat had defined life as the set of forces that resist death. With mimesis, it seems, life ceases to resist. "Here," Caillois comments, "we touch on the fundamental law of the universe brought to light by Carnot's principle: *the world tends toward uniformity.*"[25] Caillois's characterization of mimesis thus constitutes a moral allegory offering a background against which the true scope of his project for the College becomes clear. Like the male praying mantis, like those insects that turn themselves into branches among branches, leaves among leaves, the cleric too gives up self-possession, but his renunciation takes on new meaning; instead of accelerating the general tendency toward entropy, the cleric's self-abnegation reverses it, thereby producing effects of negative entropy or, to use the term Caillois introduces in *La dissymétrie,* inverse entropy.[26]

In our temperate societies, subject to much more modest seasonal variations than those of the Eskimo societies Marcel Mauss describes in his groundbreaking study of social thermodynamics, the difference between hot and cold is not as marked as hierarchical thinking would like it to be. An activist sociology can nevertheless compensate for the tepid climate by instituting artificial freezers, centers of male frigidity that would augment social production and thus counterbalance the damage done by entropy. This is exactly the function "The Winter Wind" assigns to the College. For entropy does not wreak havoc in the physical world alone. It is the principal feature of modernity. "Social life in its entirety tends toward uniformity," we read in *Man and the Sacred.*[27] And "Sociologie du clerc" has reminded us that in a "uniform society," a society in which "the distinction between the spiritual and the temporal" is no longer marked, the clerical function has no room to operate. Against secular reversibility, the College undertakes to restore a hierarchical asymmetry, to revive the difference between difference and indifference. The topography of the sacred requires a center of ambiguity; this ambiguity must still stand out unambiguously from the ambient uniformity.

In October 1938, in the wake of the Munich crisis, Caillois presented the College as a "center of energy" committed to struggling against "man's devirilization."[28] This term does not seem to be a direct allusion to the praying mantis, but it is clear that for Caillois, mimesis and castration, entropy and devirilization, constituted identical threats. The prospect of war had just offered a reminder that in the face of death all men are equal. The College took advantage of the occasion to recall that that equality does not rule out all forms of distinction. It is neither forbidden nor impossible to "maintain a certain decorum when death threatens."[29]

However, the descriptions in the essay on mimesis and the prescriptions in the manifesto of the College are only superficially in opposition. I have already noted that for Caillois, an institution such as the College, like any other clerical institution, required of its members a renunciation of self equivalent to the subjective evacuation at work in mimesis. But there is something else—and here one would almost be tempted to suspect Caillois of bad faith. His descriptions of mimesis—which are thus subjected in their turn to the attraction through resemblance whose rule they depict, and deplore—fail to mention one crucial difference. The mimetic insect, subjected to "depersonalization through assimilation to space," plays dead.[30] So be it. However, the insect can play dead only because it is alive. Yet Caillois's analysis, if only through the way it relies on Freud's speculations about the death drive, implies that there is no difference between being dead and playing dead, between actual death and feigned death. It may be, as the epigraph says, that by pretending to be a ghost you risk turning into a ghost. But the content of the article demonstrates the opposite thesis: insects play dead but do not become dead. They only look dead. The difference between appearance and identity is crucial here. No matter how mimesis is interpreted, death is a mask for life, a mask behind which life protects its difference by pretending to renounce that difference. This is why we cannot be at all certain that mimesis has entropic apocalypse as its ultimate outcome.

Caillois seems to be proclaiming the end of differences, announcing the great tide of indistinction, but it is a pretense that allows him to hold onto the one vital distinction. Life continues to distinguish itself from death; however, the distinction is no longer visible. The status of differences has changed: they have become imperceptible; they can no longer be distinguished from their effacement. The homology between the praying mantis and mimetic insects obviously breaks down here: the male praying mantis, for his part, does not merely pretend to be devoured.[31]

But the haunting notion of mimetic solicitation is reflected here, in addition, by the specter of a secret society. The College is not bound by the romantic culture of antitheses; it does not set up oppositions between contraries. The conflict between the individual and society is displaced in favor of more subtle strategies in which society, absorbed in its contentious dealings with its double, turns against itself. This confrontation takes the form of mimetic subversion: resistance is now manifested not by opposition but by one-upmanship; dissidents now constitute society's most authentic sectarians. Caillois reminds us, moreover, that "sect" and "society" may have the same etymology. "One unites only by separating," he declares.[32] Secession does not trigger a relaxation of the social bond. It has as its driving force a desire for "oversocialization." If dissidents withdraw from society, it is because they hold that society to their own lofty standard. Consequently, in a *mise en abyme* analogous to mimesis, society finds itself on both sides of a secession that is no longer in evidence.

A secret must be beyond suspicion. Strictly speaking, it must be impossible to say whether there is a secret or not; for if there were a secret, it would not be known, or else if it were known, it would not be a secret. Democracy, a political regime that functions in the glare of publicity, has always identified secrets with abuses of power. But surveillance practices, which have developed side by side with democracy, are haunted by what cannot be seen. We are told that Bentham, the inventor of the Panopticon, had a lifelong fear of ghosts.[33] Secrecy may be banished, but that will not do away with society's obsession with secrets. Thus secret societies come to constitute a major theme of democratic political fantasy.

Caillois describes the behavior of a child who is hiding some treasure. He takes "infinite care in peeling off the wallpaper, hollowing out the plaster wall, installing his prodigious deposit, then regluing the cleverly torn tapestry as best he can to make it look like an accident, or else carefully cutting it out along the lines of the pattern."[34] For that child, as for mimetic insects, it is a matter of reabsorbing a spot, dissimulating some heterogeneity behind the apparently continuous tissue of an unbroken surface. This reabsorption engenders the secret, which, according to Caillois, "derives its value from not being known": in order for it to exert its fascination, "its very existence" must remain unknown. "Power" and "secrecy" are often associated in Caillois's vocabulary, as when he refers to the false bottoms of Fantomas's Paris or "the taste for shadows and power" in which secret societies take root.[35] For secrecy is indeed a source of power, and power is all the greater when it is secret, that is to say, potential, virtual, in reserve: *en puissance.* A first reading of the historical evolution that led from the Old Regime monarchy to modern democracy may highlight the progress of entropy, of undifferentiated egalitarianism. But the same story may be read the other way around. It is not inappropriate to quote Montesquieu in connection with Caillois. In *The Spirit of the Laws* Montesquieu says: "If the pomp and splendour surrounding kings is a part of their power, modesty and simplicity of manners are the strength of the nobles in an aristocracy. When nobles affect no distinction, when they blend with the people, dress like them, and share all their pleasures with them, the people forget their own weakness."[36] Monarchy is opposed to democracy in that it displays hierarchical differences. But an aristocrat is not an exhibitionist. He is not about to reveal his difference to the first person who comes along. The trace fades: all his distinction lies in his reserve.

4

BATAILLE'S TOMB

But why the excitement? Gravediggers are honest people, certainly unionized for sure, perhaps Communists.

Jean-Paul Sartre, *What Is Literature?*

Posthumous homage, however well intentioned, cannot help but betray its debt to the rituals of necrophilia. The place and date of the present meeting, as well as its pious motive, thus give me the pretext for introducing my subject: at a barely respectful distance from Vézelay, where Georges Bataille was buried twenty years ago today, I shall speak of Bataille's tomb.[1]

Not of the grave in which he now lies, under a stone I don't think I have ever seen. No, I want to speak of the grave within him that seems to have denied him rest. My topic is not so much Bataille's tomb as the tomb of Bataille within Bataille: since it does not contain the text in which it is inscribed, it does not allow itself to be closed. A cryptological dimension discourages thematic inventory. Death no longer provides for the repose of a return to the earth. The ground itself ceases to be solid. Embedded in itself, earth falls with the tomb. "I fall into the immensity / that falls in itself," says the first poem of "Tombeau," the opening section of *L'archangélique*.[2]

Few writers can have been as profoundly seduced, captivated, and literally inspired by their own corpse as Bataille. It is not illegitimate to imagine that, when he entitled his 1929 anti-Breton pamphlet *Un cadavre*, the sentiments indicated by that title were more complex than its addressee could have imagined. Breton was of course unaware of the drafts of the open letter Bataille was thinking of sending him: I am writing you from a distant country, Bataille declares, from "the region where one at last sniffs out one's own corpse," a region where one is compelled to "borrow humor *for a price* from one's own corpse."[3]

The surrealists' Freud was the theoretician of dreams and the liberator of sexuality; Bataille's is the postwar Freud, the theoretician of collective psychology and the death drive. For Bataille, however, the libido is fundamentally necrophilic, and it reveals itself without exception as the most insistent—if indirect—manifestation of the death drive: the love of death is the only thing stronger than death itself. An illustration in *The Tears of Eros* represents a prehistoric statuette in which one may choose to see either a woman's body or an erect phallus. As an emblem for Bataille's reflections, a "plastic pun" of another type suggests itself, one that would equate female genitals with a tomb. Moreover, reading the figure painted at the bottom of the well at Lascaux, Bataille finds that man's tomb is humanity's cradle. A sort of telluric incest is symbolically accomplished through fantasies of sexual inhumation. "I fall into the immensity / that falls in itself." And a few lines later the first poem of "Tombeau" continues: "To love is to love to die." In 1929 "The Language of Flowers" had already put forth as a "nauseating banality" the proposition that *"love smells like death."*[4]

NIETZSCHE AND DON JUAN

Nothing seems to approximate the schema of interdiction and transgression more closely than the Don Juan legend, with its conclusion in which the shatterer of interdictions risks his life in a ceremonial feast where he defies the Commander. A hot spring (pleasure, sex), a cold spring (the law, death): Don Juan and the Commander personify the nonsynthetic adjunction of the interdiction-transgression apparatus around which Bataille's thought develops. Nothing better illustrates the definition of eroticism as "approval of life even unto death" than Don Juan's attitude when he refuses to repent for having lived life to the fullest because he may be at the threshold of death.

And yet the Hegelian injunction Bataille uses as the epigraph to *Madame Edwarda*, an injunction requiring the spirit to have the strength to "maintain the work of death," remains alien to Don Juan to the very end. Even in death, Don Juan approves of a life that disapproves of death. And here undoubtedly lies the reason for Bataille's oddly lukewarm interest in Don Juan, whose name, for example, does not appear even once in a book that he titled *Erotism.*[5] And if the marquis de Sade takes Don Juan's place, it is not simply because Sade is a Don Juan who writes. The fact that Don Juan does not write is part and parcel of his refusal to take into account what Bataille calls the "paradox of pleasure": literature reserves for itself the pleasure of pleading guilty.

The classic Don Juan is a healthy creature; there is nothing especially perverse about him. He is first and foremost a conquistador. Blanchot sees in him "a myth of modern times": "a superb hero, a man of the sword and of courage, a man who introduces the vivacity and the energy of the day into night."[6] According to the doctrine of *Erotism*, desire is undoubtedly the operative force behind alterations of identity, transgressions of personal barriers, the impersonal growth of life that undermines individual discontinuity. Don Juan, however, maintains his dignity. Furthermore, what do we really know about his sex life? The fact that we are dealing with a theatrical character brings into play from the outset imperatives of decency that keep the depiction of his exploits to a minimum. Nevertheless, the considerations of propriety imposed by the conventions of the theater are not the only reasons for this discretion. The logic of the character itself excludes any allusion to the sort of tableau in which the erotic novel specializes. Of the women he has seduced we know only the number. This unbridled collector does not linger over the joys of the moment. Like a woman, Bataille writes, the possible requires that one pursue it to the end. Don Juan is not a man of furtive pleasures, of indirect or equivocal possessions. But does one go to the end once and for all? Whatever the case, he has decided that, since a woman stays the same after sleeping with him, any redundancy would disrupt his accounting system. Having two women at once would pose the same recordkeeping problems, as would shared possession of one (or—all the more so—two). With any shared arrangement, one would no longer know on what list to set them down. Don Juan wants all women, but all to himself, and one at a time. The economy of his desire, maximally distributive, never bogs down in details. One entry apiece. The number is not attributable to polymorphous desire but to monomaniacal normalcy.

As for necrophilia, any suspicion of it is ruled out. "*Vivan le femmine*": Don Juan wants them alive. His libido finds nothing attractive in the ambiguities of the repulsive. The paradox of pleasure leaves this partisan of the identity principle cold. The sex organs are not, for him, included among the "forbidden horrors" that Bataille later describes to the College of Sociology as constituting the "sacred" kernel of a communication induced by "interrepulsion."[7] We know to what extent Don Juan is sensitive to the *odor di femmina*. But to say that "love has the odor of death," to assign sexuality to the region in which "one sniffs out one's own corpse," would be to attest to a deplorable lack of taste. Bataille quotes the passage from *For Whom the Bell Tolls* in which Pilar explains to Robert Jordan how to recognize the smell of death. Imagine, she says, an "odor of the wet earth, the dead flowers, and the doings of that night."[8] Don Juan's sense of smell is definitively resistant to this sort of mix. He would never fantasize female genitals as the metaphorical equivalent of a tomb. And especially not the tomb that awaits him. The loves of Hamlet and Yorick are not his style. A cemetery does not dampen his appetite, but it does not whet his appetite either. What Bataille calls "joy in the face of death" does not play any part in Don Juan's practices. In the sadologist Maurice Heine's medicolegal anthology of sexual crimes, compiled under the title *Tableau de l'amour macabre*,[9] the libertine from Seville does not appear. Don Juan, the man of desire, provokes the Commander. But the reciprocal proposition is not true: the Commander does not provoke the slightest desire in Don Juan. Independent zones are assigned to the object of desire and the object of horror. Women and the old man do not evolve in the same space; they never meet. The attraction of pink owes nothing to the repulsion of black.

And yet, what remains of an interdiction if it gives rise to no desire for transgression? Can one conceive of a transgression that would be indifferent to interdiction? According to Bataille, such indifference explains why the Don Juan character does not live up to his legend. A pre-Copernican self-satisfaction makes him imagine himself as the center of his own legend, but the satellite figure of the Commander is blind to what his greatest charm comes from: nearly all commentators on the myth agree in recognizing the Commander as the pivotal figure.[10]

On one of the rare occasions when Bataille speaks of Don Juan, he contrasts him with Nietzsche (in the chapter "Nietzsche and Don Juan" in the posthumous text "Sovereignty"). In Bataille's view, Don Juan, a rationalist libertine, honors the pleasure principle and the reality principle combined. For pleasure, he has women. As for reality, his confidence in it protects him against superstitions: it exempts him from experiencing "the fear most people have of the dead." I call a dead man a dead man. This attitude changes when the statue responds to Don Juan's invitation. Ironic skepticism turns into defiance. Don Juan is no longer the same: the one who said yes to women is not the same as the one who says no to the Commander. "In a first movement, Don Juan is content to ignore the fear that most people have of the dead: he is the Commander's killer, but the irony of his invitation is not a sacrilege if nothing is sacred to him. But when the statue walks into the house, the evidence is clear, and Don Juan no longer defies that which he had the strength to ignore, he defies that which towers over him. He passes from levity to a consciousness of *law*, when the hand of the statue chills him and, thunderstruck, he shouts *No* to the one who, in vain, commands him to repent." Death, that unreality, strikes him without obtaining from him the slightest sign of what a Hegelian would call "recognition." The absolute master has the last word. Don Juan, however, does not subscribe to it. Passing from denegation to negation, beyond the pleasure principle and the reality principle combined, Don Juan at this moment approaches a Nietzschean attitude. Bataille writes: "The feeling of Don Juan, certain that hell is swallowing him up and not yielding, is in my view comparable to the surmounted terror, which will never cease terrifying, that Nietzsche links to the certainty of the death of God."[11] The first version of these lines was even clearer: "It is to the extent that it exceeds the dryness of libertinage that Don Juan's attitude is close to Nietzsche's. I cannot help comparing the state of Don Juan when he knows that hell is engulfing him and yet remains unyielding to the fright that Nietzsche linked to the revelation that God himself is dead."[12]

But Bataille goes no further. His pairing of Don Juan and Nietzsche stops here. For the Nietzschean madman, while he is frightened by the death of God, at the same time accuses himself of being responsible for that death. He pleads guilty before the absence of a judge, an absence of which he is the cause. There is nothing of the sort in Don Juan, who to the very end refuses to acknowledge receipt of a sentence that overwhelms him. This sentence, Bataille writes, "overwhelms him *from the outside.* Whereas moral exigency never ceases to weigh upon Nietzsche *from within.*"[13]

The lines from *Inner Experience* in which Bataille defends the image of a Don Juan without complexes are often quoted: "Useless—psychological—chatter about 'don juanism' surprises me, repulses me. Don Juan is in my eyes—which are more naive—only a personal incarnation of the festival, the carefree orgy, which negates and divinely overturns obstacles."[14] There were endless turn-of-the century arguments over why Don Juan did not settle down—whether he was homosexual or impotent, whether he hated women or loved them more than they deserved. Bataille counters these decadent sophistications with a more "naive" reading: Don Juan or the unreserved orgy. But is this the right term? Is there really room, in the theory of eroticism, for a simple celebration, for an unambiguous orgy, one that is merely "successful," without complications, a picnic in the country with no false notes, naive and natural through and through, an orgy that would be purely and simply a return to nature, unpolluted by Sunday emanations of religious sacrifice? There is more. This appeal on behalf of a rose-tinted sexuality concludes a brief analysis of Mozart's *Don Giovanni* in which Bataille retains only the opera's darkest episodes, those in which the hero confronts the Commander, when his "yes" to women gives way to the "no" he addresses to the Commander.

For Bataille is less naive than he claims. Don Juan holds his attention only after the women have left the stage. Don Juan—Don Juan the seducer—is undoubtedly too "naive" to be interested in the Commander. But it is precisely because of this excessive naïveté that Bataille does not manage to be interested in Don Juan: it is the Commander who arouses Bataille's interest in Don Juan. It is the Commander who in Don Juan interests Bataille.

As Bataille notes in "Sovereignty," "Don Juan's libertinage goes beyond the delight in which the sexual prohibition is lifted: it is from the breaking of the law that assures the dead of the horror-stricken respect of the living that the figure of the 'seducer' has drawn its greatest charm."[15] Could he have stated more clearly that he himself has been "seduced" not by the way Don Juan behaves with women but by the way he behaves in the face of death? Bataille admits to being openly seduced only when Don Juan, forgetting the *odor di femmina*, finally flares quavering nostrils over his own corpse, as Michelet did in the latrine where he went to breathe in inspiration.[16]

DON JUAN'S TOMB

Perhaps a supplementary step is called for here.

Bataille's *Story of the Eye*, a kind of erotic *Pieds nickelés*,[17] is deliberately placed under the sign of Don Juan. The second part of the narrative takes place in Spain, where, after Marcelle's death, the young heroes find it more convenient to "avoid the bother of a police investigation." Sir Stephen awaits them on the other side of the border, ready to fund the next phase of their excesses. They are first seen in Madrid, at the bull ring, where they witness the death of Granero, who is enucleated by a bull's horns. This accident plunges the trio into trances that continue to haunt them through the following chapter, after they have left Madrid for the southerly sensuality of Seville. The theater of the five concluding chapters, Seville is the birthplace of Don Juan. But the events of the story are situated with even more precision: they occur not simply in the city where Don Juan was born, but in the church where he was buried. A plaque indicates the location of "the tomb of the church's founder, who the guides claimed was Don Juan."[18] This convergence is reinforced even further in the second edition of *Story of the Eye*, to which Bataille assigns a fictitious date and place: "Seville, 1940."

The reference to the commemorative plaque on the porch of the Church of Charity constitutes, to my knowledge, the first mention of Don Juan in any of Bataille's texts—a detail that is not without interest. Thus, for Bataille, Don Juan first appears in the form of a dead man. This scene reverses the traditional cemetery scene: the dead man is not the one whom those familiar with the legend were expecting. The tomb was supposed to be the Commander's; however, Don Juan has taken his place.

In 1936, in "The Sacred Conspiracy" (*Acéphale*'s manifesto for its namesake "secret society"), Bataille returns to Don Juan's tomb. The decor is no longer that of a church, but Bataille nevertheless proclaims (in a very un-Don-Juan-like formula): "We are ferociously religious." The context, moreover, is still Spanish: *Acéphale*'s manifesto is datelined from Tossa, where Bataille had gone to meet the painter André Masson. While Bataille was contemplating some figures drawn by him as possible emblems for the periodical, Masson played a recording of *Don Giovanni.* Bataille unhesitatingly identifies the phantasmic composition that arose from the unexpected encounter between Mozart's music and Masson's figures: "At this very moment," he notes, "I am watching this acephalic being, this intruder composed of two equally excited obsessions, become the 'Tomb of Don Giovanni.'"[19]

The convocation is a fatal one for Don Juan. The intruder is not Don Juan himself (that rationalism which refuses to lose its head) but his tomb: *Acéphale*, an intruder like the Commander, is Don Juan's tomb. We know that Bataille placed the Acéphale enterprise under the sign of Nietzsche. This surpassing of Don Juan by way of his own tomb prefigures what "Sovereignty" later describes as the surpassing of Don Juan by Nietzsche.

MARX AND DON JUAN

Bataille's Don Juan thus oscillates oddly between the two positions to which the legend had shown him to be the most allergic: in *Story of the Eye* he is dead, while in *Blue of Noon* he is a necrophiliac.

Blue of Noon has been called "Bataille's *Don Juan*" for good reason.[20] Yet it is difficult to see Bataille's hero, the dark Troppmann, as the personal incarnation of celebration, of the unreserved orgy, who denies and divinely reverses, and so on, that Bataille insists on seeing in Don Juan, at least in the fragments of *Inner Experience* collected under the homonymous title "The Blue of Noon." Of all the characters of Bataille's novels, Troppmann is the one haunted by the most unpardonable, the most melancholic of necrophilias.

Troppmann is never presented explicitly as a Don Juan figure. Or rather (since the narrative is written in the first person), he never presents himself as Don Juan. But on three occasions he provokes, invites, or is visited by someone he calls the Commander: this second person authorizes the Don-Juanization of the first.

The first invitation occurs in the very brief Part One. One of the aphorisms that it comprises refers to events described in singularly cryptic terms. "Several days ago (not in any nightmare, but in fact), I came to a city that looked like the setting for a tragedy. One evening—I mention this only to laugh more cheerlessly—I was not alone as I drunkenly watched two old pederasts twirling as they danced (not in any dream, but in fact). In the middle of the night the *Commendatore* entered my room. That afternoon, as I was passing his grave, pride had incited me to extend him an ironic invitation. His unexpected arrival appalled me."[21]

The second reference to the Commander comes at the beginning of Part Two, during a conversation between Troppmann and Lazare. Back in Paris after having been abandoned by Dirty in Vienna, and manifesting a need for intimacy by which he himself is the first to be astonished, Troppmann lays bare the complications of his emotional life before the "dirty virgin" of the far left. Revealing his impotence and his necrophilic obsessions, he also describes a scene that took place in Vienna after Dirty's departure. He had gone back to his hotel; a summer storm was brewing; just as he opened the window to air out the room, a long black streamer half-detached from its pole started flapping in the street. Troppmann breaks off to ask: "You know about the black tablecloth on the supper table when Don Giovanni comes in?" Lazare: "What has that got to do with your streamer?" "Nothing, except that the tablecloth was black."[22]

This episode is repeated in the following chapter, in a scene that leaves no ambiguity about the character whose arrival is announced by the black tablecloth: not Don Juan but the Commander. The scene also makes it clear that the Commander is not an ordinary intruder: his intrusion is desired. Troppmann has invited him, and not for the first time. Xenie has come to take care of Troppmann, who is bedridden; as soon as she opens the window to air out his room, he is gripped by a wave of anxiety. "A tormented shadow abruptly fell out of the sunny sky, shaking and snapping in the window frame . . . In my daze, I thought that the man I called the *Commendatore* had come in. He would appear whenever I invited him."[23]

The difference in tone between *Story of the Eye* and *Blue of Noon* is obvious. We move from the picaresque unselfconsciousness of vacations to the existential pathos of the Revolution. From *Les pieds nickelés* to a cross between Dostoevsky and Heidegger. From the Spain of a thuggish Morand to a Spain that is already Malraux's.[24] The Roaring Twenties are over. The political innocence of *Story of the Eye* becomes flagrant once the tenor of the Spanish episodes in the two novels is compared. There is no indication in *Story of the Eye*, for example, that Spain was still ruled by a monarchy in 1922 (Granero's death occurred on May 7 of that year). In the section of *Blue of Noon* that takes place in Barcelona, the Catalan insurrection of October 1934 is not just background material; quite the contrary: the characters do the impossible in order to weave their own history into the weft of this fabric. Political angst has even caused bullfighting to disappear from the Spanish territory.

The resemblance between the novels' closing scenes is thus all the more striking. In each instance, a crisis associates a sexual outburst with the proximity of tombs. But even here the difference reappears at once, for the tombs bear very different connotations. In *Story of the Eye*, the tomb in question is Don Juan's—not a high spot of Marxism-Leninism. Whereas even though Trier is Marx's birthplace rather than his place of burial, the tombs of *Blue of Noon* can in many respects be associated with him. The scene does not end until his name has been pronounced. Returning to the streets of Trier with Dirty, Troppmann has Marx in mind. "I thought of little Karl Marx and of the beard he had, later, when he grew up. He was underground now, near London."[25]

The homology of the novels' decors must not be allowed to obscure their functional differences. Don Juan's tomb is not the occasion for the characters' first trance in *Story of the Eye*, whereas throughout *Blue of Noon* Troppmann has been incapable of possessing Dirty. He himself interprets his impotence as a necrophilic manifestation: he cannot possess her because she is not dead. It is at the edge of a tomb, this anti-Portnoy's promised land, that he finally penetrates her: "The earth beneath that body lay open like a grave; her naked cleft lay open to me like a freshly dug grave."[26] The date of the event explains why the day is auspicious: it is November 1, the day of the dead.[27] In other words, whereas Don Juan is the dead man in *Story of the Eye*, in *Blue of Noon* he is alive (but not well). Still, he revives only to become a necrophiliac; he emerges from his own grave only to make merry beside Marx's.

The twists Bataille inflicts on the legend do not spare the Commander, as we see during the night in Trent recounted in Part One of *Blue of Noon*. The *vecchio infatuato* responds indeed to Troppmann's invitation, but not by putting an end to the orgy; instead, he takes part in it. The Commander no longer bears any resemblance to an enforcer of laws: far from exacting a payment due, he pours oil on the fire, ups the ante in debauchery, and functions as an *agent provocateur* to push Don Juan toward lawbreaking. His approach sets off something like a sexual state of emergency, in which transgression takes on the force of law, and in which expenditure becomes the major imperative: the Commander institutes a terrorism of pleasure.

Bataille's Don Juan scenario thus modifies the legend on two crucial points: the Commander is contaminated by sexuality, and Don Juan by death (he becomes a necrophiliac). The conjunction of these two functions culminates in a later novel, *A Story of Rats*, whose narrator, Dianus, is also obsessed by a Commander with whom he is seeking to come into contact, like K. with the castle, or Marlow with Kurtz, through his daughter: "And the hope never left me, even here, that I would grip the stone hand of the Commander."[28] This father in fact occupies the position of primary seducer. As a "dead man" he is at the origin of Don Juan's desire. He is Don Juan's Don Juan, the original tempter who infiltrated Don Juan's libido with the necrophilic perversion.

The Don Juan–Commander duo ordinarily corresponds, as we have seen, to the interdiction-transgression apparatus. Don Juan represents celebration, unrepentant expenditure. Conversely, the Commander imposes respect for interdictions: he represents the world of seriousness, work, savings, salvation. The legend assigns him the task of announcing that the party is over, that the moment of reckoning is at hand. None of this is found in Bataille's Commander: no sooner does he appear than the orgy can begin.

But what are the implications of installing transgression in the place of interdiction?

THE XXX STORY (POLITICS AND SEXUALITY)

Don Juan's grave is politicized when it becomes Marx's. But this is not the only accessory that is charged with political connotations as it passes from *Story of the Eye* to *Blue of Noon*. The black streamer in Vienna, for example, echoes the sheet Marcelle suspends from her window in *Story of the Eye* ("the sheet promptly smacked in the gusts").[29] But the streamer in Vienna is a political sign: it was hung, as Troppmann explains, "in honor of Dollfuss's death."[30]

The assassination of the Austrian chancellor was a milestone in the rise of fascism in Europe. Starting with the riots in Linz and Vienna that coincided with the far-right uprisings in Paris in February 1934, Austria was increasingly threatened with an *Anschluss.* Because he opposed this prospect, Dollfuss was assassinated by pro-German Austrian Nazis on July 25, 1934. In the novel, Troppmann arrives in the Austrian capital the next day. The reference to Dollfuss not only makes it possible to date the scene; it also inscribes the scene within a system of political references.

As this political dimension belongs to the first appearance of the Commander in *Blue of Noon,* one might reintroduce the opposition between *Story of the Eye* and *Blue of Noon* within the latter novel itself by contrasting the apolitical Commander of Part One—the Commander of the night in Trent—with the politicized Commander of Part Two.

The night in Trent is undated. Part One, in which it appears, is undated. And it is difficult to join the two parts of the novel. Both are written in the first person, but these are heterogeneous first persons that give the impression of belonging to two unrelated textual systems. The first evokes a sexual obsession closed in on itself (whom is this first person addressing?). Through its function and tone (especially through the stress its first person lays on the desire to escape fiction, insisting that what is being said is not fictitious), it recalls the "Coincidences" section (Part Two) of *Story of the Eye,* "Coincidences" that here would precede the novel instead of coming after. In contrast, Part Two is presented in a sustained narrative style; moreover, as if for greater clarity, it is paired with Troppmann's recital of the events to Lazare.

Can a date be assigned to Part One? Can its relation to Part Two be spelled out? For this we need to go outside the novel itself. We have to abandon Troppmann for Bataille. From June to November 1934, Bataille kept a daily summary calendar of his meetings and travels. On May 22 Bataille received a letter that Laure had sent him from Bolzano; on May 23 he left Paris to meet her in the Dolomites, where she was vacationing with Boris Souvarine. He arrived in Bolzano that evening; the next day he went to Mezzo Corona, where he found Laure. They left for Trent (which is sometimes transcribed as 30, French *trente*). They set out to explore the Dolomites, it seems, from their base in Trent at the Hotel Bologna: they go to Andalo and Molveno. On May 28, a telephone call to or from S: Souvarine? Sunday, May 29: an excursion to Mezzo Corona, return to Trent: "buffet 30 statue of Dante, dinner at the Paon, pastry and choc[olate] cake. the little one is moving. Stavisky." Why does Bataille mention Stavisky, who died in January, nearly six months earlier? May 30:

"bath this morning on the tel[ephone] convince L[aure] to telegraph. the sacrifices and the two burials. dinner at the Paon. w[alk] and early return." The following day he arrives (alone? with Laure?) at the Innsbruck station, where he sees (and notes) "black streamers." No mention of a trip to Vienna or of Dollfuss' assassination.[31]

What date can be assigned to the events of the night in Trent?[32] When and where did Bataille invite that Commander? Who was he? Must these questions be answered? Must they even be asked? What makes the diary interesting is that it shows the proximity of the events to which the two parts of *Blue of Noon* are related. The Commander's two appearances are almost contiguous, as if the one were only the shadow of the other, or its echo: the night in Trent and the streamers of Vienna (or Innsbruck) are inseparable. The sexual Commander and the political Commander appear in the course of the same journey, no more than a few days apart; in sum, they are the two sides of a single scenario, its recto and its verso.[33] On the Italian side of the frontier, the Commander (sexual version) suddenly shows up in the hotel room in Trent when, on the Austrian side, the assassination of one of the last representatives of democracy in central Europe makes imminent the arrival of what we may call his "political" version.

IMPOTENCES

The simultaneity of the political and erotic motifs in *Blue of Noon* is worthy of note. Without ever being conflated, they go hand in hand, side by side, one echoing the other.

A further example of this simultaneity is found in the Troppmann-Lazare couple. At first glance, their incompatibility seems to offer an allegory for the incompatibility between politics and sexuality. Yet even if we were to accept this reading, these contradictory terms—sexuality and politics—would be defined by the same attribute. Each is characterized by impotence: Troppmann's impotence is sexual, Lazare's is political. Troppmann's sexuality, which always operates in proximity to death, is in many respects an allegory for the revolutionary energy that has likewise been flirting with death at least since 1933, since the advent of the totalitarian Holy Trinity known as Hitler, Stalin, and Mussolini.

Blue of Noon, a new *Armance*, is first of all a novel of impotence. Part

Two, which constitutes the narrative body of the novel, opens with a scene in which Troppmann is confessing his sexual impotence to Lazare. That scene is followed by a conversation during which Lazare confesses her political impotence, both directly and indirectly (through the intermediary of Monsieur Melou). She is throwing away her militancy on a socialism of despair condemned to gamble on its own defeat (on its own corpse, Bataille would say). Melou is the one who exposes her position. Given "the dead end to which history is being led," given "the collapsed socialist expectations," he explains, Lazare is drawn to the "heroic solution": that of joining the last pockets of working-class resistance, "thereby dooming ourselves to an inescapable and fruitless death." The same outcome is implied in the episode during the Catalan uprising, when Lazare tries to convince the insurgents to break into a prison instead of attacking a weapons depot to seize arms for the workers. It so happens that Troppmann is the only one who approves.[34] He senses that Lazare is all the more committed to the revolution because the revolution is committed to an impasse, that she is in solidarity with the workers' movement precisely to the extent that this movement is condemned to "an inescapable and fruitless death." The movement has one foot in the grave already; it is on the point of "burying itself." We know that Simone Weil, on whom the character of Lazare is modeled, was a militant along with Bataille in Souvarine's Democratic Communist Circle. In a note, Bataille comments on her positions: "So it seems that S. W. has been led to play the role of describing the impasses socialism has encountered, and of condemning it to die in a street fight or a penitentiary."[35]

These positions do not differ fundamentally from those expressed by Bataille himself in texts dating from the same period (which was the most intensely politicized phase of his life). All his contributions to *La critique sociale* posit as a certainty the imminent victory of fascism. The question he raises is not how to prevent the triumph of fascism but what to do in a world in which fascism has triumphed. The events related in *Blue of Noon* begin a few weeks after the February 1934 uprisings. The "taking of the Concorde," on February 6, had struck him as the portent of catastrophe, and his detailed account of the following days attributes an important role to the international configuration in which the Paris events are subsumed: the Nazi takeover in Germany, the threat of civil war in Spain and Austria. Like Lazare and Monsieur Melou, Bataille sees "no way out": "From all sides, in a world in which it will soon be impossible to breathe, the fascist noose is drawing tighter."[36]

However, this "absence of a way out" offers a unique opportunity for revolutionary consciousness to ascend to a realm that can only be called Don-Juanesque (or rather Nietzscheo–Don Juanesque): in this realm, a Marxism without hope, a Marxism suddenly permeable to the tragic, gains access to what Bataille soon comes to call joy in the face of death. The year before (September 1933) Bataille had described the disorientation of the workers' movements that were being subjected, in "the three servile societies" (Germany, Italy, and Russia), to "the most imperious masters of all those who had ever reduced them to submission." Such disorientation presumably cannot open onto any practical perspective; it can lead only to anguish. But anguish has become the revolutionary affect par excellence, the distraught summit of revolt; it is infinitely more revolutionary than any strategy, any planmaking optimism. Revolutionaries no longer have a choice, can no longer draw back in the face of an uncertain future. "As is the case with any anxious passion, it [revolutionary consciousness] is liberated and expanded by the consciousness of possible death."[37] Don Juan does not recoil, either, as death approaches. But at the edge of the grave, facing the absolute master, he gives Leporello his leave.

After the events of February 1934, Bataille planned to write a book titled *Le fascisme en France.* From his draft I have excerpted three propositions: (1) "The liberal world in which we still live is already a world of old men who are losing their teeth, a world of appearances"; (2) the Western workers' movement, "moribund and wretched today, is almost unable to struggle any longer except against itself"; (3) but still, owing to the contamination of class consciousness by unhappiness of conscience, "it has become possible—moving beyond those forces that are already subjecting all men everywhere to their empire—to belong in ecstasy *to death.*"[38] This last proposition is the concluding sentence in the manuscript of *Le fascisme en France.* Bataille abandoned that project in order to write *Blue of Noon,* the novel in which, over and above the self-liquidation of the workers' movement, the protagonists Troppmann and Lazare are on the side of death. The condition of possibility for this political and tragic Don Juanism is thus the establishment of a totalitarian regime, one that has subjugated all humanity. For Bataille, transgression will always presuppose a completed totalization; it is a matter of a post-totalitarian (or postrevolutionary?) gesture that can be accomplished only on the basis of a totalitarian state of affairs or the anticipation of such a state (the postulate of the end of history). Transgression takes place only above all, after all. And even over all, *surtout*, precisely in the sense in which Bataille speaks of an overall fascism, a superfascism. Don Juan brings himself up to Nietzsche's level only when he says no to everything.

But who is the Commander?

DON JUAN AND COMMUNISM

The overall project to which the posthumous dossier of "Sovereignty" corresponds confirms the totalitarian version of the Commander. "Sovereignty," undertaken immediately after Stalin's death, in March 1953, is first of all a reflection on Communism, "which is its [sovereignty's] most active contradiction."[39] Let us recall that Bataille developed his parallel between Don Juan and Nietzsche precisely as part of this project.

"The Commander," Bataille writes, "would triumph only if his murderer acknowledged him as being in possession of the truth."[40] At no point did Bataille acknowledge the truth of fascism. This is not the case for Communism: for Bataille, Marxism had a monopoly on reason from the time it lost its revolutionary affect in the early 1930s. Consequently, unlike the pre-Nietzschean Don Juan of the legend, Bataille's Don Juan provokes a Commander whose truth he acknowledges. "The attitude of the communist," Bataille writes, "is in fact the major position, to which anticommunism opposes only a line of insignificant positions."[41] Before the greater reason of Marxism, anti-Communism can appeal only to a narrow, lesser rationality. Thus for Bataille it is a matter not of opposing Marxism but of surpassing it. What can be done in confronting someone who is right? It is not a matter of justifying oneself before that person, still less of being right in contradistinction to that person; one must accede, owing to that person, to increased culpability. Communism is necessary to Bataille's Don Juanism because it is the only doctrine that ensures an increase in guilt.

The argument with the proletarian Commander in "Sovereignty" has as its real object the relations between literature and Communism interpreted as the destiny of the modern world. The final section, which was intended as the conclusion, is thus called "The Literary World and Communism." In the literary realm, Bataille limits his focus to Nietzsche and Kafka. *Literature and Evil*, published in 1957, raises the same issues anew within the framework of a discussion of Sartre's theses on commitment.

Bataille's starting point is a double postulate according to which action alone has rights and literature does not have practical truth as its aim. The problem of literature, therefore, is to know in the face of whom, deprived as it is of any right, it agrees to be guilty.

Communism, according to Bataille, introduced into the "consciousness of the most sensitive men" an unprecedented rift between "what they love and what they affirm."[42] Left-wing intellectuals, Communists or fellow travelers, generous souls who are sensitive to the rights of others, are inspired by a desire for social justice that keeps them from defending the values (of distinction) to which their bourgeois origin makes them cling (a "painting," a "poem," a "passion," an "excessive joy"). "Values that don't have their place close to mine shafts [do not] deserve to be defended."[43] These people do not defend their own values, nor do they adopt the (working-class) values they are defending. Hence the rift between their affirmations and their tastes. But Bataille goes further in analyzing the reasons that keep bourgeois intellectuals from asserting their *right* to love what they love, their right to defend an aesthetic of distinction. The official reason is the urgency of other tasks: working for social justice, bringing literacy to the proletariat, righting class wrongs, and so on. Bourgeois tastes will remain objectively impossible to defend so long as the harm done by the class struggle is not overcome. But behind this official justification Bataille suggests a different one: those tastes would lose their savor if they were defended. If they were defendable. If they became a right. In other words, men of taste are with the Communists because Communism alone makes their tastes impossible to defend. Members of the middle class, greedier, clenched in their own anguished self-centeredness, seek to universalize the distinctive values of their class. Fellow travelers, in Bataille's view, do just the opposite: the proletarianization of the universe is the unexpected opportunity that absolves them once and for all from defending the singularity of their own tastes. Not because they are innocent, but because they no longer have to defend themselves for being guilty.

"Up to now I have spoken of Nietzsche; now I shall speak of Kafka."[44] A few lines after this declaration of intent, the manuscript of "Sovereignty" breaks off: the discussion of Kafka that it announces will be part of *Literature and Evil*.[45] Here Bataille returns to the question raised in a French Communist periodical shortly after the Prague coup: "Should

Kafka be burnt?" He begins by making the question less provocative: How else might a Marxist regime use Kafka's work? "The idea of burning Kafka—even as a hypothetical project, a joke—on the part of the Communists was logical—and even exceptionally logical."[46] But Bataille's whole effort is aimed at bringing this implication of a Communist logic into convergence with the logic of Kafka's work itself. We recall Don Juan's death: flames erupt everywhere, the Commander plunges him into the inferno. But with what is Don Juan burning? With what was Kafka burning? The dilemma recalls what are said to be Kafka's last words, addressed to his doctor: "Doctor, if you don't kill me, you are an assassin." Mysticism was dying for want of dying. Kafka was burning to burn. His only problem was the origin of the flames. Would they come from within or from without? He asked for fire, but did not want to take charge of it. Were the Communists to respond to these last wishes more faithfully than Max Brod? One may suppose so, if one grants Bataille's conclusion its full weight: "If the adult gives a major sense to childishness, if he writes with the feeling that he is touching a sovereign value, he has no place in Communist society."[47] According to Bataille, this exclusion is the perverse and paradoxical reason why Communist society corresponds better than any other to the secret wishes of a writer like Kafka—who always harbored a profound desire for a society that denied him the right to exist.

In Bataille's eyes, Kafka's example emblematizes the movement of modern literature, which awaits the advent of Communist society because only a Communist regime guarantees that literature will never establish a secure place for itself, that it will never reach the promised land. This schema unifies the set of studies constituting *Literature and Evil.* Literature, which is childhood rediscovered, is by the same token obliged to plead guilty. Speaking of Baudelaire, for example, Bataille says that the poet "chose to be guilty, like a child." For rediscovered childhood is childhood that has lost its primal innocence. This guilty childhood, which might be called a grown-up childhood, is the one with which literature is identified. The pleasures of such a childhood are indefensible. But condemning them does not imply giving them up: the demand for guilt goes without repentance. The guilty party is impenitent. Obviously, Bataille's whole analysis is rooted in a metaphor. Kafka had nothing directly to do with Communism as such. Still, in the contradictory negotiations undertaken between Kafka's work and the paternal sphere, Bataille sees an allegorical anticipation of the process to which literature is exposed in the Communist world: Kafka "did not want to oppose the father who had even taken the possibility of living from him."[48]

RETURNS OF THE PRODIGAL FATHER

The superego appears like a rat, sensual, cruel.

Jean Laplanche, *L'angoisse*

The model for Bataille's earliest sociopolitical analyses is naively Oedipal: at the heart of the capitalist system, the proletariat is in the position of a son whose father prevents him from satisfying his own desires. Bataille develops this equation in summarizing an article on "family life" that he and Jean Bernier were preparing for *Contre-Attaque:* "The basis for social morality in the capitalist regime is the morality imposed by parents on children."[49] The same idea is expressed in a text intended for inclusion in "La notion de dépense" (The Notion of Expense): "The contradiction between the prevailing social conceptions and society's real needs brings devastatingly to mind the narrowness of judgment that makes the father oppose the satisfaction of his son's needs."[50] Yet the father in question is responsible, not repressive. He does not stand in the way of his son's "real" needs; on the contrary, he does everything he can to satisfy those needs that have to do with the son's own good, with his future. But the father remains deaf to the son's phantasmic needs, the ones that lead to unproductive expense. This father, precisely because he is good, opposes only what makes his son "feverish."

The class struggle reenacts the struggle between generations: proletarian energy is repressed by the paternalism of bourgeois power. This homology leads to an identification—one that is just barely metaphorical—between the working class and human genitals. The identification is particularly apparent in "The Solar Anus": "Communist workers appear to the bourgeois to be as ugly and dirty as hairy sexual organs, or lower parts."[51] Many of the political positions Bataille adopted are modeled on this schema, which sees the proletariat as a cauldron of untamed energy. The resultant solidarity with the proletariat owes nothing to a concern for social justice or for economic rationality. It is a libidinal solidarity: all those, whatever their class, who wish to extricate themselves from the bourgeois regime of castration find themselves necessarily led to join the ranks of the working class. A "form of intellectual activity, not yet castrated and domesticated, is linked by the force of things" to the current "uprising of the lower classes."[52]

According to this schema, the class struggle pits an infantile proletarian sexuality against a desexualized capitalist maturity (adult genitalization transforms sexuality into a productive expenditure that is equivalent to its desexualization). But this Oedipal account soon becomes ensnared in a more complex game. Bataille never completely abandons his fantasy of a proletariat, or rather the fantasy of an oversexualized underproletariat: in 1948 this schema still governs his reflections, inspired by the Kinsey report, on the links between the criminal underworld and sexuality.[53] It has nevertheless been altered in one detail: the position that this sexualization confers on the proletariat in the Oedipal schema. The uncastratable son is transformed into a lubricious father. The wild child of the first schema is metamorphosed into a sort of prodigal father, an Ubu-like Commander who has a monopoly on transgression. Here we should recall that the Kafka article identified the Communist world with the paternal sphere.

In 1927—when *Story of the Eye* and "The Solar Anus" appeared, and while their author was undergoing psychoanalysis with Adrien Borel—Bataille recorded a dream, then jotted down some associations:

> In the street, in front of the house where we lived in Reims. I am leaving by bicycle, paved street and tramway tracks, very awkward for the bicycle, paved street you don't know whether to ride on the right or the left. Proliferation of tramway tracks. I narrowly miss a tram but there is no accident. I would like to arrive at the place where after a turn there is a smooth road but from here on it is undoubtedly too late and the admirable smooth road on which you ride then go back down with built-up speed is now paved. Indeed, when I turn the road is no longer the way it was before they are redoing it but to redo it they have transformed it into a huge trench out of which come some very large [missing word}. I notice these strong supports but more and more I see them in precarious forms first that they are formed with barrel carcasses of disjoined wood in circles that will have to be filled with earth, then more and more the disjoined barrels to be set up. They are proceeding as follows extremely brutal and virile and even frightfully black cellar workers arrive to set up the long, thin,

> shaky barrel. At this moment it becomes frightfully dark; I move about in the form of an American gentleman. In order to set up the barrel it is necessary to pull on thick black ropes of soot from which animals are hung, like hideous huge rats, by their tails but which threaten to bite, but they have to be killed. The cellar workers take great pleasure in their contact with these unspeakable things which they are stringing up joyfully but the American visitor in the suit risks getting spots on himself and getting bitten and he is more than a little disgusted and even terrified. However, he holds up with difficulty the bloody viscous fish or dead but threatening rats at the level of his face.[54]

The structure of this dream lends itself to the bipolar schema of the class struggle: the proletarians appear as underground workers, midway between the gravedigger and the old mole. The workers of Mallarmé's "Conflit" were already laborers, diggers in the dirt; here, they belong to the variety of the species found in Reims, men who work in cellars. Unlike Mallarmé's prose poem, this dream does not relate any explicit act of aggression. The presence of workers is enough nevertheless to bring to bear a threat. The dream does not say (nor does the dreamer) whether this threat is desired or not. But we see someone taking the risk of soiling himself through contact with what "The Solar Anus" calls the lower, dirty, hairy parts of society. Moreover, in this visiting "American gentleman" who quakes in fear for the integrity of his suit it is not hard to see a prefiguration of Troppmann, with the tanned hands and light-colored clothes that he wears in the middle of a revolution.

Oddly enough, the problematics of the class struggle, so apparent in the manifest content of the dream, is totally absent from the associations that Bataille appends to it; an Oedipal problematics appears in its place. The "cellar workers" are not even mentioned. "When I wake up," Bataille says, "I associate the horror of rats with the memory of my father administering a punishment in the form of a bloody toad into which a vulture (my father) is plunging his beak." We know that "Coincidences" in *Story of the Eye*, contemporaneous with the dream narrative, sketches a painful, obscene, repulsive portrait of that father, a tragically grotesque portrait that is not lacking in grandeur. We must presumably look to this portrait to find the operator of the substitution in question. Bataille's father, who was blind, lived in a darkness comparable to the darkness imposed on the cellar workers by their underground environment. This blindness, moreover, has a sexual dimension, since Bataille, at least in his fantasy, attributes it to syphilis. "However," he adds, "the very contrary of most male babies, who are in love with their mothers, I was in love with my father."[55]

This sexualization of the paternal figure does not diminish any of its authority. Its obscenity only renders its imperious aspects more virulent. But what makes the dreamer feel guilty? Let us note that Bataille says nothing about the fault for which he was being punished. Does it have anything to do with the suit? But why would a suit be guilty of being clean? One soon has the impression that the imperative corrects only because, naively, that is what it wants to do. It seems that the lesson administered to Bataille is not so much aimed at the son's good as at the executor's pleasure. The paternal agency here no longer represses the child's sexuality; on the contrary, it imprints the violence of its own sexuality on the child. No doubt the dreamer already feels threatened by the ("hideous") rats that the cellar workers are handling. However, the pinnacle of horror is reached only at the moment when, in this story of rats, "joy" (joy at confronting the rats) and "great pleasure" appear on the workers' faces ("The fact is, you see," said Proust as quoted by Bataille, "I need enormous rats")—joy and pleasure experienced by the "extremely brutal and virile" proletarians through their handling of these unspeakable living creatures. The young bourgeois in the guilty suit is terrorized by the pleasure of the Commander he desires: guilty owing to his pleasure, guilty of his pleasure.

Bataille returns to the scenario of the Oedipus complex in "The Critique of the Foundations of the Hegelian Dialectic." The Oedipal dialectic begins with the formation of the son's desire for his father's death. The son wishes for the disappearance of the repressive agency that opposes the satisfaction of his own desires. However, this referential aggressiveness is only the initial stage in a process that leads the son toward the revelation of the truth of his desire. He soon discovers that it is for himself that he desires the death he was projecting onto the other. The son desires his father's death, Bataille writes, but his own aggressive wishes have "repercussions on the son's personality: he tries to bring down castration on himself" in reaction to "the shock of his own death wishes."[56] Don Juan has to kill the Commander if he wants his phantom to reduce him to nothingness in return. The decisive episode in the destiny of the aggressive drive is the moment when it turns back on itself, when the drive turns back on its source, spills back onto its subject. The circle is completed in castrational pleasure: if Bataille's Oedipus complex passes, in the classic fashion, through the death of the father, this is not because the son wants to secure exclusive possession of the mother for himself; it is because only a dead father can inflict on him the punishment he desires.

We know how Freud presents the (masculine) fantasy—"I am being beaten by my father"—as derived from a primitive fantasy—"I am loved by my father"—by way of a degenitalizing sado-anal regression: the chastisement is not only "the punishment for the forbidden genital relation, but also the regressive substitute for that relation."[57] A father strikes his child. The punishment set into play by this fantasy, an indissoluble blend of eroticism and guilt, is upheld by the anachronism of a logic that excludes all difference between pleasure and its punishment, between punishment and its pleasure. Punishment ceases to be referential at the very instant when it has no other justification besides punishing the pleasure that it procures, that is, producing the pleasure that it punishes. It punishes a pleasure that would not have occurred without it. Bataille does not spell out why his father chastises him, in his dream. But there may not be any reason. The most impenitent of guilty parties are those guilty of no fault, those guilty ones whose whole crime stems from the pleasure they take in the chastisement that punishes them for it.

Thus at the dark heart of the general economy and of the notion of expenditure there is a story of rats, in which a father gives himself over to the homosexual and incestuous rape of his son. This motif could be pursued in several directions. It will suffice here to recall to what extent it breaks with the simple Oedipal outlook of the initial schema. There Bataille was exhorting bourgeois intellectuals to line up on the side of the proletariat so as to escape from the regime of castration that is the law in their class of origin. The positions and movements of the final schema are no different, but their motivations are strictly reversed. The bourgeois intellectual continues to turn toward the proletariat, but the goal is no longer to evade castration; on the contrary the goal is to seek it out, as the object of desire. But it is also the case that castration no longer intervenes to punish a prior sexuality; rather, it constitutes the test that introduces the body to the regime of sexuality. And the proletariat, by this token, instead of incarnating a sexuality that would expend itself in complete ignorance of castration, constitutes the imperative and obscene agency that sexualizes the man in the suit by marking him with a glorious cut.[58]

5

UNSATISFIED DESIRE

At the beginning of *Inner Experience*, Bataille refers somewhat ironically to the "laudable concern of creating a book." *Guilty* is not really a book—and even though it consists of notes written on a daily basis, it is not really what we usually call a diary either. Rather, it is an experimental document, a protocol of spiritual exercises undertaken in the context of a nonreligious mysticism and based on various meditation techniques. *Guilty* is the rapid, contemporaneous recording and transcription of an experience whose disquieting shock waves affected Bataille throughout the war years.

Bataille, who wrote a great deal, always manifested a peculiar negligence with regard to books. The shorthand style he uses in *Guilty* transcribes something infinitely more urgent than the project—laudable or not—of writing a book. He does not set out to systematize his thought or develop a narrative; he does not try to demonstrate, persuade, or carve out a place for himself. Instead, he jots down—transcribes on the spot—an experience as elusive as it is urgent, as imperious as it is ungraspable (he refers to "fingers that do not take hold"). If the term "writer" means simply a person who produces books, then perhaps Bataille does not belong among the ranks of the great writers. And yet the rigor of his often anxious, sometimes insolent indifference to literature positions his writings among the major events in twentieth-century language: a throttled, ragged voice struggling in the labyrinth of language.

"The date I start (September 5, 1939) is no coincidence."[1] *Guilty* does not belong to the category of works we call war literature. Nevertheless, the experience it transcribes is linked to current events in a way that is both essential and strange. For Sartre, the war provides the opportunity to adopt a militant seriousness, to commit himself to the production of meaning. For Bataille, the war is accompanied by an impression—conceivably a scandalous impression—of lightness. He does not go to war; he lives war. There is nothing of the soldier or activist about him. "Heroism," he notes, "is an evasive posture." War, a primary form of ignorance about the future, entails first of all the suspension of plans. A catalyst of anguish, war condemns human beings to the irremediable disorientation of the labyrinth, to a glorious intoxication in the face of life's incompleteness. Not that Bataille takes war lightly; rather, war takes him lightly. He no longer speaks of revolution, which is a determination to make disruptions meaningful. In war, the law of struggle, ontological discord, is laid bare. The unbearable lightness of being: war is one of the names for what Bataille elsewhere calls agony.[2] "These feelings are alien to 'men of war,'" he writes. "War is an activity that meets their needs. They press ahead in order to avoid anguish."

Why the title, *Guilty?* Bataille often puts the word in quotation marks, as if he were citing or borrowing. The term in fact refers to the world of Kafka (whose name appears several times in the book). The lightness with which Bataille experiences the war recalls the offhandedness with which K., in *The Trial*, neglects to take care of his own affairs, even though they are quite serious matters. We know nothing at all about the initial accusation. But the behavior of the accused makes up for this lacuna, substituting an undeniable and unrepentant failure to assist someone (himself) in danger. K. wastes his time in childish pursuits (this is Bataille's term, in the chapter on Kafka in *Literature and Evil*), does not take his difficulties seriously enough—or rather he forgets them, paying less attention to his lawyers' vanity than to their secretaries' charms. He does not take himself seriously enough.

The notes out of which *Guilty* is constructed show that Bataille is prey to the same methodical distraction. Guilty: "As I approached the summit . . . everything got confused. At the decisive moment there's always something else to do." Guilty: "Start out . . . forget it . . . don't conclude. As far as I'm concerned that's the right method and the only one able to deal with objects that resemble *it.*" Guilty: "I've often thought that at the summit of existence there could be only insignificance." Guilty: "Blouses undone, afternoon laughter, the sun shines down on me with deadly laughter, rousing a wasp's stinger in me."

A ladybug alights on a piece of paper where Bataille has outlined (no doubt during one of Alexandre Kojève's lectures) the architecture of the Hegelian system. The insect wanders from chapter to chapter, from category to category. Somewhere else, a train pulls into a station. What does it all mean? These random events are wounds inflicted on the system. They distract from the conclusion. In a completed universe, accidents go unnoticed. Incidents, anecdotes distract the world from its end. Bataille returns to this notion again and again: in a completed universe, these nonevents would have no claim on our attention; they would carry less weight than the system that brings completion. Such nicks in a narrative are inductors of incompleteness. In picking them up, the seismograph of *Guilty* registers the light shocks of nonmeaning.

(What happens, pure happiness, is insignificant. Thus philosophy will always prefer sadness, which at least has the advantage of meaning something, or else—but it comes down to the same thing—which suffers from being unable to mean anything. Sadness addresses the need for meaning, respects it, satisfies it. It is understood and shared. People understand each other through sadness. Sadness is a medium for collective immersion. It sounds the keynote of all communions. But Bataille argued, against Camus, that happiness does without hope. Pure happiness is not gregarious; it is not shared. The lesson of the "gay science" holds that the truth of a trace lies in the smile that effaces it, in the lightness of the laughter that dissolves it.)

When Bataille wrote the first sentence of *Guilty*, he had been dispersing his energy on a variety of projects for some ten years. Starting in the surrealist era, he had been an active figure in the Parisian literary avant-garde. He had directed journals *(Documents, Acéphale);* he had taken part in the activities of various political and literary groups such as Souvarine's Democratic Communist Circle, Contre-Attaque, and, just before the war broke out, the College of Sociology. The surviving articles, manifestos and lectures from this intense, agitated, and productive period make up the first two volumes of Bataille's *Oeuvres complètes,* a thousand pages all bearing witness to an astonishing lucidity, audacity, and provocative power. Curiously enough, there are no books. Bataille's disparate prewar texts, which he himself neglected for more than thirty years, lay buried in obscure journals and were rediscovered only after Bataille's death.

Bataille suffered from his lack of recognition. The powerful and influential intellectual trends of the past twenty years owe him so much (owe him indeed, paradoxically, so much of their own influence) that we ourselves may have some difficulty believing that his work received so little acknowledgment in his own day. The aesthetic of formlessness developed in the *Documents* articles, the general economy contained in the notion of expenditure, the interpretation of fascism he developed in 1933—these early texts did have readers, but very few. The College of Sociology represented Bataille's attempt to break out of his isolation and earn recognition for the seriousness of his thought. By exposing his views in a systematic way, Bataille thought he might finally command respect for the notions around which his system and his obsessions revolved (the ambiguity of the sacred as a simultaneous focus of attraction and repulsion, the way experience puts the subject at stake, the sacrificial dimension of knowledge). But then the war broke out. And at this level, too, the war put an end to Bataille's project: he had hoped that the College of Sociology would bring him some of the recognition he thought he might already have earned. Once the war had started, however, he put the matter behind him.

On September 5, 1939, at the age of forty-two, Bataille set down in his notebook the opening line of what was to become *Guilty.* The difference between *Guilty* and Bataille's prewar texts can be described in topographical or geographical terms. His prewar writing had had a Parisian focus: the texts had to do with the intellectual life of the avant-garde and its discoveries, its passions, its quarrels. In contrast, most of the notebooks that went into *Guilty* were written in the country. After coming down with tuberculosis, Bataille took medical leave and moved to Vézelay. In *Guilty,* in a succession of aphorisms, a regular rhythm summons up the countryside—hills, clouds, the sun's movements, nights, and the sky—in quick, sketchy phrases. Set alongside more abstract notions, this rhythm captures one component of the experience and gives his mysticism a romantic, rustic note. But there is yet another way to characterize the difference in locale. Bataille's prewar texts were open letters or lectures, tracts or manifestos, texts that are quite forcefully addressed to an audience: their second person form is often the imperative. The notes in *Guilty*, however, are part of a much more complex communicative strategy. Their addressee is harder to decipher.

The manifesto Bataille wrote for the College of Sociology was called "The Sorcerer's Apprentice."[3] It began with a theorem: "The Absence of Need [Is] More Wretched than the Absence of Satisfaction." Kojève, the Hegel scholar, had described the impasses to which the desire for recognition led, a desire that for him constituted the definition of man: desire, that is, lack of satisfaction—desire rather than its satisfaction—is what allows man to assert himself, to distinguish himself from animals. In an appendix to *Guilty*, Bataille included a shortened version of a letter he had written to Kojève after one of Kojève's talks at the College of Sociology. In the revision process, Bataille significantly modified the letter's import, in a way that sheds light on the rupture caused by the war. In the first and longer version, Bataille's starting point is Kojève's hypothesis about the end of history.[4] There is nothing left for man to do; in a sense his fate has already run its course; history is over ("except for the dénouement"). What is he to do now with his freedom—that is, his negativity—if he has nothing more to use it on, nothing to deny, nothing to transform? The first version of the letter offers an optimistic response. All man can do with his newly unemployed freedom is to try to get it recognized. When the time for transforming the world is over, when political and technological action have played out their role in history, negation of the world goes beyond art and religion to take unproductive forms. The Popular Front had reduced the work week and launched a broad-based politics of leisure. In the first draft of his letter, Bataille sketches out a populist version of the notion of expenditure: unemployed negativity has a role to play on the terrain of what he calls "using free time." But the second version of the letter is far less positive. In revising the text for its inclusion in *Guilty*, Bataille leaves out any suggestion that the desire for recognition might possibly be satisfied. It is out of the question that unused negativity could ever be acknowledged. The experience of negativity (or of desire) is now bound up with a radical solitude. "No one, in fact," he writes to Professor X, "could 'recognize' a height that is as dark as night. A few facts—such as the exceptional difficulty experienced in making myself be 'recognized' (on the simple level at which others are 'recognized')—have led me to assume the hypothesis of an irrevocable insignificance, seriously though cheerfully."[5]

Might Bataille have put behind him, in leaving Paris, what Kojève had called the struggle for recognition? *Guilty* is the transcription, the communication, the at once distracted and rigorous recognition, of what is not recognizable. Of the negligible character and ultimate insignificance of what allows itself to be recognized. An experience that detects what is lost in communication. "These notes link me to my fellow men like Ariadne's thread, and everything else strikes me as futile. Still, I would not want any of my friends to read them." Not long afterward, Sartre would connect the experience of shame with the feeling a subject has when exposed to the gaze of others. Bataille here associates friendship and guilt in a similar way: I recognize my friends by the shame I experience at the idea that they will read what I write.[6] Friends are by definition indiscreet: I cannot imagine a friend's reading what I write without feeling shame. Anyone who makes me ashamed of writing is my friend—anyone who makes the friendly gesture of reading what I did not write for him.

Bataille himself is probably responsible for proposing *A Tale of Gratified Desire*, a title associated with a Blake poem, for the 1953 English translation of *Story of the Eye*. He had already quoted this poem in *Guilty*, one section of which is called "Gratified Desire": "In a wife I would desire / What in whores is always found / The lineaments of Gratified Desire."[7] (He quotes the same lines again in his essay on Blake in *Literature and Evil.*) But this desire for satisfaction, formulated in the conditional ("I would desire"), is never itself satisfied. "Desire is eager never to be satisfied." True desire is desire for desire, and not for its own satisfaction. True desire is the experience of the emptiness of satisfaction.

In Bataille's work, eroticism does not accompany the fullness of sexual communion. The absence of satisfaction is its crucial feature. Sexuality is first of all the experience of what separates human beings. "I know that satisfaction does not satisfy." The sentences of *Guilty*—which are often fragmentary, suggesting the beauty of ruins ("incomplete successes")—sing a hymn to incompleteness that culminates in the final alleluia, a suffocated version of the Song of Songs. Here the two appendixes included in *Guilty* (which is the second volume of the *Somme athéologique* [Atheological

Summa])—the letter to Kojève and *L'alleluiah*—find their common ground.

Guilty is the first book by Bataille I ever bought. An erroneous reference in an introductory work on existentialism written, I have been told, by a Jesuit, had caught my attention: "J'enseigne à tourner l'angoisse en délire [I teach the art of turning anguish to delirium]." It took me years to discover that this was a typographic error. But I was at an age at which *délire* is more promising than *délices* (delight). *Inner Experience*, from which that quotation came, did not turn up in any bookstore. But one store did have *Guilty*, by the same author. The paper was yellowed, even though the pages had not been cut. I had the impression I was buying an old book, a volume from another era. Written before I was born. And yet, between the publication of the book and my purchase, only fifteen years had elapsed. Bataille was still alive. I have had that book for thirty years.

Around the same time, I spent several days in the Auvergne, on a farm whose new Parisian owner wanted to reconstruct the keep around which it had been built. The former owner, a relative of the new one, I think, had just died. The books that had been left lying around in several rooms suggested that the owner had been a cultivated woman: there were English novels, fine editions, books that had won literary prizes. What was *Guilty* doing in that collection? I never found out. The town nearest this hamlet was Billom. I later learned that Bataille was born there. He passed through Billom during the exodus, and certain fragments of *Guilty* were written on the spot. No other book has ever given me such a powerful impression of being impregnated with the atmosphere, the humidity, of war.

6

ON EQUIVOCATION BETWEEN LITERATURE AND POLITICS

Never, it seems, were political concepts subject to more ambiguity.

Zeev Sternhell, *Neither Right nor Left*

In June 1989 French voters were handed a list of candidates for the European Parliament running on the ticket of Jean-Marie Le Pen's far-right National Front party.[1] Those with the patience to read as far down as the thirtieth name came across a certain Jules Monnerot, identified as a "founder of the College of Sociology." Was this a clever ploy or a foolhardy stratagem? Did the reference to the College of Sociology win any votes for the party of the far right? Did it cost them any? How many voters—and how many of Le Pen's voters—had any idea what the College of Sociology was, or had been? In any event, the institution in question, a sleeping beauty that erudite sorcerers' apprentices had been struggling for some years to awaken, finally made its entrance into the world of real politics. And, dissipating all ambiguity, it confirmed the worst suspicions.

Accusations of ideological ambiguity appear with the very earliest published references to the activities of the College. For example, in *Europe*, a journal situated more or less on the left, René Bertelé calls Roger Caillois's positions "equivocal." He does not doubt the honesty of the writer's intentions. Nevertheless, he asks, what would happen if Caillois's texts fell into Hitler's hands? "It should be reasonably brought to Roger Caillois's attention that he is running this risk."[2]

The adjective "equivocal" and its semantic neighbors "ambiguous," "ambivalent," and so on, are symptomatic of an uneasiness that shows up time and again in the vicinity of the College. And, in a way, the intentions behind the use of these terms are beside the point; it does not much matter whether the College is being criticized for ideological ambiguity or defended against such a charge. The heart of the matter is that the word "ambiguous," itself equivocal, serves as a touchstone. Let me offer a couple of examples. The first comes from a supporter. In his biography of Bataille, when Michel Surya deals with the period during which the appeal of fascism was at its height in France, he never mentions (or anticipates) any accusation without adopting a defensive posture: superficial appearances notwithstanding, nothing is more alien and more vigorously opposed to fascism than Bataille's thinking, and its manifestations through the *Acéphale* group and the College of Sociology.[3]

Ambiguity is likewise the key word in Carlo Ginzburg's indictment of the ideology that Georges Dumézil had in common—according to Ginzburg—with the members of the College. For instance, after recalling Bataille's interest in the relations between death (and sexuality) and the sacred, and Caillois's interest in the relations between the sacred and power, Ginzburg comments: "In both cases, these themes implied an extremely equivocal attitude towards Fascist and Nazi ideologies." As for Caillois's musings, in "The Winter Wind," about how useful a new ice age would be for the selection of an elite, to Ginzburg's ear (and he is not mistaken) they "had an even more equivocal ring."[4] Finally, after stressing the ambiguity of the structure of the College and the heterogeneity of its participants, Ginzburg mentions, and espouses, what he sees as Michel Leiris's reservations about the equivocal project of a "sociology of the sacred" focused on contemporary reality.

Surya and Ginzburg come to opposite conclusions, but their postulate is the same. Surya congratulates Bataille for avoiding ambiguity, while Ginzburg criticizes him for being steeped in it, but they both agree that ambiguity is to be condemned. Is the equivocal merely a cloak for a univocal fascism? Bataille put his name to a book called *Guilty:* is that enough to make him a criminal? In their response to Ginzburg's article, Giampiero Moretti and Rocco Ronchi deserve credit for not denying the ambiguities that surrounded the College and in which it reveled. But their acknowledgment is not an accusation. Moretti and Ronchi do not reduce the ambiguities in question, as Surya does, to a cover for a sort of "essential" antifascism, of an esoteric but irreproachable variety, nor do they reduce those ambiguities, as Ginzburg does, to a mask for a deplorable profascism that does not even have the courage to speak its name. The ambiguities of the College are not a cover for anything. They are real ambiguities. As such, as ambiguities, they are at the heart of what the College was about.[5]

For Ginzburg is right on one point. There are ambiguities, many of them, in Bataille's work. In Caillois's case the ambiguities are even more numerous, and more disturbing. As a collection of equivocators, the College is a real gold mine. And among the equivocators I am not even counting the infamous Pierre Libra: his Maurrasism is actually quite unambiguous, and that is no doubt why he faded from the landscape after contributing his signature to the first manifesto.[6] (The least one can ask of an ambiguity is that it be ambiguous.)

In *Neither Right nor Left*, Zeev Sternhell drew up a devastating inventory of French contributions to Nazi ideology. His concluding chapters make it clear that much of what interested the College fell within the "nonconformists'" zone of influence—for that is what the antidemocratic ideologues of the day were called.[7] Moreover, this is not particularly surprising: Sternhell's tableau makes it clear that the antidemocratic ideologues, despite their vaunted nonconformism, were not so far from the spatial presence indicated by the Fascist newspaper's title, *Je suis partout:* "I am everywhere."

The calendars of various members of the College are sprinkled with revealing addresses, meetings, names: Arnaud Dandieu, Thierry Maulnier, Pierre Drieu La Rochelle, Bertrand de Jouvenel. In 1935, Henri De Man's *L'idée socialiste*—De Man being the most representative European ideologue of the generation—appeared in French in a joint translation by Henry Corbin (who had translated Heidegger) and Alexandre Kojève (who would later be a speaker at the College and whose seminar on Hegel and death attracted those who would make up the next generation of intellectuals). But the "connotations" denounced by Ginzburg come into play most clearly at the thematic level. The sociologists of the College, like the extremists in the "neither right nor left" movement, reject the privileged place Marxist theory grants to economics; they counter by asserting the primacy of the symbolic (or of myth, in Georges Sorel's sense). For both groups, denunciations of societal breakdown and the fragmentation of democracy are inspired by an insistently aestheticizing and organicist vision of society and politics: a vision of infusing bodies with souls, of reanimating a spiritless world.

The most disturbing similarities lie in the strategy these groups adopt toward fascism. In this realm, ambiguity is no longer just an effect of connotation; instead, it is used as a weapon. As Sternhell shows, among many French nonconformists, opposition to fascism (that is, to foreign fascism—Italian or German) is never direct. It takes the form of a mimetic subversion that appropriates the enemy's slogans and twists them to its own ends; it purports to outflank the enemy on his own terrain, to fight him with his own weapons.[8] Now, a counterattack that identifies with the aggressor constitutes a literally equivocal resistance, resistance by way of equivocation. It shuffles the cards, making it impossible to distinguish a potential aggressor from his victim. This derealizing strategy of beating the enemy at his own game is behind *Acéphale*'s "superfascism" *(surfascisme);* the prefix *sur* (as in "surcharge") has only to be transmuted into an *a* (as in "ahistorical") for *Acéphale*'s position to be represented as a form of afascism.

The initial thrust behind this logic of identification with the adversary was provided by Thierry Maulnier. In his preface to the translation of Moeller van den Bruck's *The Third Reich*, after emphasizing the "specifically anti-French" character of German nationalism, Maulnier went on: "Even if we have to be separated from the new Germany by a conflict against which no sense of fraternity can prevail, I feel it is opportune to say quietly that we feel closer to—and more readily understood by—a German national socialist than to a French pacifist."[9] A struggle to the death, but without rancor (and above all without contempt): this is the virile form of love for those most distant from us. Respect for those who do us the honor of making us their enemy. If we are noble, we are closer to those from whom we are separated than to our nearest neighbors. A domestic version of the same ambivalence is found in the editorials Blanchot was writing at the time: in place of generous admiration for the enemy and glorious identification with the aggressor, we read of the nausea that a Frenchman feels among his own kind, his revulsion at seeing whom he resembles. Blanchot writes: "So long as the French do not grasp the value of the terrible paradox that obliges them to be French against France and nationalists against the nation, they will not understand what kind of effort is required of them for their own liberation."[10] Maulnier's logic is rooted in the experience of identification with the other; Blanchot's grows out of the experience of nonidentification with oneself. As soon as it can be said that Léon Blum embodies France, France becomes such an object of disgust for every true Frenchman that even the most nationalist German cannot hate her more violently. One would have to have a very poor view of France indeed not to despise her. It follows that the rare individuals who deem it their duty to love her are at the same time those in whom her current state inspires the deepest horror. According to this logic, France's enemies (those who reject the France embodied in the political parties, the France of the Jew Léon Blum, and so on) are those who serve her most proudly. Love of France is defined by hatred of France.

Jacques Lacan earned his medical degree in 1932. He wrote his thesis about the mechanisms of delirious interpretation on which this very sort of paranoiac quid pro quo relies. An actress is attacked by a female admirer—Lacan calls her Aimée—at the stage door of a theater. The admirer, carted off to the police station, justifies what she has done by accusing her victim of persecuting her. Lacan shows that Aimée's jealous identification with, and admiration for, the actress is the condition that has allowed her to transform the latter into a persecutor: in striking the actress, Aimée is striking out at "the single object of her hatred and her love," that is, herself. The actress is not the true object of Aimée's aggression but rather the intermediary through whom she is striking, symbolically at first but also in reality, since the attacker's behavior has serious consequences for her own life, namely, internment. Aimée's story thus is grounded in the paranoia of self-punishment; this female version of the Baudelairean "Heautontimoroumenos" is at once her own torturer and her own victim.[11] A few years later, in 1936, while he was working on the theory of the mirror stage, Lacan argued that paranoiac reflexivity of this sort is rooted in the aggressive drives of alienation. Constitutive of the ego, alienation impels a subject to be his own rival: I have to choose between him or me even though he is I, we are one and the same.[12]

The effects of amorous hatred are perceptible even among the audience at the College. In December 1938, after the Munich agreements, Bataille summed up the costs of the Czechoslovakian crisis during a talk on the structure of democracies. His presentation, the text of which has not survived, was followed by a free-for-all, no doubt occasioned in part by the presence of Julien Benda, the most hated French writer of the day.[13] Even the audience seems to have had trouble keeping the speakers' voices straight: it was not clear whether they were mouthing love songs or chants of hate. Everyone agreed that democracy was to be condemned. However, since the logic of paranoid identification implies that one is the enemy of what one loves to excess, it was impossible to decide whether the object of condemnation was democracy as such or democracy in its prevailing state of decay. This ambiguity can be discerned in Bertrand d'Astorg's account of the meeting, published in *Les nouvelles lettres.* According to d'Astorg, the discussion took some unexpected turns: "The strange thing was that one could not tell whether the speakers were perfidious antidemocrats or if they were defending a personal conception of an ideal democracy."[14]

This sort of equivocation was not unusual. Writing for *Cahiers du Sud,* Pierre Missac had denounced the values defended by Caillois in "The Winter Wind," adding that he was no longer astonished by the author's receptivity to fascism. While he was reading the proofs of his article, someone informed him that he was mistaken: Caillois's sympathies actually lay with the Communists. Missac did not change a word in his text, but he added a correction in a footnote. Fascist. No, Communist. In any event, he added, it doesn't matter a whit. Fascism and Communism are contraries, but in a world given over to paranoid duplicity, contraries turn out to be one and the same thing.[15]

Once again, ambiguity is at the heart of the matter. Ambiguity defines the object of the College's reflections: the sacred. The sacred reunites what a narrow logic separates as contradictory. At once high and low, right and left, pure and impure, it attracts and repels, inspires respect and provokes transgression. Ambivalence is the means by which the sacred distinguishes itself from a profane realm subject to a conformist logic unable to conceive of contraries that are not opposed to one another. "The two poles of the sacred are generally opposed to the profane world," Caillois writes. "When faced with it, their antagonism shrinks and tends to disappear."[16] Following the same logic, Bataille describes communism and fascism, "during the same period and in the same society," as "two competing revolutions, hostile to one another and to the established order."[17] When differences are heated up to the point of contradiction, it becomes possible to ignore what separates them and to weld opposites together, if not in their concrete content—which has been rendered irrelevant in any case by the high temperature—then at least in the form their extremism takes. The fascist and Communist revolutions (like German and French nationalism, according to Thierry Maulnier) are mortally hostile to each other. They are in communion, nevertheless, in their extremism: that is, in their way of surpassing the classic contradictions, in their hatred of the prosaic logic that seeks to require a choice between hate and love. Since extremism is by definition situated beyond all positions (beyond nationalism, beyond Marxism, and so forth), all extremists may be in communion (or imagine themselves in communion) beyond what separates them, that is, precisely beyond the narrowness of the identity principle.

In this sense, the double negation of the slogan "neither left nor right" is not a centrist neutralization; rather, it exacerbates contrarieties. It is not a question of reversing one's colors, of switching parties, of leaving the Communist party—as Jacques Doriot did—for the fascistic PPF (Party of the French People). It is not a matter of leaving one position in order to take up another, but of moving to a different space altogether, a space of direct action, of vital—or mortal—engagement. The only serious players are the sublime dissidents, those who break altogether with the regime of political parties, who go beyond the fences of parliamentary representation. One has to lose one's seat. Blanchot describes the logic of this step beyond in a well-known appeal to dissidence: what counts, he says, "is not reiterating the popular slogan 'neither right nor left,' but being authentically opposed to right and left alike. It becomes obvious, under these conditions, that authentic dissidence is one that abandons a position while maintaining hostility toward the contrary position, or rather while accentuating that hostility. The true communist dissident is the one who gives up communism not in order to take up capitalist beliefs but in order to define the conditions of the struggle against capitalism. Similarly, the true nationalist dissident is the one who sets aside the traditional formulas of nationalism not in order to embrace internationalism but in order to combat internationalism in all its forms, including the economy of the nation itself."[18] Frenchmen, once more into the breach, yet another effort if you want to be extraparliamentary. The tension of ambiguity must not be relaxed for a second. Ambivalence must not be allowed to lapse: your "no" to Communism must never be a "yes" to capitalism; your "no" to nationalism must never be a "yes" to internationalism. Your refusal must never allow itself to be inscribed on a ballot. It must remain unrepresentable. It must never allow itself to be seduced by the trap of positions. Outside the Chamber of Deputies, do right and left still exist?

Bataille often quotes a passage Nietzsche attributes to the Madman in *The Gay Science:* "Whither are we moving? Away from all suns? Are we not plunging continually? Backward, sideward, forward, in all directions? Is there still any up or down?"[19] For Bataille these words mark what I have called "the storming of the Concorde." In 1938, in "The Obelisk," Bataille has Nietzsche's Madman utter these words in the Place de la Concorde, that is, in a politically equivocal space, the place of ambiguity itself, the extraparliamentary site where opponents of the right/left opposition and its staging in parliament (the distribution of seats according to electoral representation in the Chamber of Deputies on the other side of the Seine) had converged in February, 1934. Bataille chooses this public space, where blood had flowed for the cause of "neither right nor left" during the antiparliamentary riots of February 6, to have Nietzsche's Madman generalize disorientation. For Bataille does not limit his rejection of the classic oppositions either to the right or to the left. Bataille's storming of the Place de la Concorde is not as restrained as that of the extreme-right Croix de Feu. The place is the same, but he is playing a different game. And in "The Sorcerer's Apprentice" Bataille ignores the Chamber of Deputies in favor of the lovers' chamber.[20] We move toward infinity. From limited disorientation to generalized disorientation.

It might be said that the move toward infinity that marks the passage from Blanchot's editorials to Bataille's political tracts is a move away from politics. A little equivocation brings one closer to fascism, a great deal establishes one's distance from it. Raised to this power, the step beyond transgresses not only the system of parliamentary representation but that of representation in general. In this sense, if political ambiguities are reprehensible, it is precisely because they are limited, because in politics there is no true ambiguity, because political ambiguity is always superficial, always a cover for something else (fascism). Political ambiguities are thus reprehensible because they are not ambiguous enough, because they fall short, because they remain superficial: lift up the cover, and a proper name comes into view. From this standpoint, it is significant that Sternhell respects (although he does not thematize) the separation between the realms of literature and politics.[21] He quotes liberally from the political writings of Drieu and Brasillach, but never from their novels. And yet the writers of that era would have protested almost unanimously against such a separation of literature and politics. Their passion for ambiguity required precisely the conditions that suspend all divisions between politics and literature. When equivocations are political, they are undoubtedly dangerous and perhaps even worthy of condemnation; but would they be equivocations if one had only to label them literary in order to render them innocent? Would we continue to take the plunge if we knew for sure that unrestricted falling were a viaticum for literature?

The theory of fascism is a key element in the heterology that Bataille established in the early 1930s. This theory has as one of its nerve centers the economy of waste: the first manifestation of power is in effect the separation of the clean from the unclean, the proper from the improper. But in the case of fascism the founding gesture, the exclusion of the unclean, does not entail any valorization of what is excluded. "Consequently," Bataille comments, "no erotic activity can be associated with cruelty."[22] Bataille often associates fascism with sadism; but his denunciation targets not so much sadism itself as the desexualization of a sadism appropriated by politics. Fascism does not sanctify those whom it excludes: it suppresses coolly, without emotion, and the sacrificer does not identify with his victim. The exclusion practiced by fascism is an exclusion properly so called, properly carried out, impeccably administered, without desire and without equivocation. Hence the importance of cleanliness, sanitation, political salubriousness, in its thematics. This moralizing hygienics, emphasized by Sternhell, is equally essential in Bataille's schema. The fascist appropriation of the social body begins with an ethics of the clean body, a condemnation of base materialism.

Bataille's heterology inverts this pragmatics of waste. His erotics celebrates the prefix *ex-* in words like "excess," "existence," and "excrement": evacuation is its most expressive moment, its most tender punctuation mark. Praise of rot follows from this—for the experience of rot is constitutive of the existential structure of man.[23] This logic leads Bataille (in "The Solar Anus," 1929) to sketch out a scatological portrait of the proletariat-as-hero in which he exalts Communist workers, who "appear to the bourgeois to be as ugly and dirty as hairy sexual organs, or lower parts";[24] for Bataille, of course, this description is complimentary.

Yet at the time of Contre-Attaque (that is, in November 1935, during the campaign in favor of the Popular Front), the same Bataille wrote a polemical speech, the only mass-oriented political address he ever produced: after denouncing the "distraught rabble" who were in power in the parliamentary democracies, he launched an appeal to antifascist insurrection: "Against this garbage, we must oppose *direct* imperative violence, *direct* construction of the basic force of an uncompromising authority."[25] This garbage. *Sic.* This is Bataille speaking. Georges Bataille. To whom does the word apply? It is no longer a matter of eroticizing refuse, the wretched of the earth. Turned back against the bourgeoisie, the compliment becomes an insult. Yesterday's philoproletarian scatologist is now campaigning for an anticapitalist hygienics: the word "garbage," deprived of any glorious connotation, implies a one-way exclusion. Its nonconformist connotations become apparent in the lapse from ambiguity; political literalization is accompanied by a lowering of semantic intensity, a loss of textual energy. Unlike Carlo Ginzburg, I prefer Bataille when he is equivocal.

The primary locus of ambiguity, in Bataille's heterology, is in the identification between waste—garbage—and power, an identification that power, by definition, refuses to acknowledge. Indeed, this blindness is its characteristic feature. Power is the blind spot of the heterogeneous; it is what, in the heterogeneous, resists heterology. It may be the object of a heterology; it can never be the subject. Yet power is not nonknowledge, either; it resists nonknowledge and knowledge alike. Nonknowledge is a blinding form of self-consciousness; and whereas nonknowledge entails awareness of nonknowledge, power is ignorance that is unaware of itself. Self-consciousness, for Bataille, is always consciousness of the self as a self-that-is-dying, and it is precisely in opposition to this consciousness, and to the internalization of death that it implies, that power is constituted. Because it maintains itself by suppressing consciousness of death, power turns its back on the tragic. In Bataille, power is represented in the figure of the "armed lout";[26] its attributes are brutish naïveté and ignorant foolishness.

Bataille calls this resistance to tragedy sadism, reversing the sequence proposed by Freud in "Instincts and Their Vicissitudes." Whereas Freud generates sadism as a stage in a process of sexualization, Bataille describes the desexualization of sadism. Freud takes the instinct to master as his starting point, while for Bataille that same instinct is the end result of the process he is depicting. For Freud, the instinct to master is a desexualized drive: pure aggressiveness (nonequivocal, nonsexual), it is indifferent to what it denies (what it destroys, assimilates, and so on). In Freud's account, this instinct progresses, via masochism, toward a form of complex, sexualized sadism that is only masochism turned inside out, masochism by proxy, masochism that produces suffering through identification with the suffering inflicted on the other. With Bataille, the trajectory is reversed: the primary experience, that of (masochistic) identification with the victim, evolves toward an increasingly pure, decreasingly sexual form of aggressiveness, an aggressiveness without identification that he calls sadism (though he does not link this concept to Sade's work).[27]

The metamorphosis of the images of sovereignty dramatized by Christianity constitutes the narrative matrix of this scenario. Bataille evoked these images on several occasions in his lectures at the College, most notably in the session on power. Christianity was inaugurated by a sacralizing exclusion: this inaugural sacrifice produces identification with the victim. "Jesus let himself be treated like a criminal and reduced to the condition of a tortured body, thus identifying with the left and immediately repellent form of the sacred."[28] But the word that labels the right and appealing form of the sacred, the word *rex* of the inscription *INRI (Iesus Nazarenus Rex Iudaeorum)*, will gradually lose the derisory value it had when it appeared on the instrument of torture, and in the end it will wholly and irreversibly obliterate the tortured body. The history of the church is the history of this repression: the inaugural sadism is deeroticized; the sinister, lefthand forms of the sacred are rectified; infamy is supplanted by glory.

In the same lecture, Bataille refers in passing to the imposition of the *fascio* on the prow of Mussolini's locomotives. "The fascination with fascist symbology," Ginzburg comments, is expressed in "his contrast of the fasces portrayed in Italy 'on the bellies of locomotives' and the crucifix, associated, *à la* Frazer, to a 'haunting representation of the king's execution.'"[29] The symbolic weight with which Bataille invests these railroad emblems may in fact appear disproportionate: they would make fascism (even more than Nazism) appear to be the first seriously aggressive attack ever mounted on Christianity. "It is only in the past few years," he says, "that the crucified figure has been threatened in Germany and in Italy by images of power that exclude any idea of tragedy, any idea of killing the king. Moreover, the Italian *fascio* as it is seen on every locomotive's belly is in this respect more charged with a precise meaning than is the swastika."[30] Bataille merely reports: fascism is the first form of sovereignty that has ever succeeded in escaping entirely from the Christian genealogy of power. Its own unique form of sadism finally repulses the repulser; Mussolini is no Dianus; there may be kings who die, but Mussolini for his part kills, and he does so without identifying with his victim. He holds authority and does not seek expiation; he governs innocently. The *fascio* is an appropriate emblem for him: it is the weapon of the executioner, a technician who inflicts death without risking death himself.

But the unilateral character of the executioner's operation makes identification difficult. According to a story told by Caillois, the members of the *Acéphale* group agreed unanimously to seal their fraternity with a human sacrifice: everyone was said to have volunteered for the role of victim, no one for that of executioner. The anecdote is emblematic. When one declares, as Bataille did, that it is better to be Prometheus than Jupiter, when one signs one's name as Dianus, when one identifies sovereignty with self-mutilation, and when one uses as an epigraph in text after text the passage in *The Phenomenology of Spirit* where Hegel says that "the life of Spirit is not the life that shrinks from death and keeps itself untouched by devastation, but rather the life that endures it and maintains itself in it,"[31] one may be open to a diagnosis of obsessional neurosis and thereby exposed to a variety of insults, including those of the Marxists; but the charge of fascism would be difficult to sustain.[32]

The issue of the relation between Nazism and Christianity comes up repeatedly in Ginzburg's article. Here the College is no longer the principal focus; it is mentioned only in the conclusion, to reinforce the charges leveled against Georges Dumézil's *Myths and Gods of the Germans* (1939). Dumézil had incorporated some references to contemporary Germany into his monograph on the religion of the ancient Germanic peoples: Ginzburg reads these passages, wrongly, as support for Nazi ideology.[33]

Pointing to some echoes of archaic, pre-Christian Germania in the post-Christian Third Reich, Dumézil constructs a sharp antithesis between the Germanic world and Christianity. And he adds a second antithesis, identifying two archaic systems—pseudo-Hellenic neopaganism and proto-Germanism—between which, as he saw it, Nazism had wavered before finally choosing the second. In other words, Dumézil suggests that Nazism grew out of a twofold rejection, first of Christianity and then of Hellenism. Thus the occasional references to classical antiquity in Nazi literature are of little interest. "The 'neo-pagan' propaganda of the new Germany," he writes, "is certainly an interesting phenomenon for the historian of religions; but it is voluntary, in some degree, artificial."[34]

On the question of neopaganism, Dumézil's views are close to Bataille's. In 1936, in a special issue of *Acéphale* titled "Réparation à Nietzsche," Bataille denounced Alfred Rosenberg, who had attempted to link Nazi militarism with Nietzsche's tragic Hellenism. In the lead article of this issue, "Nietzsche and the Fascists," one paragraph explicitly deals with what Bataille calls "A 'Hygienic and Pedagogical Religion': German Neopaganism." At issue are recent attempts to establish a specifically German church by exploiting "the opposition of primitive religious forms to Christianity." Dumézil views these religious experiments as voluntaristic; Bataille finds them hygienic. "The account of the role played in Hitler's Germany by a free, anti-Christian enthusiasm, which gives itself a Nietzschean appearance, thus ends," he concludes, "on a note of shame."[35] Bataille may not take the neopagan construct seriously; still, unlike Dumézil, he does not bring Wagner's face into focus behind the pseudo-Nietzschean cardboard cutout; the surface manifestations of Hellenism conceal not Germanic roots but religious conformity. Greek or Teutonic, it is all the same to Bataille: simply a cover. An alert anti-Christian will never fall into the Nazi trap. At least that is what Bataille was saying in 1936. Two years later, when he lectured on power at the College, he said exactly the opposite, as we have seen: for the first time in its history, Christianity was seriously threatened in Germany and Italy.

In attempting to assess Bataille's position, we are reminded of Bertrand d'Astorg's dilemma after the democracy debate. Is this a perfidious anti-Christian speaking, or someone defending an ideal conception of Christianity?[36] We have entered a zone of particularly intense ideological ambivalence. Is Bataille for or against? For or against what, moreover? One day, in the name of anti-Christianity, he reproaches Nazism for remaining within the Christian zone of influence. Another day, in the name of opposite values, he declares that fascism has left the Christian realm behind. He himself is the first to acknowledge the ambiguity—and in the very same contexts Ginzburg pinpoints. In the middle of the lecture on power, he interrupts his argument to say: "Discussions of this sort, furthermore, are in danger of introducing many ambiguities; in fact, it was possible last time to take what I had said as a sort of apology for Christianity."[37] He thought he had spoken as an anti-Christian, yet his discourse was heard as an apology. Who was mistaken? Bataille himself, or his listeners? Bataille would have liked to dispel the ambiguity. He wanted to speak ill of Christianity. But his words escaped him, and his listeners heard something else. As though he always ended up being attracted by what he wanted to reject. As though attraction came across each time he sought to express repulsion.

What is important here is not the choice between these two positions. Words are slippery, and powerful texts do not allow themselves to be pinned down. Bataille has more than one voice, and, besides, his is not the only voice at the College. The reticence and reservations that Ginzburg mentions (Leiris's and Benjamin's, to which we might add Klossowski's, and so on) are important, but we have to remember that they came from within the College. At the beginning of his article, Ginzburg declares, quite correctly: "The rejection of solutions does not necessarily mean that the problems are nonexistent or irrelevant."[38] And yet Ginzburg's diatribe is unsatisfying. It leaves the reader to wonder just where the relevance of the problems taken up by the College might lie. It is not hard to understand why Benjamin contested some of Caillois's pronouncements in print; it is more difficult (and more interesting) to explain what he was doing at the College, what led him to compromise himself to the point where he was prepared to speak out on such an ambiguous matter.[39]

The College cannot be detached from its ambiguities. One can follow in Boileau's footsteps and inveigh against ambiguity. Assert that only what is clearly expressed is well conceived. Put all controversial subjects on the index. But here it is not language per se that is ambiguous; it is the subjects that language addresses: relations between the sacred and death, between sex and death, between power and the sacred. Minerva's bird flew off at dusk. For the enemies of ambiguity, this was a mistake. It should have gone to bed early. Respected the rationalist curfew. The owl is guilty of continuing to think after sundown. When one is facing the unknown, encountering the future through one's own ignorance, thinking is forbidden. Picasso was engraving his blind Minotaur at the time.

At the heart of Bataille's definition of power, the impossibility of self-knowledge is inscribed: the law of power escapes anyone who exercises it. Thus heterology is above all an effort to circumvent that blind spot, to open the black box and overcome the resistance of power to knowledge.

Jean Paulhan describes a strategy of the same order in his May 1939 talk on sacred language. As he tells his listeners at the College, he has set out to examine proverbs as utterances presenting the same characteristics of "distinction, effectiveness, ambiguity with which we were trying to characterize the sacred."[40] During a three-year stint in Madagascar, from 1908 through 1910, Paulhan had studied the ritual rules of recourse to proverbs in verbal exchanges; he was especially interested in accounting for their rhetorical efficacy. What is the origin of the unanimously recognized authority that allows the use of a proverb to bring virtually any discussion to an end? More generally speaking, where does the power of words come from? How is it that certain words or groups of words (proverbs being one example) can exercise authority over people's hearts and minds without regard to their semantic content or truth value? With these questions, Paulhan was attempting to take ethnological categories developed in the context of archaic civilizations and apply them to the modern world. For Paulhan, political slogans are the contemporary equivalent of Malagasy proverbs: their rhetorical effectiveness is independent of their semantic content (as Bataille would have said, they do the job).

But Paulhan's lecture is not so much a presentation of a theory as an account of a failure. Although the mysteries of proverbial effectiveness continued to escape him, he explains, he noticed that he had begun to speak in proverbs, almost unwittingly taking on proverbial authority. Yet he is not a triumphant sorcerer's apprentice. "There is nothing more humiliating," he observes, "than to be able to do something perfectly without being able to understand it." What interests him most in this situation is its negative epistemological side: less what he ends up performing than what this prevents him from knowing. In the absence of victory, the lecture is quite precisely an attempt to use narrative to master a peculiar defeat, that is, to survive it and resist it. "The rout of intelligence," Paulhan says, "is also something which interests intelligence."[41]

Moretti and Ronchi make it clear that the College's concerns revolve around a critique of science, and they are right to emphasize the College's determination to "submit reason to the requirements of the sublime."[42] Heterological knowledge is in fact a form of paradoxical knowledge, resembling what Paulhan calls the rout of intelligence. Heterology is not just another science. It is a science that incorporates the negative clauses on which the epistemological contract relies: as in the Bluebeard story, there are doors that scholars promise not to open. Every will to know is accompanied by a refusal, a will not to know. Heterology begins where science stops respecting its contract; it is the science of what science does not want to know, the science of what exceeds knowledge. The science of epistemological residues.[43]

Bataille and Caillois carry out this epistemological transgression in different ways. With Bataille, it takes the form of subjective engagement, implying a hermeneutic risk on the part of the experimenter. With the more formalist Caillois, it is rather a matter of going beyond the contradiction between order and disorder toward a kind of structuralist construction of a complex or general order within which disorder itself has its place, an order that—as Caillois's theory of festival shows—would bring disorder itself into the order of things, producing an order capable of disorder. Thus Caillois's undertaking is not so much an irrationalist liquidation of rationalism as a surrationalist surpassing of rationalism: reason has to account for its interdictions, for its limits; it has to take into account what it rejects and what rejects it. The affinities of thought and light do not justify the suspension of vigilance at nightfall. Caillois parted company with Breton after a quarrel over Mexican beans. Caillois wanted to know why they jumped. Breton was afraid that if he opened one up he would destroy the mystery. Yet who would want any part of a miracle that could not be questioned? The object of heterology is a "marvelous that is not afraid of knowledge."[44]

The concept of ambiguity is central to existentialism. But the ambiguity in question is not a consequence of the imperfections of language or the limits of human consciousness; it is a concept that defines the structure of existence. Existential ambiguity is at the heart of various postwar works, such as Simone de Beauvoir's *The Ethics of Ambiguity* and Maurice Merleau-Ponty's *Phenomenology of Perception.* For Merleau-Ponty, ambiguity "is not some imperfection of consciousness or existence, but the definition of them."[45] Ambiguity is also the essential dimension of the theory of history presented in Raymond Aron's 1939 doctoral thesis. Aron argues that the relativity of historical knowledge "is due to the ambiguity of the intellectual development and the incompleteness of the evolution"; ambiguity, he says in a later text, is the very "substance" of history.[46]

Reviewing Aron's thesis in *La nouvelle revue française,* Bernard Groethuysen stressed the paradoxical implications of an axiomatics that turns historical discourse into the discourse of a science no longer capable of knowing. And if knowledge is ruled out, this is not, as the traditional argument went, because past events are unrepeatable and because one can no longer summon up the battle of Waterloo to decide which witness was right and which one was wrong. On the contrary, it is because history takes the present as its object that it is no longer in a position of knowledge. The irruption of the present on the horizon of history is responsible for producing, in the realm of scientific discourse, structural effects of blindness identical with those accounted for by Paulhan. For the present is historical (although perhaps this was easier to see in 1939 than it is now) when the experience of the present is identified with uncertainty about the future, that is, with the presence of the unknown. "Something is happening, and we don't know what it is," Groethuysen says.[47] In this sense, the ignorance about the future to which Bataille so often refers defines not an imperfection but the very form of historical experience. It is in the nature of the present to be ambiguous and to imply a risk that is at once hermeneutical and existential. Under these conditions, the desire for unambiguous thinking maintains a utopian ideal of thought without history, or history without risk. Certainly not all ambiguities are equivalent. Certainly there is not even any such thing as an innocent equivocation, an impeccable ambiguity. But to denounce equivocation and ambiguity as such is to adopt a positivist stance that borders on a categorical rejection of history and language.

To come back to Jules Monnerot, it would be exciting—and enlightening—to learn what strange logic led a former Communist student from

Martinique, the author of the declaration presented on behalf of the French West Indies at the International Writers' Congress for the Defense of Culture in 1935, to present himself fifty years later as a candidate on a cryptoracist platform. But that story, to make sense, would have to be told with more pointed narrative tools than equivocation.

Since Le Pen did not succeed in getting thirty of his candidates elected, the College of Sociology will not be represented in Strasbourg.

FEAR AND TREMBLING IN THE AGE OF SURREALISM

She exhausts, she kills, and it only makes her all the more beautiful.

Alfred de Musset, *The Cup and the Lip*, act 4, scene 1

Caillois's work is hard to categorize. But not for the same reason as Bataille's, Blanchot's, or even Sartre's: Caillois does not mix registers of discourse, does not oscillate between theory and fiction. Instead, his work is hard to categorize because of the perverse way he chooses to play, almost exclusively, on the less literary of those two registers: the theoretical. The reasons for this choice are essentially negative and defensive. At the heart of almost all Caillois's essays, whether they deal with sociology or aesthetics, with morality or the philosophy of nature, we encounter the same horrified fascination with imagination—imagination conceived not as a preserve of freedom, an escape hatch allowing a momentary respite from the demands of reality, but as an implacable force of ontological equalization, complicitous with the Freudian death instinct, a power of dissolution that is not limited to psychic life but that threatens all distinctions, including the ones separating the psychic from the physical, the inside from the outside, the self from the not-self, the subject from the object. Caillois's preference for theoretical writing over fiction may be related to a fear that, were he to give in to his penchant for revery, he would find himself swept away by the indistinct tide of the imaginary; perhaps his choice is explained by an implacable resistance to everything that, in literature, is not resistance to imagination. Just as Odysseus has himself tied to the mast of his ship so he can listen to the sirens while maintaining his vigilance, can enjoy their song without succumbing to it, Caillois clings to the theoretical position as if it were a guardrail allowing him to approach the imaginary without yielding to it, letting him navigate the dire straits of fiction without succumbing to the temptation of Saint Anthony.

These defensive origins may explain why it is so difficult to situate his work within the typology of theoretical writings. There is something heterodoxical, oblique, disquieting, and even occasionally hypocritical in the relation to knowledge that Caillois's writing puts into play. In his essays, erudition tilts toward destabilizing adventures that function quite differently from a search for truth. Caillois was one of Jorge Luis Borges' first French translators. In order to exorcise the temptations of fiction, he adopted the mask of science in a way that recalls Borges' imaginary encyclopedias. But the science in question is unrecognizable; it seems to have become its own double. This resistance to fiction exposes theory to the shadowless glare of unreality; it inoculates theory with the fictive virus against which theory was supposed to immunize.

It is difficult, moreover, to assign a precise origin to this strangeness, to decide whether it corresponds to a judgment on the work that emanates from within the work itself or from without, whether this judgment is added to the work or is part of it, whether it bears upon the work or bears the work in itself, whether the reader attributes this strangeness to the work or whether the work conveys the strangeness to the reader—for the work itself is only an insistent meditation on the vertigo of the unsituatable, the vertigo of a subject prey to the distancing effects of a writing that eludes him, a writing without subject, a prehuman grammatology. From *The Necessity of the Mind* to *The Writing of Stones*, Caillois's work strives to formulate the *cogito* of those "emphatic exiles who no longer know what to do with themselves":[1] psychasthenics, subjects dislodged by space, expelled by space, replaced by space.

The Necessity of the Mind was not published until after Caillois's death. With just one exception, Caillois never made any reference to this autobiographical essay, which was his first book, written when he was twenty years old. However, the posthumous discovery was not the only surprise held in store by the publication of these youthful memoirs from beyond the grave. *The Necessity of the Mind* does not merely exhume a Caillois one did not expect to meet, a Caillois who is at once adolescent and autobiographical. It casts a retrospective light on his earliest published texts (especially the best-known ones, his essays on the praying mantis and on the psychasthenic dimension of mimesis)—an unsuspected autobiographical light revealing that the praise of impersonality encountered in these essays is rooted in the most highly personal of contexts.

The surrealists, who idolized woman, preferred to see her as deadly. They wanted her to arouse in them a fear and trembling that would amplify and sanctify the emotions of which she was both source and object. In *Manhood*, Michel Leiris describes how he reacted angrily one day when his father refused to share his admiration for the passage in *Alcools* where Guillaume Apollinaire, in keeping with the surrealist theory of beauty, establishes fear of woman as the fundamental aesthetic affect. "This woman was so beautiful, / She frightened me."[2] Caillois does not quote these lines, but one suspects that, consciously or not, he is offering a variation on the same passage from "1909" when, citing one of his own poetic texts in *The Necessity of the Mind*, Caillois evokes "women so beautiful as to inspire fear."[3] Indeed, both Caillois's autobiography and Leiris's invoke muses that are similarly overwhelming in terms of the effect of terror they produce. *Manhood* is dominated by the figure of Judith, who decapitates Holophernes after allowing him to degrade her. In *The Necessity of the Mind*, the praying mantis—a Judith of the entomological realm, for the male who takes his chances with her will not come out alive—seems to be what seduced Caillois onto the shifting sands of autobiography. Many other texts from the same period attest to a strong oral masochism (in the pages of *La terre et les rêveries de la volonté* [The Earth and the Daydreams of the Will], dedicated to Leiris, Gaston Bachelard diagnoses what he calls a Jonas complex). Caillois shared with Dali a taste for cannibalistic objects and invisible architectures, a taste that culminated in the veneration of the urban orifices of what a well-chosen catachresis calls the mouths of the subway. Shortly afterward, when Leiris and Caillois set up the College of Sociology, along with Bataille, these individual fantasies converged in the figure of Acephalus, the decapitated Don Juan.

Caillois published two versions of "The Praying Mantis." The first appeared in 1934 in the surrealist journal *Minotaure*, with illustrations. But the one included four years later in Caillois's first book, *Le mythe et l'homme*, is better known. The publication of *The Necessity of the Mind* allowed the first version to be rediscovered. It constitutes the book's fifth chapter and is reprinted as such; unedited, the text even keeps the footnote from *Minotaure* announcing that "these pages . . . make up the fifth chapter of a work to appear . . . titled *The Necessity of the Mind and the Continuity of the University*."[4] In this first milling of his meditations on the praying mantis, Caillois also declares: "I will speak of my personal adventures later." Only the posthumous publication of *The Necessity of the Mind* has given us access to these adventures.

Caillois was born in northeastern France (Reims); his relation to the praying mantis, a creature more commonly found in the Mediterranean region, was for a long time dependent on books and legends. He saw his first mantis in 1928 when he was fourteen, one day during a vacation on a southern beach. That same day, a woman approached him and made sexual advances.

Caillois's brief notations invite the reader to wonder, on the one hand, about the conjunction between the mantis and autobiographical discourse and, on the other hand, about the repercussions of this conjunction on the text in which it is produced. Indeed, it is difficult to avoid an impression of defeatism when one sees a man choose to expose his first person, choose to expose himself in the first person, in front of a legendary maneater. And what the material history of the text relates, what happened to the text itself between the time Caillois wrote it and the time he published it, is, literally, the defeat of the first person, since the versions published by the author in his lifetime eliminate all personal references. It is as if the first person of the autobiography *(The Necessity of the Mind)* had been gnawed away, dissolved from within, before being absorbed and assimilated by the third person of the study on the praying mantis *(Le mythe et l'homme)*. It is difficult, here, not to speculate on this double disappearance, the coincidence that inflicts on the author's first person the fate that befalls the masculine partner of the tragic loves he relates. A strange *mise en abyme* turns the utterance back on the enunciation, applies the fate of its subject (who, once the female has been penetrated, does not reappear alive) to the text itself (which, once written, does not appear). The female's devouring (outside the text) of her sexual partner is echoed by the text's devouring of its foretext. It is as if the meeting with the mantis had the effect of depersonalizing Caillois's voice: his first person, at least his literary first person, did not survive *The Necessity of the Mind.*

In *Le mythe et l'homme*, Caillois borrows Nietzsche's definition of myth; it is what gives voice to the "*orgiastische Selbstvernichtung.*"[5] This *orgiastische Selbstvernichtung* comes into play on two levels in the essay on the praying mantis: first, with the self-annihilation of the male who disappears during the act of copulation; and, second, with the depersonalization proper to mythic enunciation. From mantis to myth, from mantis as myth to myth as discourse, the passage is seamless. The form of Caillois's discourse is homogeneous with its thematic content. The praying mantis superimposes a mythic depersonalization onto the impersonality of the myth. In other words, the myth finds an adequate allegory for itself in the orgy to which the male mantis must take recourse in order to efface himself, in order to put himself in parentheses.

A posthumous text always has an autobiographical aura. Death, intervening from without to determine the text's final form—making it a text whose author did not have time to sign it, a text to which he did not have the possibility of subscribing—is responsible for an alteration in its textual status; death moves the text from the register of signs to that of events. However, the posthumous status of *The Necessity of the Mind* does not stem from a biographical accident. It is not posthumous because its author died before or right after finishing it (so that he could not have supervised the transformation of the manuscript into a book). The text is complete; it is definitive. Its author dotted its final *i*'s and crossed its *t*'s. He could have authorized its publication. He did not. He withdrew the text from circulation. The posthumous book is also an inaugural book; it is the first one Caillois wrote. But he buried it almost as soon as he had finished writing it. And as soon as its author was buried, the text resurfaced.

Here ends the analogy between the text's destiny and that of its subject, between the fate of *The Necessity of the Mind* and the fate inflicted by the praying mantis; the analogy in fact recaptures only part of the text's history. For if it is an interesting fact that Caillois did not publish his autobiography, it is no less interesting that he never destroyed it. If *The Necessity of the Mind* had really disappeared, there is every chance that we would have known nothing at all about it. *The Necessity of the Mind*, which never appeared, never completely disappeared, either: the book was held in reserve. According to a strategy that would no longer evoke the fate of the male praying mantis but rather the mimetic ruses of the insects that

Caillois studied in his contemporaneous essay on psychasthenia, the first person was simply withdrawn from circulation, taken out of service. Confronted with the praying mantis, the text ensured its own survival by playing dead as long as its author remained alive.

The Necessity of the Mind is not, properly speaking, an autobiography. It is rather, in the strong sense, almost in a chemical sense, an essay—an assay—in self-analysis: an exercise in the analysis of the self, an experiment in dissolution or decomposition conducted in the first person on the first person, the narrative not only of a crisis but also of the plunging of the self into crisis. On this basis, it can be compared to essays by writers who, like the Sartre of *The Transcendence of the Ego* and the best passages of *Nausea* and *The Wall*, were also seeking, at around the same time, to depsychologize consciousness, to describe a consciousness purified of all subjectivity, what Blanchot somewhat later called a "consciousness without me" (and even, more strangely, a "me without me"), a consciousness that would belong to no one. But *The Transcendence of the Ego* is a phenomenological essay.[6] The paradox of *The Necessity of the Mind* stems precisely from the fact that in this self-analysis Caillois asks the first person to account for the transcendence of the ego and even to trigger it.

The high point of this crisis of depersonalization is no longer simply (as with the praying mantis) the disappearance of the ego, but (as in mimesis) the fascination of the ego with a world from which it is absent, in which it has no place.[7] *The Necessity of the Mind* is the autobiography of a subject who is literally possessed by his own absence: a posthumous first person that allows the subject to save himself in his absence, holding himself absent but in such a way that he is present to his own absence, bearing witness in his absence—but in the first person nonetheless—to his own absence, as if he had managed to distance himself without losing sight of himself, as if his absence only confirmed the first person rather than denying it. Syntax does not lend itself readily to the sort of semantic strabism that leads to formulas such as the following: "I wanted to cross the frontier of my skin, to live on the other side of my senses." Caillois admired Montesquieu for inventing, in *Persian Letters*, the art of "pretending to be a foreigner in the society in which one lives." *The Necessity of the Mind* stems from an autobiographical revolution that, like Montesquieu's sociological revolution, would allow a subject to make himself alien to the body in which he lives, alien even to the life he lives.[8]

The Necessity of the Mind owes a great deal to *Nadja*. No doubt it will one day become obvious that autobiography was the preeminent literary genre of surrealism. And in saying this I am not thinking of the surrealists who ended up growing old enough to write their memoirs. On the contrary, the surrealist autobiographical essays are all youthful works, attesting to an insolent immaturity; they are surrealist first of all, one might say, by virtue of their precociousness—for their authors had rarely reached the minimum age required for undertaking that sort of exercise. This is true of André Breton's autobiographical texts, not only *Nadja* but especially *Communicating Vessels* and *Mad Love.* It is true of *Manhood* as well: Leiris was not quite thirty when he started to write that book. As for Caillois, he almost needs a special dispensation for his youth: he was not yet twenty when, absorbed by the feminine body, he began to draft *The Necessity of the Mind.* Autobiography, in this instance, does not bequeath the experience of a lifetime; it is an exercise in inexperience. The first person rushes up in the first line, effaces itself as it exposes itself, expends itself—the first head to fall under the epistemological cut.

UNDER THE HEADING OF HOLOFERNES (NOTES ON JUDITH)

> The keenness of my love for you makes me lose my head,
> and that is as it should be: if one worried about one's head,
> one would no longer go anywhere.
> Quills are at the bottom of the scale. Can you not see that
> a quill has no access to purity until its head has been cut off?
>
> Calligraphy sample, Iran, sixteenth–eighteenth century

In 1946 Gallimard put out a new edition of Michel Leiris's autobiography *Manhood.*[1] Leiris reframed the 1939 text for the occasion. He shored it up with a corrective dossier at each end. The first, placed as a preface at the head of the volume (in the English translation it appears as "Afterword: The Autobiographer as *Torero*"), reevaluates the postulates underlying the initial autobiographical project: Leiris plows under the hopes of earning bulls' horns with which he had earlier sought to justify his exhibitionism (it does not suffice to expose oneself in order to expose oneself to anything and everything). At the other end of the volume, in the position—if not the form—of an afterword, the author added a handful of notes, each correcting a specific point on which he had changed his mind. The second edition thus leaves the text intact (otherwise it would lose its authenticity as a document), but it dates the text by means of reference points indicating that, in relation to the first version of the autobiography, "I" has become another. Cut off from himself by the war, the author no longer recognizes himself in the first person of his self-portrait. Six unhappy years have introduced some slack. The subject stands apart from its support. It comes unstuck. The real autobiography begins.

The passage of time is not responsible all by itself: the war and the

Occupation have a lot to do with the demystification of elements Leiris now calls "maniacal" in his desire to make literature an act. A writer never exposes himself, as a writer, to a literal death threat; anyone who chooses to write has given up running any real risks "except outside his art."[2] And if Leiris considers himself more committed in 1946 than he was before the war, this is because at least to a limited extent he is committed not literarily but "materially."

He continues to be obsessed by masculinity, which he still measures in terms of risk, but he now acknowledges that he had overestimated the risk presented by women. Two examples: in the 1939 text, he had declared himself unable to make love without immediately anticipating the tortures to which love might expose him; in 1946 a note offers a correction on that point. The correction has to do with his fear of physical suffering, which has not decreased (nor has the shameful certainty that his behavior is unheroic) but which has changed context. "The period of police terror imposed by the German occupation" has made him realize that torture chambers do not slam shut exclusively on Romeos.[3] And although there may be danger in frequenting too many beds, the choice of this theater nevertheless remains, in itself, a refusal to take risk to extremes: the hand that issues the certificate of manhood is no longer exclusively feminine.

The interpretation of the Judith figure is corrected in a similar way. Leiris had associated that female image (which is one of the poles, along with the Lucrece figure, around which *Manhood* is organized) with "the image of that punishment simultaneously feared and desired: castration." In 1946 his view has changed: "Today, I would no longer explain this in psychoanalytic terms and by invoking castration. Instead of a punishment both feared and desired, I would refer to my fear of committing myself, of assuming responsibilities—whence my tendency, counterbalanced by an inverse desire, to evade any virile determination—a general attitude I adopted with regard to life (which can only be lived on condition that one accepts death) and an attitude of which what I feel about physical love is no more than a particular case."[4]

Leiris—who has just read Sartre's *Being and Nothingness*—reinterprets his fears in terms of a much more existential psychoanalysis than the one to which Doctor Borel had subjected him: sexuality no longer has the last word.[5] Masculine resolve is still at issue, but the threat hanging over it is no longer sexual. Ever since the Gestapo showed that one could punish effectively with no love involved, Judith has been the emblem for any situation requiring commitment. Risking a little bit of one's own body within a woman's body ("I love not knowing what the future holds," Bataille used to say) is no longer the only way to lose sight of oneself. Once the terrain of truth has been displaced from the sexual to the political, commitment replaces castration. In this sense, the politicization of the 1946 text is first of all a desexualization of risk.

JUDITH OR SALOME

But is Judith a sexual figure? In the original context of Jewish resistance to Nebuchadnezzar, her image was exclusively religious and political. The book of the Bible (generally considered a work of fiction) that recounts her principal exploit makes no mention of sexual relations between her and Holofernes. And tradition maintains more or less unanimously that the chroniclers said nothing on the subject not because they were overly discreet but because nothing had happened. Judith's chastity even led the church fathers to make her a prefiguration of the Virgin, the canonical prototype of militant virginity. No doubt she was not unaware of her charms, which she knew how to use to approach and attract a brutish soldier, but good wine plunged the lout into a sleep from which love never had the chance to awaken him. Judith shared his table, not his bed. The Bible brings her out of Holofernes' tent as intact as she went in. She must not be confused with Yaël, still less with Mata Hari.

This chaste scenario is the one Leiris borrows from the Larousse dictionary as an epigraph to the chapter of *Manhood* titled "Judith." However, that does not prevent him from evoking a "murderous" Judith a page or so later, the "murderess of the man with whom, the moment before, she has gone to bed." Leiris may well have seen the dictionary entry as an expurgated version, like the *Histoire sainte* of his childhood; in the latter case he did not doubt for a moment that only pious censorship, *ad usum delphini*, could account for the absence of any "licentious" details. The turn-of-the-century atmosphere undoubtedly has a lot to do with this sexualization of a Judith who is more and more contaminated by Salome. Leiris's Judith is in fact a syncretic figure in which Holofernes' heroic killer is fused with Herod's daughter, "an implacable and castrating child (she demands the severed head of the prophet, although she loves him)." These two women have identical claims to fame. They both caused the death of a man: in Judith's case a man she had provoked into desiring her, in Salome's case a man who had refused to desire her. But the source for the "patriot prostitute," as Leiris calls Judith is not the Bible but Maupassant's "Ball-of-Fat."[6]

For Erwin Panofsky, the amalgamation of Judith and Salome constitutes a particularly clear-cut example of modern ignorance of iconography. In his introduction to *Studies in Iconology* (published in 1939, contemporaneously with *Manhood*), Panofsky challenges the identification of a painting by Francesco Maffei (a seventeenth-century Venetian) that a conservator had labeled *Salome* because it depicted a woman, armed with a sword, bearing a man's head on a platter. Now, a structuralist might say that there are two ways of bearing a head: from the bottom or from the top. You either hold it up (so that it lies with the cut-off neck resting on a supporting surface) or else you hold it down (and then it hangs by the hair or is wrapped up in a bag or a cloth).[7] This binary choice ought to suffice for identification of the murderess: if the head is suspended, it is Holofernes', being carried out of the tent by Judith's servant; if it is lying flat, it is John the Baptist's, which Salome has had brought in on a platter. But the language of icons is subject to incorrect "pronunciations." Certain figures violate the rules of agreement between the subject and its attributes. This is the case for Maffei's beheader, beside whom a man's head is lying on a platter. Still, a grammatical error of this sort should not affect the reading of the icon. The woman has a sword in her hand, and, as Panofsky shows, as long as she holds onto the sword, a Judith, even a head-bearing one, remains a Judith. As far as any iconologist can remember, no Salome has ever taken up her weapon.

SLEEPING WITH THE ENEMY

The account of the night Judith spends in Holofernes' tent takes up two pages and reminds us that Leiris initially conceived *Manhood* as an erotic text. His narrative conflates the two phases of Judith's relationship with the enemy general. Whereas one might presume that she slept with Holofernes first and cut off his head afterward, Leiris's metaphors superimpose these consecutive acts. Musing before Lucas Cranach's painting, he lingers over the man's head, "a bearded ball she holds like a phallic glans she could have sundered merely by pressing her legs together when Holofernes' floodgates opened; or which, an ogress at the height of her madness, she might have cut from the powerful member of the drunken (and perhaps vomiting) man with a sudden snap of her teeth."[8] Holofernes' destiny had already inspired Freud, in his 1918 essay "The Taboo of Virginity," to make the identical equation: "Beheading is . . . a symbolic substitute for castration."[9] But in Leiris's description, Holofernes' head is detached not after he has reached sexual climax but at the very moment when climax conflates head and sex: the acephalization is not the result of a postcoital retaliation; it is part of the ejaculation.[10]

Leiris was not the first to conclude that, without sexual relations, something was missing in Judith's story. In "The Taboo of Virginity" Freud had congratulated Friedrich Hebbel, his most famous predecessor, for restoring the logic of events along with the sexual relations between Judith and Holofernes in his own *Judith* (1840). In condemning this logic, biblical censorship made the sequence of events incomprehensible. Still, not every woman who spends the night with a man decapitates him the next morning. To be explicable, the passage from Judith's sexual relations with Holofernes to the latter's decapitation requires a supplementary fact: Judith's virginity. It is not enough for Judith to sleep with Holofernes; he must also be the first man with whom she has slept. A woman cannot forgive the man who has been the first to introduce her to the pleasures of shame, to the man who makes a woman of her. Freud calls this a brilliant insight.[11] Now that the biblical story resembles a Zola novel, now that it can be explained without invoking a divine mission or Israel's status as a chosen people, it finally means something. In the explanation of the murder, sexuality has replaced God.

When Judith's virginity was called into question, reactions were heated. Jean Giraudoux used Hebbel's hypothesis in his own *Judith*, staged by Louis Jouvet in 1931, just at the time Leiris was beginning to capture his own ego on notecards destined for *Manhood.*[12] At the time, Paul Claudel was ambassador to Washington. It took several days for newspapers to cross the Atlantic. On November 19 he learned from *Le Temps* with what sauce Giraudoux, his precious colleague from the Quai d'Orsay, had just seasoned the Bible story. He did not read the play. Reading the critics was enough. He wrote at once to Darius Milhaud: that play, he declared, "adds blasphemy to smut. Judith is one of the pure, lofty figures of Israel, and the Church venerates her as a live prophecy of the Holy Virgin. I shall not allow her to be insulted by a miserable wretch without protest." On December 16 he informs Milhaud that the predicted reprisals have taken place. "To avenge the pure and sublime figure of Judith, I have just completed a fairly long poem that I shall probably send to *Les nouvelles littéraires.* Judith is the flower of God's Wisdom, whom the Jewish mystics called Shekinah. The little town besieged on the mountain is the fortress where all those who believe in the God of Israel stand fast. Nebuchadnezzar and Holofernes are the vast materialistic legion in the midst of which we are floundering. Judith's weapon is goodness and charity, as indicated by two striking lines of the admirable text. Holofernes' head is the periodic bounty that the Church exacts of heretics, by detaching from the body that which gave it life. Finally, it is to Judith that the Church addresses this solemn praise: *Tu gloria Israël! tu honorificiancia populi nostri.* You'll be able to do a lovely piece on the subject."[13]

There are important differences between Hebbel's *Judith* and Giraudoux's. In both plays, Judith is a virgin when the curtain goes up and is no longer a virgin when it falls. In both plays, too, the murder of Holofernes is a consequence of the sexual relations she has had with him. But nothing in Giraudoux evokes the taboo of virginity. In contrast with the Freudian thesis, in Giraudoux's play there is nothing sinister about Judith's wedding night. Nothing in the language Giraudoux uses hints at what Freud called the "narcissistic injury which proceeds from the destruction of an organ." What Giraudoux's Judith holds against Holofernes is not what took place but what followed: the letdown. Not the penetration but the withdrawal. She kills Holofernes not in retaliation for what happened but as a way of preserving the event. Hebbel's Judith kills Holofernes because she hates the man who made a woman of her; Giraudoux's Judith kills him because she loves him (she kills the man with whom she has just discovered love). Seeing him asleep, watching him snore, she is afraid that day will break on a life in which there will be no more room for what the night has revealed to her. Giraudoux's *Judith* is thus the story of a young woman who discovers love in the arms of the enemy. She had been promised to the Minotaur; she finds herself confronting Don Juan. And if she ends up killing him after all, it is in a gesture of supreme tenderness; it is because she refuses to allow the experience to be trivialized through contact with everyday life.[15]

Like Hebbel's, Giraudoux's Judith breaks free of holy writ. This is the sense in which Claudel can term the play "Voltairean." What happens inside the tent concerns only those who were there. Holofernes leads Judith to find refuge in a space sheltered from the sacred: no god, no religion, no chosen people, no historical mission has access to it. He removes her from the rabbinical concept of the chosen, the elect. Afterward, she revolts against the idea of her own eschatological instrumentalization, refuses to identify herself as a blind and passive tool of a mission that transcends her. Thus the third act and last focuses on the conflict between two interpretations of Holofernes' murder. When she leaves the tent, Judith tries to impose her version, which is profane (sexual or amorous), against the rabbis who want to stifle it under their sacred version. But she ends up giving in. She has to give up her authorial rights. She is deprived of the interpretation of her act. The act belongs to her, but its meaning escapes her. And the play ends with the triumph of the story's historical meaning, the invention of the edifying legend that turns Judith into a sort of Joan of Arc, the elimination of everything that might hint at what Leiris calls scabrous details: Judith, according to Scripture, came away from Holofernes' bed a virgin, for God made him impotent ("God weakened him suddenly, and he did not take her!"[16] The rabbis take an act that Judith had wanted to make irrecoverable and force it back into the bosom of the synagogue (similarly, at the end of *Dirty Hands*, the Communist party recovers the historical meaning of Hugo's murder of Hoederer by amputating its sexual dimension).

JUDITH, OR THE THIRD PERSON

As originally published, *Manhood* was organized not around the decadent twinship of the Judith and Salome figures but, by way of Cranach's diptych, around the much more canonical pairing of the two "strong women" of the humanist tradition, Judith and Lucrece. Leiris presented them as opposites: Lucrece, or the weakness of the (feminine) object, versus Judith, or the weakness of the (masculine) subject. But this is a symmetry imposed after the fact.[17] Leiris himself had to acknowledge that, given the associations clustered about Judith, the Lucrece rubric remains on the thin side. This inequality itself results from a deeper dissymmetry. Lucrece's relative paleness stems from the fact that in the account of her misfortunes there is no opening where the autobiographer can slip in (at no point, for example, does Leiris suggest that he identifies with Tarquin, that he sees himself as Lucrece's rapist: the Leiris-Tarquin equation is somewhat improbable). However, if the first person is more easily introduced into Judith's story, it is not because of Judith herself; it is because of Holofernes, or at least what is left of him: the "Judith" chapter is followed by "The Head of Holofernes," a section that has no counterpart on Lucrece's side. This redistribution of the biblical legend and its recentering around Holofernes are logical consequences of the fact that *Manhood*, unlike Hebbel's play and Giraudoux's, is not a book about Judith. It is an autobiography. And not Judith's.

By detaching itself, Holofernes' head indeed marks the point of departure of the autobiographical project. Under the (indirect and paradoxical) invocation of Judith, this head is what wins Leiris over to the use of the first person. And if Leiris is right when he says in his 1946 clarification that what is at stake here is not simply a masochistic sexual obsession with Holofernes' fate, it is nevertheless hard to believe that this transcendence of sexuality is brought off in favor of politics, as the postwar autocritic would have it. An identification with Judith might well have initiated a credible political engagement. But Leiris identifies with the beheaded Holofernes, and this identification (like Mallarmé's identification with Saint John, or Blanchot's identification with Odysseus in his reading of the Homeric episode of the Sirens' song) marks the origin of his book.

Thus it hardly matters that Leiris confuses a chaste Judith with a depraved Salome. The values emblematized by these two figures are relegated to the background by the effects they induce. The women are made into muses for the elocutionary disappearance of the autobiographer; they serve as inspiration for the autobiographical caesura; they allow the first person to detach itself; they allow the subject to expose itself as a self-that-is-dying.[18] Because it capitalizes on Holofernes, this first person takes the phantasmic material that was initially distributed between Judith and Lucrece and recenters it on the Judith-Salome pair. By the same token, Judith herself, not just an object in her own right, becomes the intermediary without which the autobiographer would not have had a chance to put on Holofernes' mask.

Here, too, there is nothing especially innovative about Leiris's move. As Maffei's painting would suffice to prove, the ignorance of the iconological tradition to which the Judith-Salome amalgamation attests has its own tradition, and—as is obvious from the impressive gallery of beheaded egos Louis Marin parades before us in *To Destroy Painting*—this tradition is peculiarly related to that of the self-portrait (from Alessandro Allori, who, in *Judith and Holofernes' Head*, lends his own features to Holofernes and gives Judith those of his mistress; to Michelangelo Merisi Caravaggio, who, in response to Giorgione painting himself as a conquering David, reverses roles and represents himself as a decapitated Goliath).[19] Reframed within this tradition, the identification with Holofernes can no longer be reduced to a masochistic weirdness exclusive to a neurotic bourgeois male named Michel Leiris; it has an exemplary power that inaugurates and structures the self-representative exercise as such. A castrating mimesis: the mirror cuts. I recognize myself in a mirror that reduces me to a head. Marin's commentary can be displaced without modification from Allori's and Caravaggio's painted self-portraits to the written self-portrait of *Manhood:* "The problem of truth separates the head from the body . . . Not only does the mirror, with its surface effect, pass between the painter and his model (himself), not only does it split the subject of the act of painting into an 'I' and a 'you,' but *it passes between the head and the body*, between the place of looking and the place of gestures, between the representation to be painted (the idea, the design, the subject) and the act of painting (the body and the hand that inscribe the reflection in the mirror onto the canvas). The mirror . . . poses the theoretical and technical problem, indissolubly theoretical and practical, of beheading and re-heading, of decapitation and recapitation." And also: "The painter inscribes himself in the painting under the double sign of the gaze and the caesura of that by virtue of which it is a gaze, the head."[20]

As if he were taking his place inside the life-size cardboard figures with cut-out heads used by carnival photographers, when Judith and Salome beckon, Leiris rushes head first into autobiography; he thrusts his first person into the hole. He yells: castration. Then he reconsiders: I am committing myself. Autobiography produces the same effect as Judith: it detaches the head from the body, distances from himself the one who undertakes to represent himself.

This homology between Judith and autobiography presides over the famous passage in which Leiris, right at the beginning of the "Judith" chapter, describes the autobiographer's *caput mortuum:* "I cannot say, properly speaking, that *I die*, since—dying a violent death or not—I am conscious of only part of the event."[21] What gets the autobiographical enterprise going is what will also always cut it off from its end; autobiography is triggered by the encounter with the imaginary, by the (impossible) experience of what escapes it, the experience of what eludes its grasp, the grasp of the first person; in this sense, it is the enterprise of a subject who is forbidden to reach its end. He will commit himself to the enterprise only on condition that he not see the outcome. Autobiography grabbed by the tail:[22] it is, literally, broached by what breaches it—*entamée*, in all senses of the word, by the dictum "You will not reach your end." "You will not say everything." But this prohibition on saying everything is not sexual. For it is not *ad usum delphini* that I cannot say that I die. Rather—to remain in the realm of marine creatures—it would be *ad usum Sirenarum*. The encounter with the imaginary subjects the autobiographical game to the law of unfinished siren songs. In this sense, the preface added to *Manhood* in 1946 adds nothing to the text that it purportedly corrects: it is in effect because I cannot say that I am dying that no bull's horn will be inscribed on the surface of the text. Odysseus must become Homer. And Holofernes must become Leiris in order to narrate in the first person the unreality to which his encounter with Judith condemned him.

On the occasion of the reprint edition of *Manhood*, Blanchot wrote "Gazes from Beyond the Grave." The essay is reprinted in *The Work of Fire*, a collection of articles describing literary inspiration as the movement of someone who in his writing strives for impersonality, depersonalization, effacement of the first person before the third.[23] It would seem that, owing to the exclusively autobiographical character of its inspiration, Leiris's work ought to have challenged the validity of such a law. The autobiographer's intention was to protect himself against such depersonalization; that much is clear. But the work itself is there to attest to his failure. Blanchot comments on a passage of *Aurora* in which, after identifying the third person with death ("all the vague chastisements and monstrous threats which the word HE could hold for me"), Leiris deplores the fragility of the protection afforded by the first person against the dangers of that grammatical Judith: "For here I have come to cathedral Death, to this third person singular . . . whatever the words I utter and whatever this 'I' which I put forward."[24] But this setting forth of the "I," including its detachment by means of quotation marks (achieving the separation of the

"I" that is set forth and the one that is setting it forth), constitutes precisely the autobiographical precipitation, the apotropaic advance that brings about the detachment of a head. Thus autobiography itself is what produces the transcendence of the ego: like Judith's sword, it is the instrument of a bracketing, an evacuation, a subjective reduction that, in phenomenological terms, is as radical as it is capital.

According to a well-known anecdote, it was while he was looking for illustrations for *Documents* (of which he was managing editor at the time) that Leiris happened onto the reproduction of the diptych by Cranach that would serve as the frontispiece for *Manhood.* But Cranach is not the only link between *Documents* and autobiography. Most of the articles Leiris published in that journal set the stage for *Manhood.*[25]

Documents automatically gave pride of place to features that evoked metamorphosis, morphological transgression, some gap in the reproduction of forms. Leiris's contribution to the final issue of the journal ("Le 'caput mortuum' ou la femme de l'alchimiste" [Caput Mortuum, or the Alchemist's Wife]) sets up what might be called a distorting mirror stage; it is a meditation before various types of *acephali,* images of headless—or rather, faceless—bodies. The article accompanies a series of photos, taken by William Seabrook, of an "effaced" woman, her head wrapped down to her shoulders in a sheath of black leather that depersonalizes her. Leiris comments in highly laudatory terms on this censorship, which, by deindividualizing the small other, gives body to a sort of large other. The individual cost of this anonymity, this *in vivo* generalization, is not completely overlooked, however. Leiris notes that the woman "suffers under the leather"; she is "annoyed and mortified," and this, he points out, "must satisfy our desires for power and our fundamental cruelty." But this conscious and even labored sadism is overturned in the last paragraph; in a reversal for which the reader is left unprepared, the anonymous woman, woman "*in general,*" is described as "masked like an executioner."[26]

Sadism or masochism? And what happens to sexual difference in this case? Is the sex of Acephalus subject to the same ambiguities as that of the angels? Could that female Acephalus be a Holofernized Judith? Let us settle for noting here that their masochistic streak is what allows these fantasies to open the way to autobiographical inspiration.

Leiris turns Seabrook's photos into a set of peculiar stations of the Cross, associating them with a mystical Arabic narrative that culminates in a moment of terror: a dervish who was expecting to see the face of God finds himself confronting "his own face." This conclusion constitutes a rather unexpected moral in the context of the fable it illustrates. The images of headless women are formative of the function of the "I." These photographs of a head that does not see itself establish the paradoxical matrix of a relation to the self. According to Bataille's equation, man is what he is lacking: thus it is the absence of a head that broaches autobiography. The subject of autobiography is not the one who stubbornly insists on effacing the other, but the one who loses face, who in the depths of himself encounters the faceless other, recognizes himself in the without-self of the third person. Such is literally the *caput mortuum* of the autobiographer: his alchemy aims at bringing his own face and the other's absence of face into convergence in a common horror. Leiris borrows the description of this moment from Hegel and speaks of the "empty self that gives itself as an object his own empty identity."[27] This is the beginning of kenography: the emptying of the subject is the support for the autobiographical cenotaph.

The title of Blanchot's essay, "Gazes from Beyond the Grave," refers to an experience structured according to the same model as the one Hegel describes. At issue is a dream narrative that Leiris included in *Nights as Day, Days as Night:* "I insert my head into an opening that resembles an oeil-de-boeuf window overlooking a dark, enclosed area akin to those cylindrical pisé granary lofts . . . My anxiety derives from the fact that as I lean over this enclosed area and get a glimpse of its inner darkness, I am actually gazing into myself."[28] The key word here is the verb "surprise." For the relations between the autobiographer and his inner self imply that the former feels he is an intruder within himself. A genuine autobiographer operates by acts of burglary; he must be able to prove that he did not expect himself within (he has to surprise himself penetrating himself, he has to penetrate himself by surprise, has to penetrate an interior where, the further he goes, the less he knows his way around, the less he recognizes it as his own). He has been ordered to undertake the mission of rejoining his body. He enters without knocking. And he experiences the anguish of someone who, turning in on himself, offers himself as prey to his own shadow. Someone who, by dint of envisaging himself, stares himself down.

9

POETRY FROM A TO Z

CENOTAPHS

The setting was a pathway on the grounds of Ermenonville, where the author of *Aurélia* and *Pandora*, *Aurora*'s two sisters, used to stroll in search of forgetfulness. "Where are our sweethearts? They are in the grave." Rousseau's weightier shade soon joins Gérard de Nerval's: the author of the *Confessions* died and was buried at Ermenonville. As it happens, the same estate also houses a temple of philosophy dedicated "to Michel de Montaigne." In a descriptive passage, Leiris mentions this fact in passing. To bring Montaigne's name into *The Rules of the Game*, nothing less than Nerval's patronage was required.[1] Name dropping. A name falls. Hollow.[2]

Rousseau's grave is indeed the true center of the passage in *Fibrilles* (Tiny Fibers) that describes the grounds where the marquis of Girardin, after providing the solitary wanderer a haven for his last days, would eventually shelter his ashes. And there the ashes remained, until the Revolution transported them to the Pantheon. The description occurs during a detailed analysis of a dream. Leiris is just about to launch upon a series of associations inspired by a singularly elusive garden: the dreamer, who has become the analyst of his own dream, no longer knows to what extent the dream really occurred. Perhaps he has dreamed this garden—but then he would have to specify whether in the dream it appeared "in person," as a dream garden, or whether in the dream it was not already a memory of a garden, a garden not dreamed but remembered by the dreamer, or else—a third possibility—whether the garden was not tacitly suggested in the dream, an implicit but never verified presence on the horizon of the dream sequence. But perhaps the dreamer is also in the process, after the fact and pen in hand, of giving body to the garden in order to introduce it forcibly into a dream that is no longer there to make its voice heard and to recall, if necessary, that it unfolded in the first place without that horticultural apparatus. Thus before what might quite legitimately be called the associative sequence induced by the word "garden" begins, the exact status of this inducer itself has to be determined with maximal precision: what about this garden, which Leiris no longer manages to find in the dream that had nevertheless conveyed it, a secret garden, lost without leaving any tracks, buried beyond recall in the dream at the bottom of which it is hiding as if it wished to be forgotten there forever?

Just as he is about to solicit this imponderable garden, Leiris hesitates, asks himself if he is not proposing to drag out of his dream "a secret that perhaps it lacks." (But are not true secrets the ones that are lacking?) This scruple inaugurates the description of the Ermenonville grounds, grounds that soon come to hold in turn a sort of secret lack; they constitute a landscape in which a haunting absence is ensconced. At the end of a string of frames embedded one within another ("in the leafy fullness of the park, the void of a body of water; in the void of that lake, the fullness of the earth of an island; in the more or less round fullness of that solid ground, a smaller circle drawn by poplars; in the middle of the void created by the ring thus formed, the fullness of the gravestone"), the reader is led to the cenotaph in which, below the fullness of the stone, lies "the hollow where—as Nerval says—*Rousseau's ashes are missing.*"[3]

The Ermenonville grounds do not come into play for their thematic value, as a first variation on the theme of gardens, but for their scenographic productivity: they repeat the scene of the dream that summons them up. Rousseau's remains are absent from the garden they haunt just as the phantom garden is missing from the dream that evokes it. Cenotaph and hollow dream: this scenography is a *cenography.* The thing looks like nothing at all. It functions in a void. The stage is deserted. How far does a text go? It goes to the point of not saying where it comes from. Or where it is going. The description ceaselessly elides that around which it turns;

it augments itself endlessly from the eclipse of its center. If the text authorizes itself, it is only by virtue of the lack of that on which it bears and rests. It tirelessly repeats the desertion of its core. At the heart of the text, the reader stumbles onto what Leiris has called "a real lack of heart."

At the beginning of *Manhood*, Leiris evokes his "first actual contact with the notion of infinity":[4] the label on a tin of cocoa displaying an image of a Dutch girl holding a tray on which an identical tin of cocoa has a label displaying another tin of cocoa displaying an image of the same Dutch girl, et cetera, ad infinitum. Within *Fibrilles*, Rousseau's empty tomb is not limited to reproducing the structure of the dream with the elusive garden. but, through an anticipation that is nevertheless incalculable, it miniaturizes the book still to come in which it appears: in the middle of *Fibrilles*, as we know, Leiris commits suicide. At the center of his book, the author puts himself in his own grave; the tomb into which he descends will remain empty, as the cenographic scenario requires. In order to be central, the descent had to be unsuccessful, *manquée*. What remains is *Fibrilles*, a cenotaph deprived of the ashes whose hearth it had wanted to be, nameless living ashes, the author's remains. At Rousseau's tomb, *Fibrilles* reproduces itself ad infinitum even before it exists. It mirrors itself vertiginously in the tomb where it is lacking, empty. Leiris's first published poem was titled "Nothing Is Ever Finished."[5]

A homologous mark, to come to or come back to Montaigne, traces at the heart of the *Essays* a void that hollows out, between center and cinders, a similar cenography, that of a writing that nothing fills, the fulfillment of writing nonetheless. In their initial design, the *Essays* had as their center what ought to have been the most voluminous citation in a work that was by no means short on citations, moreover an entirely unpublished citation, offered up here as a preview: a series of twenty-nine sonnets by Etienne de La Boétie. Montaigne introduces himself by introducing the remains of his alter ego. He authorizes himself through the text of another and becomes an author by augmenting himself with the works of his former half: a doubly foreign body, since this work, which was not written by the signer of the book in which it appears, is moreover a work of poetry (sonnets) inserted as the heterogeneous center at the heart of a text written, prosaically, in the language of daily life.

Montaigne's writing—he went so far as to publish this fact on his walls—took definitive shape in the aftershock of the loss of that friend for whom the *Essays*, in their first form, sought to be only a sort of tomb. A tomb that in the very first edition strangely prefigures Rousseau's tomb in the garden at Ermenonville. In the central place that is reserved for them but that they no longer occupy, under a heading that announces them—"Twenty-nine sonnets of Etienne de la Boétie"—but to which they are no longer present to respond, only the following words remain: "These verses may be seen elsewhere."[6] Rousseau's ashes too appear elsewhere: in the Pantheon. No one has yet managed to break the nullibiety, to localize the point that withstands all topography where Montaigne sent his readers off to see the poems of his friend. A farewell to poetry? The autobiographic discourse gives poetic writing its leave: the poems retreat before their introduction. Beat a retreat first. Then desert.

I should like to suggest here in a similar way that throughout his autobiographical work, Leiris never stops grieving over poetry, marking its retreat, tracking down its absence, deploring what in *Frêle bruit* (Frail Noise) he calls "the silence of the Sibyl's lair: deserted seat of an oracle whose voice has been cut off."[7] An Orpheus singing Eurydice's disappearance, Leiris sings the loss of his own voice; he prolongs the grand aria of the offstage voice. Like Montaigne with his double, Leiris bids adieu to the poet he will not have been. *The Rules of the Game:* the cenotaph of Michel Leiris, poet.[8]

One final remark about Montaigne: the words he uses to recommend the poems of his late poetic alter ego indicate that a temperamental incompatibility would keep poetry and autobiography apart, would condemn them in advance to divorce. There can be no such thing as a poet's memories, if it is true that the words of a poem are always words without memory. And what is at stake here, precisely, is husbandry *(ménage)*, a certain way of writing to husband one's resources *(se ménager)* while sharing a household *(emménager)*. Speaking in praise of La Boétie, Montaigne explains that he wrote the sonnets in question "in his greenest youth": thus they attest to a fiery "ardor" that can no longer be found in the later poems that he wrote "in favor of his wife" and that "smack of a certain marital coolness." In the third book of the *Essays*, in the chapter called "On Some Verses of Virgil," Montaigne expresses astonishment at finding a "passionate" depiction of a "marital Venus" in the *Aeneid*.[9] The love of poetry does not readily espouse the prose of legitimate conjugations.

The tone is not the writer's voice, but the intimacy of the silence he imposes upon the words.

Maurice Blanchot, *The Space of Literature*

A calling makes a poet.[10] Poets are called by the only name to which they answer; they are marked.

As for Leiris, no one has asked him for anything, and his autobiographical step returns again and again to the place marked by the absence of the mark that would have authorized this text that goes on and on remarking its absence: he did not have the calling, and that lack is the starting point for his work.

It so happened, however, that when he was about ten years old he suddenly felt that he had not only been called but specially chosen for a vocation. The angel of glory landed on him during a brief annunciation that might recall the triumphal euphoria that Raymond Roussel confided to Pierre Janet, or the Proustian experience of recaptured time, though with a difference: Leiris's experience was preliterary, scarcely linguistic, a child's adventure. This glorious suffusion takes him over for a few short minutes, brought back to life in *Fibrilles.* The scene takes place at Heist-sur-Mer in Belgium, where the family vacation is winding down. To help out with a game, little Michel was asked (or perhaps he offered) to leave the living room so that the two remaining children could choose a card from a pack. The excluded player was then called back in and had to pick out the card in question from all the others. But the conspirators, instead of choosing a card, had agreed to say that the card Michel selected was the right one, no matter what card it was. So the child succeeded again and again; going from triumph to triumph, he ended up conceding, in all simplicity and good faith, that he was possessed by a gift for divination that he had not previously had the occasion to demonstrate, or even to suspect, and that would henceforth set him apart from ordinary mortals, would position him among the most prestigious seers. If Leiris recalls this episode, it is obviously because of the cruel deflation with which it ended, once the players showed their hands. He then goes on to say: "Thinking about what I had experienced at Heist-sur-Mer when I had thought I possessed a gift that would have situated me in a singularly marginal relation to the ordinary, I have wondered for a long time to what extent an impulse of the same nature as that childish pride might have been the inspiration at the point when, having become a young man and not knowing very well what to do with myself, I wanted to *be a poet*."[11] He had thought he was possessed, when he had simply been had. The gift of the gift par excellence, the gift of prophecy and fortune-telling, a gift that would have made him an oracle, leaves behind its derisorily false appearance as only a miserable taste of ashes.

In the "Sunday" section of *Scratches*, a sequence headed "Choosing a Career" begins with a similar episode. There, the setting is a church. As soon as the person who has defined himself as "a specialist in confessions"[12] emerges from the confessional, the vicar calls him, takes him aside and tells him: "My dear Michel, I have been watching you carefully: I see that you have the signs of the vocation. I am sure that you would make a very good priest." "Little" Michel obviously does not fail to grow in contact with these signs that the recruiting curate's proselytism has just attached to his person: a sudden dilation of the ego, a megalomaniacal gulp of air is all it takes to convince him that he is "some sort of chosen person." As in the Heist episode, expansion is followed by detumescence, the return to reality. But this time, before spelling out the future to which these so-called signs are inviting him, the narrator does not wait for someone well versed in ecclesiastical practices to demystify him by suggesting that any conscientious priest would have approached the young members of his flock in just the same way. With no thought of checking to see whether the call was real or not, Leiris immediately decided to elude it, and the reason given for his refusal is worth contemplating: "Those who entered the orders were obliged to be chaste and prohibited from marrying."[13]

Talking about marriage, we have to go back to *Manhood*, where the generation of the autobiography is settled, in terms both of life and of writing, and especially in the book's later chapters, those which have virtually nothing to do with the author's childhood. These chapters are dominated by the somber figure of Holofernes, in whose shadow the poetic vocation and marriage trace their tragicomic zigzags.[14] For if in *Scratches* we saw the child Leiris reject a so-called calling that would have condemned him to virginity and celibacy, in *Manhood*, some ten years later—just after he has depicted himself as a disoriented bachelor "not tempted by anything," having "no vocational impulse whatever"—we see him presenting himself as someone who possesses "still more than a vocation, a *destiny*" that turns out to be celibacy, chastity, absolute purity (and "unsatisfaction"), a fate common to those who live as poets. The reason for this reversal? Leiris wants to avoid marriage. "I meditated," he wrote, "on Gobineau's fable (one of the *Nouvelles asiatiques*) of the initiate to whom an illustrious thaumaturge is about to reveal the ultimate magical secret, but who loses everything on the threshold of discovery because he turns back when his wife (who saw herself being abandoned) follows and calls to him."[15] (On the threshold of discovery, just as he was about to learn the last word, the omega, on the matter, just as he was about to reach point Z, was within a hair's breadth of having them show him their cards, lift the veil, and so on. It was at precisely this moment that he had to be called! That the conjugal vocation should call him by his name! Obviously, in Gobineau's story, if we follow Leiris's summary, the catastrophe stems not from the fact that the wife follows the initiate and calls out to him, but from the fact that the initiate responds to his name, that he lets himself be turned aside by the appeal. He is already divided between two bifurcating desires that condemn him to digression, to distraction.)

In *Manhood*, Gobineau's fable concludes the narrative of a liaison that Leiris has just interrupted. He draws a lesson from it: one must choose between one's work and one's life. In order to attain the ultimate revelations of poetry, it is necessary to abjure marriage ("[I was] convinced that marriage and poetry were mutually exclusive"). Leiris goes further still: he attempts to renounce sexuality. One might even suspect that the poetic vocation of which he had manifested no previous sign had arisen miraculously to spare him certain difficulties in sexual relations. For it is from that first liaison, while Leiris is engaging in the "habitation of women" that did not work for Rousseau (from whom I borrow the expression) according to the latter's own testimony, that his "first aspirations to poetry" arose, he reports: "[it] seemed to me a refuge, a means of . . . recovering a safe domain that would be all my own, where my partner could not interfere."[16] At the root of Gobineau's moral tale is the postulate of the initiate's chastity: abstention from sexual relations is the path to revelation. But only one discovery offers itself along this path: for there to be no sexual relations, it is neither necessary nor sufficient for me to abstain from them.

Between the lines of *Manhood*, the figure of the Medusa is suggested everywhere. The final chapter borrows its title from the legendary raft, taken as an allegory of life. In the opening chapter ("Tragic Themes"), Medusa had already been associated with Stella in Offenbach's *Tales of Hoffmann;* and even before that, in an epigraph borrowed from Goethe's *Faust* (in Nerval's translation, of course), Mephistopheles has warned his protégé against what, except for the hour, could be called the midday demon, the slashed-necked specter of Marguerite. Mephistopheles: "That rigid stare would 'thick men's blood with cold' and almost turn you into stone. Haven't you heard about Medusa?"[17]

Almost to stone: something a poet might say, if one takes literally Leiris's description of his own poetic vocation as "a symbolic attempt at *mineralization*, a defense-reaction," he specifies, "against my inner weakness and the collapse by which I felt myself threatened; I longed for some kind of armor, seeking to achieve in my eternal *persona* the same idea of stiffness and rigidity which I pursued poetically."[18] According to Freud, man stiffens up in front of woman not with desire but with terror: as if to resist the other's cut. The sun also rises, but Aurora is spelled Horror.

What lesson are we to draw from Gobineau's fable? Against what did its reader think it would warn him? The question is all the more compelling in that the narrative of the bachelor's poetic rigors is immediately followed ("I relaxed") by that of a matrimonial fiasco that *Manhood* calls a "base swindle" and *Fibrilles* a "double betrayal."[19] But the quantity is not what matters: this is not the first time Leiris gives up a vow of chastity in order to marry. As for his poetic vocation, while he may betray it by this marriage, it barely existed prior to its betrayal.

The word "fiasco" may seem excessive. But the author himself is the one who says that, starting from that event, that is, his marriage, he felt himself to be "still less than Holofernes' head."[20]

AND MY ALL WILL NOT COME ABOUT

> Grail whose name does not end but remains in the air and stretches out in invisible currents.
>
> Leiris, *Frêle bruit*

The difference between the real and the imaginary ought to be nonnegotiable.

The pages of *Manhood* in which the author reports the circumstances of his marriage with an equal blend of complacency and culpability are not merely anecdotal. It would be no less mistaken to see them as a simple clinical document making it possible to grasp in their unfolding the convoluted mechanisms of a masochism ready to take anything and everything as a failing. These pages are important because they put the genotext of the autobiography in place.

His marriage constitutes, in Leiris's life and in his work, the realist turning point that programs his conversion to autobiographical writing. It is probably not possible to espouse reality, which is as phantomlike, seen close up, as the Africa through which that realism has led him while endowing him with a second career. Married, he nevertheless has to leave what a text of his surrealist period, a few years earlier, had called "the land of his dreams."[21] If Leiris earlier "accorded a preponderant importance to the *imaginary*," if he wanted to escape reality, the setting up of the autobiographico-conjugal apparatus obliges him to make a break; it cuts his life in two. The nonnegotiable frontier described by the first sentence of *Manhood* lies in between: "I have just reached the age of thirty-four, life's mid-point." Life in two halves. Leiris has spent the first half running after his dreams; the second is to be devoted to the pursuit of reality. Just after the Second World War, in 1946, the preface added to the reprint edition of *Manhood* recalls the decision, both ethical and moral, to which the author held himself: a "predilection for realism" and the rejection of any "fallacious compromise between real facts and the pure products of the imagination."[22]

The marriage is thus not just an anecdote, sentimental or cynical, that could be kept out of the text and attributed to the chapter of a study on Leiris devoted to his "life." The marriage is not so much one of the events lived by the author of *The Rules of the Game* as the birthplace of that text. The place of alliance and divorce where Leiris's life and work, twins and rivals, advance and stagnate at a henceforth competitive pace, where they conjugate and impede each other, incompatible but equally insufficient for themselves and for each other.

The voyage to the end of unreality recounted in *Manhood* ends with an awakening: on the level of utterance, it is marriage; on the level of enunciation, it is the autobiography, the text of *Manhood* itself. "Dreaming and writing down my dreams, regarding some as revelations whose metaphysical bearing I had to discover, comparing them in order to decipher their meaning and deriving from them all sorts of narratives, I woke up screaming almost every night."[23] Is it appropriate to speak of symbolism? The conjugal function, even as it allows an exit from the *idios cosmos*, an opening outside of the unsharable oneiric dimension, even as it sounds the dusk of dreams, negotiates that passage to reality through a screamless awakening whose miniaturized version serves as the conclusion to several of the dreams whose narrative appears in *Nights as Day, Days as Night:* October 8–9, 1933: "but Z . . . wakes me up, informing me that I am on the verge of screaming"; July 12–13, 1940: "Waking up (with a shriek that Z muffles)"; September 29–30, 1957: "Z . . . (roused from her real sleep by the screams I am beginning to emit) calls out to me."[24] *The Rules of the Game*, whose inaugural volume is dedicated to that same awakener, in its very first chapter stages the analogous repression of a scream, the transformation in the course of which ". . . *reusement!*" is lost and found again as "*Heureusement!*"[25]

The College of Sociology cast its lot against life that would be exclusively quotidian. It was imperative to escape. The exception, that which eluded dailiness, was deemed sacred. The strength of Leiris's contribution, indicating how much he has to offer, is summed up in the wording of his title: "The Sacred in Everyday Life" replaces simple antagonism by polemical inclusion.[26] At the end of his poem "The Poet's Vocation," Hölderlin evokes man waiting "till God's being not there helps him."[27] We have to understand in the same way that, like Rousseau's ashes in the Ermenonville garden, the sacred is absent from, or, more forcefully, that it is absent *in*, daily life, like daylight absent from day. One poem from *Haut mal*, "Tragique," begins with a similar gap: "Between loves and *love*."[28] The divorce is broached by the multiplication of a plural deprived of the singular it calls for: Loves without love. *Nights as day, days as night:* the singular is what is missing in everyday life. In Latin, *divortium* also means bifurcation: *divortium itinerum*, distraction from the unique. Distraction was my Beatrice.

The same logic governs *The Rules of the Game* to the very end. Poetry is literally advertised as missing by the autobiographical prose. But, like Hölderlin in the absence of the gods, Leiris's prose comes to find in the process of mourning poetry the surprising resource for a poetic raising of the stakes. Poetry was for Mallarmé a power of negation that compels things to shrink before their own absence, to give way before their own lack: it produces a place in which the thing itself may be lacking. For Leiris, autobiography, precisely inasmuch as it sets itself up as poetry's tomb, is the space in which poetry itself becomes in turn the object of the poetic operation and absents itself in its vibratory disappearance. It embeds itself there without occupying a position of infinite regress: not poetry within poetry, but poetry without poetry, poems without poem. The singular is missing. To the end.

There is also the rule that is missing from the game it entitles. The author will have played the game, but without the rule: the rule was to be discovered and revealed in *Fibules* (Fibulas), previous volumes having announced that this one would bring the enterprise to a conclusion, would allow "the whole to shape up" (*s'ajuster:* to proceed in such a way that there is no more game), would give out the "ultimate secret," the "stubbornly coveted Grail," as if it were one of Gobineau's *Nouvelles asiatiques.* We know that, at the end of the match, *Fibules* ends up missing. *The Rules of the Game* does not lead to the recapture of any time past. Instead, a few maxims are articulated toward the end of *Fibrilles;* rules without rule. But was not *Fibules* supposed to be missing, was it not already, through its plural, condemned to miss the unique point where the scattered insights of the preceding volumes would be gathered, the point that would have ordered their plurality under its authority: why several fibulae to tie up a single rule? Still, in the place where these *Fibules* are lacking, there is *Frêle bruit,* the unique singular of the series—*Biffures (Scratches), Fourbis (Scraps), Fibrilles*—that it unties. As unique and as singular as the messageless sound, "frail noise," "fragile sound" which in "Mors" (Bit) was already saying a single thing—and "that unique thing it was saying is that it was *unique.*"[29] Unique, singular, but fated to dispersal: where the whole was to shape up, there is "nothing but dissemination, disparateness and the scarcely coherent."[30] *Frêle bruit:* shards of uniqueness, the archipelago of the singular.

My first:[31] a grail is being sought that meets all your needs. But it will never be fully pronounced: you never reach the last letter of the last word.

My second is autobiography, the art of reaching one's own end. But with distraction: one touches it, displaces it, and never finds it again.

My third: as a form of exit, just to mark what is or is not a step, that other insignificant detail: "picked up in Dublin, the outside door of 7 Eccles Street, where Leopold Bloom lived, a door that I believe to be

Georgian which—today transferred to the first floor of Bailey's Bar and placed near the toilets—closes nothing and opens onto nothing."[32]

Postscriptum: As first or last rhyme for the charade in *z* of this sort of backward *abc*, a supplementary absence: "on the credence, in the empty room, no ptyx."[33] Certain absences go without saying: seeking to verify them does them an injustice. It is nevertheless the case that, as it should be, the expression "where *Rousseau's ashes are missing*" does not fail to be missing in the text by Nerval to which Leiris refers. It is only missing, of course, literally: its spirit is there, and Leiris says he is quoting from memory. As for the page of *Fibrilles* on which the description of the Ermenonville grounds appears, he recalls having written it with an advertising banner in mind, the one that came with *Being and Nothingness* when it was first published in France. Its legend: "What counts in a vase is the emptiness in the middle."

THE USE VALUE OF THE IMPOSSIBLE

Beauty will be unsalvageable or not be at all.

DOCUMENTS

The *Documents* adventure (two years, fifteen issues) originated a long way from the avant-garde: it began in the Cabinet des Médailles, where Bataille and Pierre d'Espezel were colleagues. D'Espezel was also the director of several very official and more or less specialized reviews: *Aréthuse*, where Bataille's first articles appeared (Bataille was a specialist in numismatics at the time), and *Cahiers de la République des lettres.* In 1928 Bataille had published "L'Amérique disparue," his first major article, in the *Cahiers*' special issue on pre-Columbian America. D'Espezel was also connected with *La gazette des beaux-arts*, which was backed by the art merchant Georges Wildenstein. With d'Espezel as intermediary, Wildenstein went on to finance *Documents.*

Numismatics, as *Documents* collaborator Jean Babelon later defined it, is the science of "coins that no longer circulate except in the speculations of scholars."[1] It is also concerned with medals—coins that have never been in circulation. The numismatic passion verges on avarice: the numismatist loves money but only because, like Molière's Harpagon, he likes to hold onto it, touch it, look at it. He does not enjoy spending. His is a strange, disinterested love of money: it is love of something that makes anything possible, once it has been cut off from what it makes possible. A love of frozen, off-limits currency, money that is simultaneously on display and held in reserve. The numismatist has a passion for units of exchange that are not exchangeable. He requires that these conductors of exchange value be out of circulation themselves. Money leaves the Paris Exchange to be recycled, two blocks away, on the rue de Richelieu, at the Bibliothèque Nationale.[2]

DOCUMENTS AS DEFINED BY THE CHARTIST SCHOOL

It was Bataille who came up with the title *Documents.* For the journal's founders (Bataille, d'Espezel, Wildenstein), the term seems to have had a programmatic value; it was virtually a contract. However, as d'Espezel and Wildenstein saw it, Bataille—who was to be in charge, for practical purposes, as "general secretary"—had ceased to respect the contract even before the journal was fully launched.[3] As early as April 1929 (after just one issue had been published), d'Espezel sent Bataille a humorous but pointed warning: "The title you have chosen for this journal is hardly warranted except in the sense that it gives us 'documents' on your state of mind. That is a great deal, but it is not quite enough. It's really critical to get back to the original intentions behind the journal, as you and I presented them to M. Wildenstein."[4]

Bataille uses the word "document" to present his thesis for the Ecole des Chartes, "L'ordre de chevalerie." The sole value of this medieval text, he says, is documentary. "The poem has no literary value, no originality; it is of no interest except insofar as it is a peculiar old document on chivalric ideas and dubbing rites."[5] Was there a consensus, in keeping with the Chartist notion of a document, that *Documents* would publish only texts that had neither literary value nor originality? If so, d'Espezel's concern is understandable, for Bataille published his own texts in *Documents,* as well as texts by Leiris and others; as d'Espezel realized, whatever their literary merits, these texts unquestionably displayed a certain originality.

ETHNOGRAPHY

Among the rubrics listed in the journal's subtitles, the trinity "Archaeology/Fine Arts/Ethnography" occupies a central position.[6] Each term refers to an independent domain: ethnography is geographically independent and archaeology historically independent of the tutelage of the fine arts. But this relativization of Western aesthetic values is exacerbated by an even more radical relativization, that of aesthetic values as such, a relativization that is highlighted by the choice of the term "ethnography" as opposed to "primitive arts." The term has the value of a manifesto: it announces that *Documents* is not another *Gazette des beaux-arts*, and definitely not a *Gazette des beaux-arts primitifs*.

Documents takes opposition to the aesthetic viewpoint as its platform; the opposition is implied in the journal's title itself.[7] By definition, a document is an object lacking in artistic value. Lacking in or deprived of, depending on whether or not it ever had any. But it comes down to the same thing: an object is either an ethnographic document or a work of art. This binary opposition gives the term "document" its anti-aesthetic connotations even when it is used without qualification. Leiris uses the term quite innocently, without any hint of wordplay, in reviewing a book of anthropological photographs for *Documents:* "France still did not have a book intended for a broad public offering a selection of purely ethnographic documents and not simply a series of artworks."[8]

And although he does not use the word "document," Carl Einstein sets up the same opposition in his review of one of the most important displays of primitive art of the day, the exhibit of African and Oceanic art organized by Tristan Tzara and Charles Ratton at the Pigalle Theater Gallery: "This art must be treated historically, and no longer considered solely from the standpoint of taste and aesthetics."[9]

USE VALUE

> "Our modernity makes a constant effort to defeat the exchange."
>
> Roland Barthes, *The Pleasure of the Text*

Except for one article by Bataille and another by Babelon, the perverse interest of numismatists in the material support of exchange value leaves no lasting traces in the *Documents* table of contents.[10] Use value comes to the fore right away; it is the axis of reflection for the ethnographers grouped around Georges Henri Rivière, the assistant director of the Trocadéro Museum of Ethnography.[11] But the ethnographers and the numismatists disagree not only about values; they also differ over how to approach the issue of objective (one ought to be able to say "objectal") support for the values in question. The ethnographers resist turning tools into aesthetic objects, while the numismatists support the aesthetic exemplification of coins that are not in use. Display windows may restore the fortunes of devalued coins, but they decrease the stature of abandoned tools.

Marx's name does not appear a single time in the pages of *Documents.* But the debate over museums that is pursued in the journal offers close parallels to the opposition between use value and exchange value that comes up at the outset in *Das Kapital,* in connection with the analysis of merchandise. The critique of merchandise also comes to serve as a framework for the common front between ethnographers and dissident surrealists that gives *Documents* its specific character. A significant faction within the avant-garde of the period—which is the period of resistance to the first wave of modernist formalism—is indeed motivated by a desire to return, even to regress, to what might be called the primitivism of use value. And each of the competing trends offers its own critique of formalist decontextualization in the name of use value.[12]

Marx's description of use value in the early pages of *Das Kapital* is familiar. "The usefulness of a thing," he writes, "makes it a use-value."[13] This usefulness, or use value, is thus inseparable from its material support. It has no autonomous, independent existence. But by the same token, this property of a thing is realized only in its use, its consumption, that is, its destruction. Use value does not outlast use; it disappears as it comes to fruition. It is a value that the thing cannot help losing. Exchange value, on the contrary, is not an intrinsic, exclusive property of the objects whose exchange it allows: by definition, it must be common to at least two objects. But more importantly, an object acquires or loses exchange value owing to a delay in consumption. Exchange value is deferred use value. A commodity is an object whose consumption has been delayed, an object set aside, literally placed out of use, in order to be introduced on the market and exchanged. The same principle of diversion that defines markets also applies to museums: objects enter a museum only after they have been detached from the context of their use value. This principle of diversion—the aesthetic (if not mercantile) added value of what is placed out of use—is thematized by the *Documents* ethnographers in their discussions of museums.

“Poterie,” a short piece by Marcel Griaule, provides a good example of the way thinking about museography was recentered around use value. Griaule denounces the formalism of the “archaeologists” and the “aesthetes” who will admire “the form of a handle” but will pointedly refrain from studying “the position of the man who is drinking.”[14] If we see only the form of objects—that is, if we see objects alone—we no longer see how they were used, or even that they were used. In other words, taking use value into account implies being on equal footing with the object. Instead of looking at a water jar, we must enter into the object’s space; we must put ourselves in the position of a person drinking.

André Schaeffner’s article on musical instruments offers the most elaborate critique of a museography in which objects put on display are rendered pointless, disaffected through decontextualization, reduced to rubble. Griaule asked museums to introduce the phantom of a man drinking, alongside a water jar. For Schaeffner, an isolated musical instrument is an abstraction. It needs to be accompanied. Photographic and phonographic documents must be included so that the instrument can recapture its concreteness, evoking the position of the instrumentalist who plays it, the sound or sounds it produces, and so on.[15] Yet a whole range of musical performances takes place without any instrument except the (mortal) body of the musician; these performances consist in gestures that “would be annihilated,” Schaeffner claims, “if photography did not conserve their process.”[16] According to Marx, use value always refers, in the last analysis, to the organs and needs of a living creature. Insistence on the use value of objects on display, giving their function precedence over their form, led to the introduction of the human body into museum space, opened up the Apollonian space of the museum to the body and to needs. Body techniques constitute the conceptual core of anthropological museography.

A symbolic contract governs the notion of beauty. Just as money must not be mentioned at the dinner table, in a museum one must keep silent about the role of labor in the origins of the objects being displayed. Like money, beauty has no smell. The slate is wiped clean. This is a requirement of aesthetic elitism. True connoisseurs will not ask what those objects were doing before they became worth so much, will not attempt to find out why the objects had never been seen before they were put on display.

The *Documents* ethnologists take issue with this contract and with the suppression of use value it implies. They want a museum that would not automatically reduce the objects on display to their formal, aesthetic properties; they demand an exhibition space from which use value would not be excluded, one in which it could be not simply represented but manifested, exposed. They seek to dismantle the alternative according to which a tool is to be used while a painting is to be looked at. When a tool is admitted into a museum, it should not have to deny its origins. Instead of replacing its use value with exchange value, or display value, museum space should preserve use value, should allow that value to survive decontextualization: cut off from its purpose, it would remain use value nonetheless, use value on sabbatical. At once useful and idle. Here is a utopian space where one can have one's cake and eat it too. These are not Sunday shoes, they are everyday shoes, but observed on their day of rest. Work clothes on holiday.[17]

Seven years after the last issue of *Documents* was published, the Trocadéro Museum was shut down and replaced by the Palais de Chaillot, which was built for the 1937 International Exhibition. The following year, in the new setting, the Museum of Ethnography became the Museum of Man. In a short article in *La nouvelle revue française*, Leiris set forth the ambitions of that institution; the term "document" appears several times. "How can we proceed so that documents (observations, objects in collections, photographs), whose value is dependent on the fact that they are things gathered from life, can retain some freshness once they have been consigned to books or caged in display windows?" And he goes on: "A whole technology of *presentation* has to come into play on the heels of the technology of collection, if we really want to avoid seeing documents reduced to mere raw material for pedants."[18]

ON THE SPOT

> Painting is superior to music because, unlike unfortunate music, it does not have to die as soon as it is born . . . Music which is consumed in the very act of its birth is inferior to painting which the use of varnish has rendered eternal.
>
> Leonardo da Vinci

It is not entirely coincidental that Sartre, just back from New York after the Second World War, first formulated his aesthetic imperative with reference to jazz: works of the spirit, like bananas, are to be consumed on the spot.[19] The primitive arts (a category that includes jazz) are in fact subject to (or rather they submit to) what Proust called the tyranny of the Particular. They do not obey the laws of the marketplace; they recognize use value alone. Yet that is also what allows them to have their own requirements, all related to the fact that the primitive arts do not move around. One must not look to them to take the first step. These untransportable objects, inserted into the social fabric so tightly that they would not survive if they were extracted from it, impose the rule of being "on the spot."

Proust evokes this tyranny of the Particular in connection with the Balbec church. Since Balbec is "the only place in the world that possesses Balbec Church," this church, like Sartre's bananas, releases its flavor only on site.[20] The narrator of *Remembrance of Things Past* makes that comment from a vantage point across from the church. But at the same time, he recalls the plaster casts of statues from that church that he has seen at the Trocadéro Museum. Alongside the Museum of Ethnography, under the Third Republic, the Trocadéro housed still another invitation to travel, even if to less remote destinations: the Museum of French Monuments. Without making an ethnographer of Proust, the conjunction is revealing. Many travel plans must have been inspired by a visit to one or the other of the two museums housed in the now-vanished Trocadéro building, about which everyone said that the thing without its place is never quite the same thing. Those two institutions, whose contiguity was no doubt accidental, exhibited the same uprootedness, the same nostalgia that Théophile Gautier attributed to Parisian obelisks (dreaming of "the absent coconut palms of magnificent Africa" in the middle of the Place de la Concorde). Their shared and doubled resistance to the laws of exchange value and display value led ethnography and aesthetic reflection to the same demand for the irreplaceable, to the same nostalgia for a world subjected to the tyranny of use value. The "particular" in fact refers here to the unexchangeable heterogeneity of reality, to an irreducible kernel of resistance to transposition, to substitution, a reality intractably resistant to metaphor.[21]

An analogous articulation between the tyranny of the particular and use value is at the heart of one of the period's most important discussions of the status of the work of art in the context of its commodification, Walter

Benjamin's "The Work of Art in the Age of Mechanical Reproduction," published in 1936. Benjamin uses the language of use value to characterize the value that a work of art acquires by virtue of its uniqueness: for an object to be unique is precisely for it to have only use value and no exchange value; its value is invested in its nonexchangeability. "The unique value of the 'authentic' work of art has its basis in ritual, the location of its original use value." And furthermore, "the uniqueness of the work of art is inseparable from its being embedded in the fabric of tradition."[22] The reference to tradition indicates the ritual and cultural (rather than the economic and instrumental) nature of the use value involved here. In other words, a work of art is unique only to the extent that it can be consumed only on the spot. Thus the originality of artworks was degraded by museums well before photographic reproduction came into play (as Duthuit has shown, museums did not need Malraux to become imaginary). The problems connected with the reproduction of a work of art are only a recent avatar of the problems implied in the possibility of its displacement. The depreciation that Benjamin attributes to mechanical reproduction was present in embryonic form in museographic decontextualization. It follows, moreover, that museum space, rigorously speaking, has already begun to deprive objects of their aura; the aura indeed is attached less to the original object itself than to its ritual rootedness in a given time and place. Objects are identified with their use value; thus Benjamin can characterize "the cult value" of works of art as diametrically opposed to their "exhibition value."[23]

The triple conjunction of use value, ritual, and the uniqueness of place, which for Benjamin defines the tyranny of the particular, purges the concept of use value of any utilitarian connotations. In the essay in question, analyzing the genesis of works of art, Benjamin does not start with decommissioned factories but rather with deconsecrated churches. Thus the reference to use value does not imply any judgment here as to the practical utility of an object or the usefulness of a technique; it merely implies that a work of art takes place only in its place. On the spot. It can be neither transposed nor transported. It resists reproduction and displacement. It resists what Malraux would call the metamorphosis of the gods. Use value (value for ritual, for worship) is situated beyond usefulness (it has to do not with profit but with expenditure). This is what is meant by the tyranny of the Particular: an absolute dependence with respect to jealous, irreplaceable objects. In the final analysis, use value describes the anxious dependency of a person who cannot change objects. In Proust's case, after the Balbec church, the irreplaceable Albertine will be the one to exercise that tyranny.

And yet, in *Documents*, nostalgia for use value runs along two different paths. Among the ethnologists, it follows a secular penchant; for them, the term "use value" refers to the technological, social, and economic uses of objects (Griaule talks about jars, and the man using them is not necessarily a priest). But Leiris does not have that sort of material production in mind when he criticizes museography for transforming "a mask or a statue constructed for specific and complicated ritual purposes into a vulgar art object."[24] As it does for Proust and Benjamin, use value here tilts toward the sacred: it designates the category that Bataille later explores under the name of "unproductive use." And it is on the basis of these two versions of use value, the secular and the sacred, that the two wings of the *Documents* editorial board, ethnography and the avant-garde, go their separate ways.

Moreover, the most vigorous critique of exchange value (the utilitarian version) published in *Documents* comes not from an ethnographer but from Bataille, who takes issue with the commercialization of the avant-garde. Bataille sees this phenomenon as originating, curiously enough, in 1928 (is he referring to the publication of *Le Surréalisme et la peinture?*), when, in his view, avant-garde productions lost all use value and went onto the stock exchange as exchange values. Before that date, the avant-garde expended itself; now it is purchasing itself. It used to correspond to unconfessable, nontransposed obsessions; now it clings to display shelves ("you go into an art dealer's shop the way you go into a druggist's, in search of attractively displayed remedies for unmentionable maladies"). The avant-garde that used to dispense "images that form or reform real desires" has been Hegelianized and reduced to a simple category of art history, a period, the most brilliant perhaps, but nothing more than a period. "I defy any lover of painting," Bataille said, "to love a canvas as much as a fetishist loves a shoe."[25] For the opposition is not between science and love of art, but between love of art and fetishism, between the art lover's distance and the obsessive's haunting preoccupation. I defy a lover of modern art to eat his heart out over a canvas the way a fetishist does over a shoe.[26]

Bataille's example is a conventional one, but it is interesting nevertheless. Indeed, the shoe brings into sharp relief the gap that opens up here between Bataille's version of use value and the ethnographers'. For a shoe is actually a useful object: it is used for walking, and so forth. But the fetishist does not "use" the shoe for walking. For him, a shoe has a use value that begins paradoxically (this is what Bataille calls elsewhere the "paradox of absolute utility") at the precise point when it stops walking, at the point when it is no longer used for walking. This is the use value of a shoe placed out of service. Let us recall that it was in connection with Van Gogh's painted shoes that Heidegger charged works of art with revealing "the being-produced."[27] The use value of shoes that are detached within the painting. But Bataille's fetishist will never be detached enough from his shoe to be satisfied with a painting; without setting the shoe to walking again, he wants to remove it from the painting's idleness. Thus Bataille's Van Gogh is not Heidegger's. His is not the Van Gogh of nonattributable shoes, of shoes detached by painting, but the Van Gogh of a very different detachment, the sacrificial catachresis that overtakes him in his own body, the detachment of the ear that is connected to his body. An ear attributable to the person who goes on to spit it out, yelling "This is my inexchangeable body." An ear diverted from the exchange market. Bataille's Van Gogh rejected the spirit of transpositions: "Vincent Van Gogh belongs not to art history, but to the bloody myth of our existence as humans."[28]

NEITHER HIGH NOR LOW

The issue of anthropological documents (their collection and preservation) occupies a central place in the *Documents* table of contents. Moreover, the journal pays close attention to the remodeling of the Museum of Ethnography undertaken by Georges Henri Rivière under the direction of Paul Rivet, its director since 1927. In the first issue of the magazine, Rivière sums ups the work in progress.[29] Two months later, Rivet himself spells out the ideology behind the museum's reorganization.[30]

It is a fundamentally anti-aesthetic ideology, as we have already seen. Trocadéro is not to be a museum of fine arts any more than *Documents* is to be a chronicle of fine arts. Not for a moment does Rivière imagine competing with the Louvre. On the contrary, he congratulates Rivet for placing the Trocadéro Museum under the tutelage of the National Museum of Natural History, so that it is associated with "one of the premier scholarly bodies of the Nation while still remaining faithful to its object, ethnography." Once again, it is clear that Rivière is discussing not primitive art but ethnography. He even speaks of protecting ethnography against the fashionableness from which the primitive arts are benefiting in the avant-garde. "Following our latest poets, artists, and musicians, the elite is beginning to bestow its favor on the art of people deemed primitive and strange . . . This leads to some strange incursions in ethnography; it increases a confusion that people thought they were diminishing . . . The renovated Trocadéro might have been based on that misunderstanding; it might have become a Museum of Fine Arts where objects would be displayed on an aesthetic basis alone. A poor principle, in truth, that ends up only distracting the viewer from the painting and highlighting at random just a few of its essential elements."[31]

Thus the ethnographers take up their positions in the front lines of the anti-aesthetic crusade.[32] Rivet: "It is crucial for the ethnographer, like the archaeologist and the prehistorian, to study everything that goes into a civilization; he must not overlook any element, however insignificant or banal it may appear . . . Collectors have committed the error of those who would attempt to judge contemporary French civilization by the luxury objects that are found only among a very limited group of the population."[33] Griaule: ethnography must "be suspicious of the beautiful, which is often a rare, that is, monstrous, manifestation of a civilization."[34] Schaeffner: "No object of musical or sound production, however primitive, however formless it may seem, no instrument—whether essentially or accidentally musical—shall be excluded from methodical classification."[35] Just as the psychoanalyst has to pay equal attention to everything, just as the surrealist who writes under automatic dictation has to let everything come through, so the anthropological collector has to keep everything. He must never privilege an object because it is "beautiful," and he must never exclude another one because it appears insignificant, or repugnant, or shapeless. Nothing will be excluded, Schaeffner says. No object, however formless.

In the December 1929 issue, Leiris and Griaule each devote a short article to spitting. Are these ethnographic texts or surrealist ones? Both, according to James Clifford; they are articles of surrealist ethnography: "The ethnographer, like the surrealist, is licensed to shock." Clifford adds:

"Spit . . . denotes a condition of inescapable sacrilege. In this newly recomposed definition, to talk or to think is also to ejaculate."[36]

This definition obviously requires that it be applied to itself. The article called "Spittle," acting on its own words, has to become a sacrilegious ejaculation. When an ethnologist talks about spitting, he has to shock as much as he would do by the act of spitting itself. Hence the recourse to the right to shock. Here, then, we encounter an article (in more than one sense) of a markedly different type from any we have previously considered.

Thirty years later, after Bataille's death, Leiris uses the same change of register to characterize the direction taken by *Documents:* "The publication itself, rather than its objects of study, came to be inherently irritating and eccentric, if not disturbing"[37] Indeed, the collection of anthropological documents gave way to a different sort intervention altogether. At the very moment when, under cover of the slogan "neither high nor low," erudition claimed low culture as an appropriate object of study, something happened to it. It was soiled by contact with its own object; it became contaminated. Just as it did within the collage, the object here too failed to keep its distance; it lost its reserve, forgot itself on the page where it was mentioned. I say "a flower"—and here it comes. Things happen in the very place where they are being discussed. On the spot. Leiris's article on metaphor sets up the same irruption of the referent: the object of study becomes, as it were, a feature of publication—"this article itself," he concludes, "is metaphoric."[38] It is not yet a bull's horn, but something breaks into the page that had sought to appropriate it, something that is not in its place, something heterogeneous. Like the fly on the speaker's nose. Or like the self in the metaphysical totality. The appearance of the self, Bataille says, is perfectly shocking. That is what shocked d'Espezel. "The title you have chosen for this journal is hardly warranted except in the sense that it gives us 'documents' on your state of mind."

LICENSED TO SHOCK

But that is the point, Clifford says: the ethnographer, like the surrealist, has the right to shock.

He has just one rule: Show everything. Gather up everything. Tell it all. Nothing is out of place when things happen in the museum. The

Museum of Man will be the museum of everything that has to do with man. *Nihil humani alienum.* No object, however formless it may appear, will be excluded. Everything that exists deserves to be documented. There is a form of compassion, a movement of epistemological charity, in this penchant for little things. Science consoles the humble realities for the contempt with which they are treated by the aesthetes' elitism. Clifford concludes that ethnography "shares with surrealism an abandonment of the distinction between high and low culture."[39] And from the abandonment of that distinction it would follow that low culture no longer shocks.

D'Espezel does not share this opinion. He had not yet read the "Spittle" article.

There is something Nietzschean in this project of saying yes to everything. Wanting what is, in its totality. Saying yes, without choosing, to what one has not chosen. Reaffirming, item by item, the totality of what exists in the ontological display cases of a museum without reserve. But the eternal return of everything has a price. No one affirms the whole in all innocence.

Published in the same issue as the "Spittle" entry written by Griaule and Leiris, Bataille's "Formless" echoes those other texts with its final theorem in particular: "To assert that the universe resembles nothing and is only *formless* amounts to saying that the universe is something like a spider or a spitball."[40] Formless: it is the same word Schaeffner uses, but it has lost the humility it had in the ethnographer's text. Enlarged to cosmic dimensions like Baudelairean ennui, it now designates the unpresentable monstrosity of the whole. It is no longer a question of displaying everything, of showing what everything, including the formless, looks like; the whole, because it is formless, is invested with an undisplayable monstrosity. It looks like nothing at all. It is a whole without example. The formless (too present to be presentable) can no longer be contained. Placed *en abyme*, it destabilizes the difference between object and world, between part and whole. And, once again, the common front between the avant-garde and ethnography unravels. The same words no longer do the same jobs. The use value of the word "formless" is not the same when Schaeffner uses it as when Bataille or Leiris uses it. What Schaeffner wants is to classify even the formless; whereas for Bataille the formless "declassifies" and downgrades. On the one hand, the law of "no exceptions." On the other, the law of an absolute exception, a unique without properties.

Clifford insists on the importance Marcel Mauss's teachings had for *Documents.* But he is not referring to Mauss's major texts (on gifts, sacrifice, seasonal variations, and so on); instead, he has in mind a talk Mauss gave in 1934 (thus after the *Documents* era) on body techniques. This text touches in a number of respects on the problems of museography that loomed so large for *Documents,* although it does not address those issues directly.

Among the body techniques Mauss mentions, spitting turns out to have a prominent place. But here it is not a sacrilegious act; instead, it is therapeutic (it falls under the heading of oral hygiene). The thing can thus be done, and talked about, in a perfectly appropriate manner. And furthermore, if there were anything to apologize for, the ethnographer is on hand ready to make amends. Here is an already-forgiven, pasteurized spitball; it absolves Mauss from having to invoke in his own defense the ethnologist's right to shock.[41]

For Bataille and Leiris, however, hygiene is not an excuse. On the contrary, it is their whipping boy. As they use it, the word "hygiene" has exactly the same impact as a spitball. Men are characterized by dirtiness; thus it follows that the less clean a thing is, the more human it is. And vice versa. Leiris spells out the equation in detail. Speaking of the naked body as represented by conventional painting, he declares it "clean and smoothed over, and in a way *dehumanized.*"[42] And Bataille's claim that the big toe is "the most *human* part of the human body" implies the same equation: it is the most human part, he specifies, because it is the dirtiest, the one that is subject to "the most nauseating filthiness."[43]

Unlike the ethnographers, Leiris and Bataille are not undertaking to rehabilitate the lowly. Everything can be said. But in Bataille's "everything," there remains something unspeakable, something that cannot be avowed. Saying the unsayable involves exposing a taboo, thus exposing oneself to the taboo. And this induces an expenditure, shifts the balance of communication from the level of exchange value to that of use value. Or, to put it differently, it reintroduces the forbidden into science. Everything has to be said, that is true, but on condition that everything may not be said. The categorical imperative is caught here in a bind in which the "you must," no sooner formulated, gives rise to a "therefore you may not."

The avant-garde (let us retain this name for it) does not want any part of the license to shock that the ethnographers offer it. Ethnographer's license? But what would be a sacrilege within the bounds of mere reason?

DEVIATIONS

Griaule, Rivet, and Schaeffner criticize aesthetes for departing from the average. By selecting what is beautiful, they privilege what is rare, thus what is monstrous. Bataille's position is just the opposite. In "The Deviations of Nature," he no longer locates beauty on the side of exceptions, but rather on the side of the statistical norm: "Beauty," he writes, "would be at the mercy of a definition as classical as that of the common measure." Thus teratology (the science of nature's deviations) is the decisive component of his aesthetics. But teratology implies a reversal of relations between monstrosity and ugliness. Ethnologists reject beauty because they deem it statistically monstrous; Bataille privileges the monstrous because he judges it aesthetically ugly. His definition of the monstrous is no longer statistical but aesthetic. The monstrous is not privileged because it is rare; on the contrary, far from standing in contrast to the normal, it is now at the heart of individuality (the impossible is an everyday affair). Given the "common character of personal incongruity and the monster," the individual as such is the locus of all deviations.[44] Bataille objects to the common measure, but not in the name of romantic excess; rather, he stakes his opposition on something like a very ordinary excess, a common absence of a common measure: in "Figure humaine," the human race as a whole is described as a "juxtaposition of monsters."[45] Thus it is precisely around the concept of deviation that the greatest deviation takes shape between the two driving forces behind *Documents*, the ethnographers and the anti-aesthetes. The ethnographers want continuity; Bataille wants rupture. The ethnographers want to reconstitute contexts so that each thing will appear in its place, whereas Bataille wants documents to expose the radical incongruity of the concrete: all at once, the most ordinary beings resemble nothing at all, cease to be in their places. We may well speculate as to who was responsible for the publication, in *Documents*, of "Crise de la causalité," where Hans Reichenbach denounces a "false idealization" in determinism and adds: "Every event is a throw of the dice."[46]

This deviation (the *hiatus irrationalis*) is a key aspect of *Documents*' aesthetic ideology. With modern painting, Carl Einstein says, "we are placed outside the *normal* . . . Biological monotony has been set aside." The rapidity of Picasso's imagination "exceeds biological conservatism."[47] Modern art begins at the precise moment when identical causes cease to produce identical effects. It undoes the reproduction of likeness, the engendering of sameness by sameness, the law of biologico-aesthetic homogeneity. In other words, beauty always results from resemblance, whereas ugliness (like formlessness) resembles nothing whatsoever. That is its definition. Its space is that of abortion, of failures in reproduction. It never succeeds in elevating itself to the stage of the double, the image, the reproduction (the typical and the characteristic). It remains a special case. But the *Documents* aesthetics inverts the value judgments applied to those definitions. We are required to imagine that the reproduction of ugliness is impossible, and that beauty arises out of this failure. Beauty is no longer in any respect triumphant; it is merely the product of a failure, the result or residue of an unsuccessful reproduction of ugliness. For this aesthetics of deviation, which is above all an anti-aesthetics of the untransposable (a resistance to aesthetic transposition), it is of secondary importance that ugliness should be a failure of reproduction (nature's deviations are not the same as nature's failures); what is essential is that beauty itself should be a failure of nonreproduction. A reproduction that has not managed to fail one hundred percent. An expenditure that has not taken place without something held back. Use value has not been wholly used up on the spot. The abortion of an abortion.

DOCUMENTS: I AM NOT INVENTING ANYTHING

Documents have one additional characteristic. They restitute reality in facsimile form—not metaphorized, not assimilated, not idealized. A document, in other words, cannot be invented. It is distinguished from the products of the imagination precisely because it is not endogenous. Like social phenomena for Durkheim, documents are transcendent. I am not inventing. I have no part in this document. It has not yet been assimilated by aesthetic metaphorization. It is heterogeneous and allogeneous; it impacts, it bumps, it shocks (it has shock value) the way a trauma would. "X marks the spot," to quote the title of a collection of sensational photographs of gang wars in Chicago that Bataille reviewed in *Documents*.[48]

The advocacy of documents has to be situated within the framework of the condemnation of imagination that is an essential component of the modernist inspiration.[49] Leiris, for example, relates his autobiographical project to this condemnation. In the afterword to *Manhood*, "The Autobiographer as *Torero*," he stresses the fact that *Manhood* is not a work of fiction: it is "the negation of a novel." Comparing his autobiography to a sort of surrealist collage or photomontage, he presents it as a collection of pieces of evidence for the prosecution: "No element is utilized," he says, "which is not of strict veracity or of documentary value."[50] The same "documentary" inspiration had led Bataille to add a final chapter of "Coincidences" to *Story of the Eye:* these recollections make it possible to downplay the role played in novelistic invention by untrammeled imagination.[51]

In this sense, *Documents* is not a surrealist publication. It is an aggressively realist periodical.[52]

"Imagination alone offers me some intimation of what *can be*," André Breton wrote in the 1924 *Manifesto*.[53] But *Documents* wants neither imagination nor possibility. In its pages, photography takes the place dreams occupied in surrealist publications. And if metaphor is the most active figure for the surrealist transposition, the figure of the document constitutes its antagonist; it is aggressively antimetaphorical. With documents, the impossible, that is, the real, leaves no room for the possible.

OF A FETISHISTIC MATERIALISM

Roland Barthes concluded his lecture on "The Big Toe" with a characterization of Bataille's words: "ragged enough, brilliant enough, triumphant enough to inspire the same sort of love fetishes do."[54] A woman in the audience spoke up in objection: the reference to fetishes diminishes the impact of the words. Barthes: "You see, now we can't talk about fetishism any more. It's too late for fetishism."

It is too late indeed. The unreserved praise of fetishism found in *Documents* is undoubtedly what distances us most from that journal. For if fetishism evoked the avoidance strategies of more or less "soft," coquettish, lukewarm perversions for Barthes's listener, for Bataille the term designated the "hard" demand of the thing itself. Fetishism is absolute realism: it puts into play real desires, in real locations, with real objects. Not for a moment does Bataille set fetishism into opposition with use value, as the Marxists do (for him there is no such thing as commodity fetishism); on the contrary, when he invokes fetishism, it is always in opposition to commodity. The fetish is the irreplaceable, untransposable object. Bataille writes: "I defy any lover of painting to love a canvas as much as a fetishist loves a shoe."[55] And Leiris begins his article on Alberto Giacometti by contrasting true fetishism ("undisguised" fetishism) with what he calls the "transposed fetishism" (or bad fetishism) of works of art: "In the realm of works of art, scarcely any objects (paintings or sculptures) can be found that are capable of responding more or less to the demands of that true fetishism."[56] A transposed fetish is precisely a fetish that has been taken out of use to enter the marketplace, one that has been downgraded into merchandise. A fetish that is no longer used but collected. According to Leiris, Giacometti's surrealist objects were the first true fetishes to appear in a long time in a Parisian artist's studio. It is significant that, among *Documents*' contributors, the ethnologists were not the ones who used this concept, even though it is part of the vocabulary of the anthropology of religions.

In April 1929 Emmanuel Berl published his pamphlet *Mort de la pensée bourgeoise;* his *Mort de la morale bourgeoise* came out a few months later. Bergson, Proust, the surrealists were all caught in Berl's line of fire. In the conclusion, Berl argued in favor of a position very close to the one Bataille later called low materialism, a materialism defined by an aggressive baseness that Berl sees as the proletarian weapon par excellence, the only weapon with any clout against the bourgeoisie. Using a formulation strikingly reminiscent of Bataille's language in "Materialism," an article that had appeared a few months earlier in the June 1929 issue of *Documents,* Berl defended a materialism that would not consist "in giving ontological value to matter while denying it to everything else, but in seeking first of all, in the infinity of causes underlying a phenomenon, the simplest and humblest causes . . . Materialism is thus a certain way of depreciating. It signifies a certain taste for depreciation."[57] These are Bataille's own words: he had begun his article by denouncing the materialists who had subjected matter itself to the idealist requirement of having-to-be, going so far as to substitute for it an "*ideal* form of matter, with a form that was closer than any other to what matter *should be.*"[58]

But despite various appeals to a proletarian populism, the inspiration of this materialism is more Heraclitean than Marxist. It defines matter as what does not last; matter is exhausted as it is consumed.[59] And it does not rise again out of its own ashes. It is the without-remainder of the holocaust. It is exhausted on the spot; it does not outlive itself. It leaves no surviving traces. Not even a memory. Matter, in this view, gathers no moss: Bataille's materialism is not cumulative (hence the loss); it is a materialism of groundless difference, difference without representatives, without a future and without reserve, without sequel, without descendants, with no tomorrows. Matter expends itself wholly, leaving nothing behind: no phantoms, no heirs, no doubles. A flash—then the dark.

Henry-Charles Puech, a student of Manichean religions, published an unlikely article in *Documents* in which he represented Giambattista Piranese, the engraver of *Prisons*, as a "nihilist architect," the promoter of an architecture of disaster, motivated by "an impatience for total accomplishment, the desire that everything should come to an end, that ruin should be absolute ruin, that plenitude should demolish the taste for nothingness that governs all progress, and that man should end up under a heap of stones that might be either construction or rubble. The aims of this desire are terribly ambiguous; is it restrained by the ruin to be reproduced, or is it intensified, magnified into a burning desire to *end it all*, to sweep everything away, to construct a universe in which man would be reduced to nothing?"[60]

REPRINT

The word "reprint" does not mean the same thing for a periodical as it does for a book. A novel is reprinted because it has been a success, or because the time has come for it to be rediscovered. *Habent sua fata libelli.* With a periodical, the transposition from the aorist to the imperfect tense alters the textual status of the object, changes its punctual nature. A magazine is turned into a document. Publishing a 1990 facsimile of the 1929–1930 *Fliegende Blätter* is in more than one respect like showing a work of primitive art in a Paris museum, whether it be the Museum of Man or the Louvre. *Carpe diem.* Make haste to collect today's newspapers today.

But top honors in the reprint category go to the kamikazes, the flashes-in-a-pan of the avant-garde, the periodicals that did not see a second winter. Those that held out so briefly that they had to be called back. Reprints recover entities that had not wanted any part of survival. *Documents*, for example. Placed, as Leiris said, under the sign of impossibility, it was a journal that had no intention of lasting. Its official ideological contract consisted in an aesthetics of irrecoverability. Thus when it was reprinted, a phoenix in spite of itself, the event had something in common with, for example, the transformation of slaughterhouses into culture parks.[61] We civilizations would give a lot to be mortal. But in the age of mechanical reproduction, it is too late. We have lost faith in fetishes. This thing will not kill that one. Who today would place any bets, as Sartre's Hugo did in *Dirty Hands*, on irrecoverability? Or as Giraudoux's Judith did when she realized to her horror that the unspeakable pleasures she had known in Holofernes' bed were about to be transformed into a pious tale, an edifying legend?

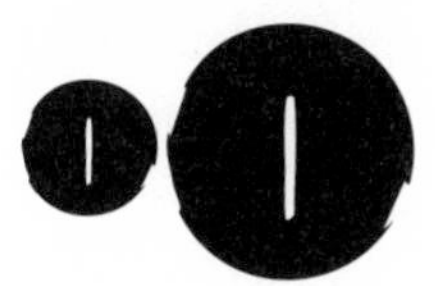

WHEN EXISTENTIALISM WAS NOT YET A HUMANISM

> All terror is futile because it has no subject. To say "my terror" in the subjective French sense is to recognize the power that terror has over me, and which, by that very token, undoes me as myself. That is why no one can conceive of mastering terror without having to flinch before it in turn.
>
> Laurent Jenny, *La Terreur et les signes*

We may well wonder why Jean Paulhan turned to the calendar of the French Revolution to find a name for the enemies of rhetoric.[1] The Terror has never been without critics, but what they generally attack, apart from its verbosity, has little to do with love of, or hatred for, language. The only justification for the historical anchoring offered in *Les fleurs de Tarbes* is the epigraph placed at the head of a chapter called "Les mots font peur" (Words create fear). The epigraph is by Joseph Lebon, a delegate to the Convention. In August 1793 Lebon enjoined the Revolutionary tribunal of Arras to begin its debates with those among the "accused individuals" who were "distinguished by their talents." In the body of this chapter, Paulhan comments: "Competence, intelligence, and skill become suspect, as if they hide some lack of conviction."[2] The Terror pursues any artifice that allows one not to say what one thinks, not to mean what one says, to avoid committing oneself to what is said; it systematically hunts down figures of speech, whatever authorizes or maintains ambiguity, indirection, reserve; in its eyes, any language suspected of not saying everything is suspect. In this sense, the Terror is opposed perhaps less to the talent Lebon denounces, less to talent as such, than to the thoughts and intentions that talent makes it possible to hide. If words are frightening, as the chapter title suggests, the words in question are not the ones actually spoken but the ones that are suppressed; what is frightening is not what they say, but what they do not say. The Terrorist thus dreams of a language in which no word could ever appear in place of another, or even in place of a thought.

In other words, to borrow an expression André Breton used in the *Manifesto of Surrealism*, the Terrorist seeks an "unrestricted language."[3] Elsewhere Breton, in "Introduction to the Discourse on the Paucity of Reality," took issue with a critic who had allowed himself to translate an image of Saint-Pol Roux—"*Breast of crystal* means: a *carafe*." "No, my gentle sir: does not mean . . . Rest assured, what Saint-Pol Roux meant to say, he said."[4] This scolding illustrates perfectly what Paulhan "meant" by terror. No one talked about what Saint-Pol Roux meant. At issue was what "breast of crystal" meant—a figure of speech, not a poet's talent. For "breast of crystal" could mean "carafe" without preventing Saint-Pol-Roux from meaning to say "breast of crystal." The two are not incompatible. But Breton mistrusts figures of speech. Might someone be insinuating that Saint-Pol-Roux has something to hide? That he does not manage to say what he wants to say, what he means? No, sir, the poet does not mean. He says.

Breton will push this anathema even further when he defines automatic writing as a linguistic regime in which both language and the person using it give up meaning anything at all. In a broader sense than the one in which Paulhan uses the word, this anathema constitutes an instance of pronounced terrorism. Historically, indeed, the Terror came into being with the Law of Suspects, which suspended the difference between a suspect and a guilty party, a difference that repeats in many respects the difference between meaning and saying, between intention and act. The Terror was inaugurated by the suspension of the presumption of innocence; a fundamentally paranoid begging of the question justifies all suspicions in advance as soon as what one is guilty of is precisely being suspected, guilty for beginning to give rise to suspicions—for example, the suspicion of not saying everything, of meaning something other than what one is saying. In one of his political speeches in support of the Terror, Robespierre declared: "Mistrust, whatever you may say, is the guardian of the people's rights; it is to the deepest sense of liberty what jealousy is to love."[5] To be suspect is to keep one's head, one's entire head, with its dreams, thoughts, desires, emotions, and intentions, a whole inner life that the opacity of the cranial case removes from the collective tax-collector's view, protects from the general will.

At the risk of forcing the issue somewhat, one could compare the aestheticization of the Terror, diagnosed by Paulhan as a feature of avant-garde practices, with the accusations leveled against psychology that became one of the specialties of the writers and ideologues of the same period; foremost among them were Malraux and the young Sartre. Corneille allowed his heroes some solitude, some time to collect themselves. But in the space of the Terror, there are no more wings to wait in, no more asides. Historical pressure is too strong for monologue. In his preface to the first Malraux volume in the Pléiade series, Pierre Brunel sees some hesitation begin to surface in Ch'en, the terrorist of *Man's Fate;* but he goes on to say that "action left him virtually no time for such a thought."[6] What I call the aestheticization of terror is this novelistic valorization of situations subjected to a law of urgency, to a sort of imperative of public safety that allows the actors neither the time nor the freedom to think. It introduces a generalized suspicion with regard to everything that offers resistance—in the name of the values of intimacy, reserve, privacy of intention—to the general will's right to see. We find an echo of this aesthetic in the enthusiasm with which Sartre encounters Husserl and Heidegger in the early 1930s; like Marxism, psychoanalysis, primitivism, or formalism for others, phenomenology was for Sartre first and foremost a way of escaping what Paul de Man later called "the psychological fallacy."[7] In Husserl, Sartre discovers a theory of consciousness that cuts off all possible paths of retreat, a theory that denies one any refuge and—by condemning one to exist—deprives one of all intimacy or interiority. "Consciousness," Sartre writes in his article "Intentionality in Husserl," "has no 'inside'; it is just this being beyond itself . . . When consciousness tries to recoup itself, to coincide with itself once and for all, closeted off all warm and cosy, it destroys itself." This is the article in which Sartre utters his famous cry of relief: "We are delivered from Proust. We are likewise delivered from the 'internal life.'"[8] Around the same time, he concluded *The Transcendence of the Ego* by proclaiming, with the same words and on the same triumphant tone that the "I" has lost "its *intimacy*"; "there is no longer an 'inner life.'"[9]

Historically, according to Hegel, the Terror marks the critical threshold of the transformation of bourgeois individuals, private subjects, into citizens; thus the many antipsychological platforms developed in the 1930s can be viewed as the epistemological equivalent of this suppression of the subjective agency. The Communist philosopher Georges Politzer wrote, for example: "Psychology is important as long as human events are considered in their relation to the individual; it is no longer of any importance where human phenomena themselves are concerned."[10] Or, to use Hegelian terms, one can analyze the psychology of a bourgeois, but the citizen should be above all that. There is only one way to be above all suspicion, and that is to be above psychology. Thus Politzer's formula opposes the individual, as the object of psychology, to what he calls human phenomena themselves. The opposition is a lexicographical and ideological constant of the discourses of the 1930s. And while it is not particularly surprising to see a Marxist theoretician like Politzer remove from his image of concrete man everything that might recall the individual, philosophers do not have a monopoly on the gesture. Malraux, for example, offers variations on the same theme in a number of public speeches: "The most important psychological fact of Western Europe," he declares in 1934 in Moscow, "is the end of individualism in its acquired bourgeois form. I believe not in the end of the individual, who is a biological fact, but in the end of individualism, which is a value given to that fact, an exaltation of the particular. I believe that we will soon witness the birth not of individualism but of Soviet humanism."[11] *Omnis determinatio negatio:* you cannot make an omelet without breaking an egg; you cannot produce a man without destroying the individual. And the same Malraux, at about the same time, defends the humanist vocation of Soviet society, which has been accused of "mistrust" with respect to mankind; he points out that "this mistrust bears only upon the individual."[12]

The decline of the values associated with psychology has a prominent place in the program of virtually all the avant-garde movements. It is the trend in sociology (the College of Sociology included), and it is also a central motif in the manifestos of the theater of cruelty. "Who ever said the theater was created to analyze a character," Artaud rages, "to resolve the conflicts of love and duty, to wrestle with all the problems of a topical and psychological nature that monopolize our contemporary theater?"[13] "The realm of the theater is not psychological but plastic and physical."[14]

The essay "On the Balinese Theater" inscribes this rejection of psychology within the framework of an aesthetics of terror: "A kind of terror seizes us," Artaud writes, "at the thought of these mechanized beings whose joys and griefs seem not their own."[15] Terror is clearly identified once again with a deprivation of intimacy; it inaugurates a regime of affective dispossession. Artaud's mechanized beings suffer from sorrow that does not belong to them, and they feel joy that is not their own.

Politzer and Artaud bring about this *Aufhebung*, this surpassing of psychology, in opposite ways. To borrow from the title of Merleau-Ponty's later work, with Politizer the *Aufhebung* tends toward humanism, while with Artaud it tends toward terror. With Politzer we abandon the first person of the bourgeois individual and of introspective psychology in favor of the "we" of collective commitment, whereas with Artaud we move toward the depersonalization of the third person, of the nonperson; commitment is a double-edged motif.

However, it is rather unusual for the demarcation between humanism and terror to be this sharp. On the contrary: many texts of the period depict humanism and terror as oddly interlocked, mutually embedded one within the other in the sinister ceremony of republican marriage evoked by Garine in *The Conquerors*, where a living man was attached to his dead companion.[16] The humanism of a living person is thus coupled with the icy stiffness of a cadaver. The motif of such a conjunction recurs in the work of both Malraux and Sartre, in passages that illustrate—at least for early French existentialism, that of the period between the two world wars—how difficult it is to separate the humanist message of existentialism from its terrorist shadow. The terrorist moment is not merely the starting point; it will always remain the inescapable inner lining of humanist generosity. Here the fellow traveler is no longer the fraternal militant; he is the terrorist aesthete. The constructivism of a communitarian honeymoon will never succeed in completely masking its frigid, inhuman accompaniment: the militant's warm anthropocentrism is defocused, veiled by a Copernican revolution that transforms the decentered planet into an earth without men.

The effects of this antipsychological terrorism are especially noticeable on the aesthetics of the novel.[17] In the critical apparatus of the Pléiade edition of Malraux's work, Michel Autrand offers several examples of the way Malraux corrected the manuscript of *The Conquerors*, systematically seeking to demotivate his characters' actions. From one version to the next, he eliminated notations he had introduced initially to give greater biographical resonance to a given character's actions: for example, in connection with Klein, the reference to "old stories," intended to flesh out his behavior within the novel, disappears in the final text. *Don't explain.* Malraux, visiting Moscow, is questioned by a Soviet journalist who asks him what he thinks will become of psychology in the U.S.S.R. Malraux's answer: "By and large, it will be behavioral."[18] In other words, psychology is reduced to behaviorism (what Politzer called third-person psychology): a descriptive psychology that is no longer concerned with the subject's self-awareness or self-consciousness, a psychology that no longer takes the subject's intentions into account but brackets off everything a speaking being may say in the first person about what she or he experiences and feels.

This rejection of psychology is at the heart of Malraux's theory of the novel. Whereas a novelist is expected to relate his characters' behavior to the logic of their personalities, to work things out so that their acts express them, are their own, are appropriate to them, to have his characters do things that are "like them," as we say, Malraux reverses the relationship. He prefers to see characters in situations that do not suit them, that are not tailor-made for them. This, for example, is why he likes Georges Bernanos' *L'imposture:* "The individuals portrayed by M. Bernanos are subject to a fatality that does not stem from their own nature . . . It is not the characters who create the conflicts here, but the conflicts that create the characters."[19] He makes the same remark in connection with Sade's novels, in which "it is not the character who creates desire for himself, but desire that creates the character, as it does in dreams. And it would be more accurate to say that desire creates the act, which is expressed by the character it calls for."[20] The character, traditional mainstay of psychological analysis, is reduced to the role of novelistic accessory: if there is to be a murder, there has to be a murderer—but this is only of secondary importance. The first person who happens along will do nicely. He is forced to take on a situation for which he was not made and of which he had no notion. Malraux's preface to *Sanctuary* develops this point so emphatically that it constitutes a sort of antipsychological manifesto: "I would not be the least surprised," Malraux writes about Faulkner, "to learn that he often thought up his scenes before imagining his characters, that the work was for him not a story whose outcome determines tragic situations, but rather on the contrary a story born of the drama, of the opposition between or the destruction of unknown characters, and that imagination served simply to bring the characters into this preconceived situation in a logical manner." The word "psychology" appears at least ten times in Malraux's preface, and each time Malraux points out, approvingly, that it does not apply to Faulkner's world. "There is no such thing as Faulkner's 'man,' or Faulkner's values, or even Faulkner's psychology, despite the interior monologues of his early books." The famous final stroke of the gong—"*Sanctuary* is the intrusion of Greek tragedy into the detective story"[21]—says the same thing: fiction is regressing to the stage of tragedy; in novels, the individual is once again dominated by powers about which psychology has nothing to say; the characters are not consulted about the situations they are immersed in or the events they have to deal with. As "mechanized" as those that Artaud wanted to put on stage in the theater of cruelty, fictional characters never have the leisure to appropriate for themselves the acts they carry out, to sign them, to have intentions corresponding to their acts.[22]

The preface to *Sanctuary* appeared in 1933. The essays Sartre devoted to the American novel a few years later contain similar formulations. The key word is still "destiny"; Sartre borrows his definition of this term from a more recent Malraux. "The tragedy of death," says a character in *Days of Hope*, "is that it halts the process once and for all, irrevocably. After death nothing can be compensated for." And Sartre comments: "In capitalist society, men do not have lives, they have only destinies." "Acts, emotions, and ideas suddenly settle within a character, make themselves at home and then disappear without his having much to say in the matter."[23] We never witness the ripening of a project, the accomplishment of dreams, the disappointment of hopes. For Sartre, too, Faulkner's characters are dispossessed creatures "whose joys and griefs seem not their own."[24] Sartre uses Artaud's words to describe Quentin's suicide in *The Sound and the Fury:* the act—and even the idea—of the suicide come to inhabit him like parasites, without consulting him, without his having much to do with it: "It is not an *undertaking*," says Sartre, "but a fatality."[25] It should be almost superfluous to specify, once again, that psychology—

which this *ars poetica* explicitly aims to exclude from fiction—is first and foremost the art of linking a character with his own acts, emotions, and ideas, attributing them to him and making him assume them. Clearly, this art has been an almost exclusive privilege of the novel and even, I might suggest, of the novel precisely insofar as the novel is the literary form that emerges when one leaves the world where destiny reigns, the classical world of tragedy.

At the meeting of the Association Internationale des Ecrivains pour la Défense de la Culture, in London in 1936, Malraux dedicated his opening remarks to "the legacy of culture." He began by quoting the words of an anarchist just released from prison who declared that only three books had stood up to the test of his cell: *The Idiot*, *Don Quixote*, and *Robinson Crusoe*. Malraux mulled over this remark. What could these three books have in common? The fact that their authors were all acquainted either with prison or—in Defoe's case—the pillory. "Each of the three," Malraux says, "wrote the book of solitude, the book of a man who comes back to find men alive and absurd, men who can live while forgetting that somewhere there are prisons and pillories."[26] This formula warrants a closer look. According to Malraux, Dostoevsky, Cervantes, and Defoe each wrote a book about a man who rediscovers men. These latter, men themselves, the *terminus ad quem* of the rediscovery process—living, absurd, forgetful men—are not particularly significant. The heart of the matter lies elsewhere: "you would not find me again if you had not lost me," as Pascal suggested. What is most important in the words Malraux uses is the boundary line they draw, a boundary that allows a man to leave himself behind, the boundary of a space—desert, prison, and so on—beyond which man takes leave of himself, escapes man. Malraux's formulation induced the terrorist retrocession toward a space in which man escapes anthropomorphism, in which he is man precisely because he is not among men, man by subtraction, man constituting an exception to the humanist syllogism: All men are mortal; but as for me, I am dead. Books like *The Idiot*, *Don Quixote*, and *Robinson Crusoe* are thus exemplary because of the conjunction of the two contradictory movements that animate them: they are books of exile and commitment, to twist the title of Albrecht Betz's study of the German intellectuals who lived in France in the 1930s.[27] As in the ceremony of republican marriage, humanist communion is coupled with terrorist separation. The return to the human is accompanied—to play on another title, this time of an essay by Philippe Sollers—by the experience of its limits.[28]

The opening scene of *Man's Fate* stages the tension implied in this contradictory movement. The text depicts an assassination. At night, in a hotel room in Canton, Ch'en kills a sleeping arms dealer. But the novel does not follow the course of the murder so much as it portrays the metamorphosis of the murderer. In communion with his victim, bound to his victim in a sort of republican marriage, Ch'en accompanies him, as it were, beyond the world of the living. The terrorist murder sets off a sacrificial identification with the victim; it offers the terrorist vicarious access to the rarefied space, the azotic space, of an earth without men, a world without life. Once Ch'en has killed, he no longer cares about life. Not that he has killed out of detachment, but, like a Theseus who does not come back out of the labyrinth or a Judith who refuses to leave Holofernes' tent, his act removes him irreversibly from the company of men. In a review of *The Conquerors*, Bernard Groethuysen defined Malraux's heroes in terms that sum it up particularly well: "Everything attracts them toward this stage of the world, a stage on which it seems that a man truly appears only when he is no more."[29]

In *Man's Fate*, various notations underline the crossing of the threshold. In the second paragraph, after some cars have honked in the tropical heat of the Chinese night, the author introduces a parenthetical aside: "(there were still traffic jams out there in the world of men—)." A similar observation is made a few pages later: "nothing but the silence and the overpowering intoxication into which he was sinking. Cut off from the world of the living . . . he was alone with death, alone in a place without men."[30] Ch'en's assassination of the arms dealer is neither a gratuitous act à la Gide nor a murder committed for profit; this act is part of a larger strategy on which the future of the Chinese Revolution depends. And yet carrying it out expels Ch'en from the world in which the Chinese Revolution has meaning.

The scene that depicts this double movement of communion and separation most eloquently is the attack on the police station by the Communist assault section whose progressive annihilation is the subject of the novel. The police have barricaded themselves inside the building; the assailants have to take over the roof. Hanging from one another's arms, they make a living chain whose last member, level with the window, can use his free arm to throw a grenade inside the room. It would be hard to find a more obvious allegory for the human roped line, the great chain of beings. Ch'en is at the top, holding onto the roof. But, as Malraux says, despite the weight of the three men hanging onto him below, "he did not escape his solitude"; "in spite of that fraternal weight which was pulling him apart, he was not one of them."[31] In solidarity but nevertheless solitary, Ch'en is the prototype of Camus's Jonas: he does not achieve corporeal oneness with those whose hands he shakes.

What is more, he somehow does not even achieve corporeal oneness with himself. Before stabbing the sleeping arms dealer, he tries out his dagger on his own arm. Malraux starts a sentence: "The pain . . ." but at once inserts a parenthesis "(he was no longer aware that it was his own arm) . . ."[32] The terrorist has left the world of men behind, and yet he is one with those others, he counts himself among the men he has left behind. His commitment detaches him from other men—and from himself. The arm that feels pain is no longer his own arm. Expelled from himself, dispossessed from his body, he suffers a pain with which he has no intimacy, like the pain the theater of cruelty was intended to produce, pain that no longer belongs to anyone, pain localized in organs that no longer belong to anyone's body.

Even without counting the gesture of self-mutilation, which Bataille would no doubt have labeled sacrificial,[33] this scene is echoed in many places in Sartre's fiction (I shall limit my choice of examples here to texts written before the war). "The Wall" is in many respects a kind of phenomenological study of a similar identity crisis. Pablo Ibbieta, the hero of this short story, has joined Dostoevsky, Cervantes, and Defoe in their cells. He has left the world of men behind, the world in which a man has a body and that body belongs to him. Instead of inhabiting his own body, Pablo contemplates it. The reversals in pronoun use, the passages from the first person to the third, convey an impression of defamiliarization with a particularly compelling virtuosity: "My body, I saw with its eyes, I heard with its ears, but it was no longer me; it sweated and trembled by itself and I didn't recognize it any more. I had to touch it and look at it to find out what was happening, as if it were the body of someone else."[34] This experience too can be described as an experience of limits; Pablo has gone beyond his own limits, he has detached himself, distanced himself from himself. Another name for this transgression might be found in the title Sartre gave his first philosophical essay, which was violently antipsychological in inspiration: the transcendence of the ego. Pablo looks at himself with a distant gaze, considers himself as if from the outside, as if there were between himself and himself a distance equal to the one separating him from any other object. He is no longer capable of thinking of his arm as his own, Malraux says about Ch'en. In the same way, Pablo no longer looks with his own eyes but with the eyes belonging to his body.

The Transcendence of the Ego is often represented as an argument in which Sartre defends phenomenology, a doctrine that the Marxists have accused of being a form of idealism. No, Sartre counters: Husserl's doctrine provides the most solid foundation possible for the idea of commitment. The phenomenologists "have plunged man back into the world; they have given full measure to man's agonies and sufferings, and also to his rebellions . . . No more is needed in the way of a philosophical foundation for an ethics and a politics which are absolutely positive."[35]

This conclusion, however, does not stem directly from the analyses undertaken by Sartre in the essay; it is only an indirect implication of those analyses. Sartre is setting up here not a first version of commitment, but a theory of consciousness that is probably, on the contrary, the most disengaged ever to have been conceived by a philosopher. He intends to correct the humanist bent that, along with various concessions to the anthropological and the worldly, led Husserl to soften his theory of consciousness. "As long as the *I* remains a structure of absolute consciousness," Sartre writes, "one will still be able to reproach phenomenology for being an escapist doctrine, for again pulling a part of man out of the world and, in that way, turning our attention away from the real problems," while, to the contrary, "the conception of the Ego which we propose" (that is, the conception that puts transcendence where Husserl had mistakenly put transcendentality) "seems to us to effect the liberation of the Transcendental Field, and at the same time its purification."[36] But the price of this liberation needs to be made clear: liberation comes at the expense of the first person; purification is first of all a purging that eliminates all subjectivity, a distancing of the ego that prefigures the description of Pablo's relations with his body in the cell where he is waiting to die. In its Sartrean definition, transcendental consciousness is, literally, consciousness that must be unable to say "I."

The thesis of commitment and the thesis of purification are thus defended simultaneously, in a pairing that constitutes yet another version of a Garine-style republican marriage. One and the same gesture destroys all reserve and engenders absolute reserve.[37] Man must never be separated from the world, but consciousness must never be attached to a subject. Nothing of man escapes commitment, but on condition that consciousness itself absolutely escapes the human. Man is abandoned to the world, but after the fashion of a scapegoat, with the hope that this sacrifice will make it possible to make an exception for consciousness, to save it, to keep its purity. In a formula that recalls Dostoevsky, Cervantes, and Defoe emerging from their cells to mingle with men, Sartre can thus write: "The *I* appears only at the level of humanity."[38]

"We call Terrors," Paulhan wrote, "those passages in the history of nations . . . in which it suddenly seems that the conduct of the State requires not insight and method nor even science and technology . . . but rather an extreme purity of soul."[39] Sartre, too, is seeking an extreme purity, if not of soul at least of consciousness. Extremism of purity is a feature shared by terrorist and phenomenological methods. And in his description of the latter, Sartre draws on a verbal formula whose strong terrorist resonances need hardly be underlined: "The transcendent *I* must fall before the stroke of phenomenological reduction." And he goes on: "The *Cogito* affirms too much. The certain content of the pseudo-'Cogito' is not '*I have* consciousness of this chair' but 'There is consciousness of this chair.'"[40] The phenomenological reduction cuts through, it lops off the first person, it precipitates "I" into "there is." And, as the descriptions offered in *The Transcendence of the Ego* make clear, this "there is" must be considered as the exact, literal equivalent of "there is no *I*."[41] I quote: "When I run after a streetcar, when I look at the time, when I am absorbed in contemplating a portrait, there is no *I*. There is consciousness *of the-streetcar-having-to-be-overtaken*, etc."[42] The phenomenological reduction amounts to a break with the first person—which, to quote the Sartrean formula once again, "appears only at the level of humanity"—a break that is marked by the passage from the first person not just to the third person but to the impersonal forms of the third person, not just from I to he but from I to it, from I to there is.

To write, Blanchot says later, is to give up saying "I."[43] And Emmanuel Levinas describes the discovery—the terror—of what he calls existence without *existant* as a deprivatization of existence: "The *private* existence of each term, controlled by the subject that is, loses this private character, returns to an indistinct form."[44] These formulas, both drawn from essays dating from after the war, were written from a profoundly anti-Sartrean perspective. When Levinas, for example, describes the discovery of existence without *existant* as the horror of the *there is*, he does so explicitly in order to contrast this horror with Sartre's "nausea." "It is of his subjectivity, of his capacity for private existence, that the subject is stripped, in horror. The subject is depersonalized. 'Nausea,' as a feeling of existence, is not yet depersonalization; whereas horror turns the subjectivity of the subject, its particular nature as *being*, inside out."[45] The solemn beauty of these pages, which will be extended by Blanchot's attacks on Sartrean humanism in the portrait of the terrorist offered in "Literature and the Right to Death,"[46] unfortunately entails a misreading of the motif of nausea. For, on the contrary, this motif gave Sartre the opportunity for one of the earliest literary experimentations on "there is," one of the first attempts to give voice to a world defined by the impossibility of saying "I," by the impossibility of personalizing existence. The impossibility, as Artaud put it, as Malraux described it, not only of suffering in the first person, but of suffering—putting up with—the first person. This is what happens on the last day depicted in *Nausea.* Roquentin, in the process of writing his journal, is overcome by a violent crisis of pronominal defamiliarization. "Now when I say 'I,' it seems hollow to me. I can't manage to feel myself very well . . . And suddenly the 'I' pales, pales, and fades out." In the next two pages of the journal the "I" does not appear a single time; it is replaced, as in the descriptions in *The Transcendence of the Ego,* by "there is consciousness of." The proposition "I have consciousness of this chair" becomes "there is consciousness of this chair." Or, as Roquentin puts it: "Consciousness of Anny, of Anny, fat old Anny in her hotel room, consciousness of suffering . . . But no one is there to suffer and wring his hands and take pity on himself."[47]

Language does not lend itself without resistance to the rendering of such an experience. To the project of giving voice to a consciousness that, as Roquentin says, "has emptied itself of me."[48] But the "there is" attempts precisely to express the uninhabitability, the *Unheimlichkeit,* of a consciousness without a subject, de-indexed, transcendental, a consciousness in which no first person would feel at home any longer. In *Was ist Metaphysik?* these are the terms Heidegger uses to characterize anguish, one of the situations, he writes, to which the expression "es ist einem unheimlich" applies. In his first translation of Heidegger's lecture, in 1931, Henry Corbin rendered that expression by a long paraphrase followed by a footnote. Here is his paraphrase: "In the everyday expressions we use to try to translate our anguish, what we give to understand is that the problem of the malaise goes beyond the limits of the person and that it affects the very basis, the indeterminate basis, of existence itself." A lexical remark by the translator then appears in a note: "It is impossible to give a grammatically exact French equivalent for the German expression *'es ist einem unheimlich,'* cited here by M. Heidegger as the everyday expression for primordial anguish. What it translates is a pure, nonpersonalized, existential malaise. Nevertheless, one cannot transpose it directly into French, where the impersonal phrasing is never anything but a fiction by which the speaking subject himself is not fooled."[49] Corbin was already anticipating the mysteries of the "there is." It is not out of the question to imagine that the "there is" sequence in *Nausea* might be attributed to Sartre's desire to take up Corbin's linguistic challenge and force the French language to do the impossible, that is, compel its grammar to produce the equivalent of the German impersonal. *Wo ich war, soll es werden.*

12

A FAREWELL TO ART

The quip attributed to Goebbels—"Whenever I hear anyone talking about culture, I get out my gun"—is usually cited to illustrate the Nazi leaders' contempt for, and brutal treatment of, everything connected with the life of the mind. Yet in the 1930s, especially in France, many politically committed writers, frontline left-wing antifascists, brandished slogans of the same stripe. In doing so, moreover, they were only following the motto of the young Marx: criticism as a weapon will never replace criticism by way of weapons. I do not know the precise context of Goebbels' remark. I do know that his gun is generally interpreted as a weapon aimed at culture. It could be interpreted differently. For example: "If you want to talk about culture, I'll show you mine." And out comes the gun.

Guns were very much in fashion in French culture in the 1930s and 1940s. The fad led a respectable number of avant-garde writers to chant their own farewells to the pen, in a kind of counterpoint to Hemingway's farewell to arms.[1] Stendhal claimed that political discussion in a novel produced as dissonant an effect as gunfire in a concert hall. Without going all the way back to Alfred Jarry's legendary exploits, the entire anti-Proustian generation—from Malraux to Breton, Drieu La Rochelle, and Sartre—was haunted by the quasi-alchemical dream of transforming its writing instruments into firearms. But what is at stake is no longer just the introduction of a firearm into a literary context, as it was for Stendhal; it is a matter of transforming the work itself into a weapon, of turning it into a work fired pointblank. As Sartre put it later, words are loaded pistols. With its dreams of bulls' horns, Leiris' tauromachic aesthetic is rooted in a similar inspiration. These writers conceive of language in a way that is decidedly unparliamentary. What they are demanding does not fall under the heading of the right to free expression, but rather, in Maurice Blanchot's oddly compelling expression, under the heading of the right to death.

The difference between pens and weapons, between literature and politics, between fiction and verbal action, belongs to the very definition of liberalism. The extraterritoriality of dreams is inscribed in the conception of liberalism according to which the practice of literature enjoys absolute freedom: this practice belongs to the realm of individual liberty and is therefore exempt from the responsibilities of what Benjamin Constant called political liberty. But this extraterritoriality is precisely (and paradoxically) the reason why the committed writers of the 1930s were so passionately insistent on distancing themselves from liberalism. They refused to allow themselves to be reified within the liberal frameworks of fiction; they wanted no part of a freedom of speech that would keep them out of the public domain. At the core of their inspiration lies a persistent rejection of the distinction between politics (which is social) and literature (which would be individual). We want to be judged not by our words, Sartre said, but by our acts.

In the move from pens to guns, from ink to blood, language gives up several of its properties. For example, it is true, on the one hand, that words (like weapons) can produce effects; on the other hand, weapons (unlike words) have no representative function. Words represent things; guns destroy things. Thus the committed literature of the period dreams of a realism that is no longer representative (as realism was in the nineteenth century) but performative, a realism in which words, instead of being signs of things that they do not touch, leave their mark on the world they describe. No grass will grow on the terrain over which the sentences of these Attilas of the pen have passed. Language, instead of allowing a distance from reality that makes the representation of reality possible, is asked to reconnect with reality and attack it. Search and destroy. And this mutation is not limited to setting performative language in opposition to descriptive language. It is not simply a matter of knowing whether words are tools or not, but whether they are weapons or not. The difference between saying and doing fades into the background, eclipsed by the identity between saying and undoing, between saying and killing, between saying and dying.

It is all the more remarkable, then, that a novel lacking any political ambition whatsoever, Gide's *Lafcadio's Adventures*, was the first to present this problematic. On several occasions the novel's protagonist, Lafcadio, expresses his scorn for what happens on paper. He is not about to wait for Goebbels; when he hears someone talking about culture, he pulls out his own version of the irreversible, which is not a revolver: Lafcadio works barehanded. "Do you know," he asks the novelist Julius de Baraglioul, "what it is I dislike about writing? All the scratching out and touching up." Lafcadio cannot bear the identity between the trace and its effacement. He requires ineradicability. Spots in the style of Lady Macbeth: indelible. If he is to leave a mark, it will have to be all at once and once and for all. It will have to be impossible for him to backtrack. For him this is the difference between literature and life: in life, as he puts it, "one can't correct what one does. It's the power of revising that makes writing such a colorless affair—such a . . ." (He leaves the sentence unfinished.) "Yes! that's what seems to me so fine about life. It's like fresco-painting—erasures aren't allowed." To paint on fresh plaster, *al fresco*, to paint on a surface that has not yet congealed, to intervene directly in the subject's life (his flesh): this is the essential motif of committed literature. At the novel's end, Lafcadio is preparing to commit the gratuitous murder that earned him the admiration of an entire generation. He is about to shove Fleurissoire off the train. And the motif of irreversibility reappears. He has no patience with literature that allows things to survive under erasure; murder is an act that precludes retouching. The scene is broadcast live. Lafcadio is thinking: "And no more right to take back one's move than at chess . . . Come, come, Cadio! No touching up."[2] Exit Fleurissoire. But once again, we have a metaphysical murder and not a political crime. *Lafcadio's Adventures* is not a novel of commitment. Lafcadio is a terrorist without a cause. Can he be imagined as a militant? After he got his Party card, Gide started referring to Nathanaël as "comrade," in *Fruits of the*

Earth. But not until Malraux's Kyo in *Man's Fate* does a Lafcadio figure become a political terrorist.

Two motifs of the literature of this period bear prime responsibility for the antiliberal aspect of its inspiration. The first is authority; the second, community. Democratic society is accused of being afraid of the first and inhospitable to the second. War, an unfavorable climate for liberalism, appears as the providential remedy for this dual deficiency: it ought to make it possible to restore them both.

Authority is understood here as a linguistic phenomenon, a sort of verbal aura that, like the stage presence of an actor, emanates from the voice of one person rather than another. It can be recognized by the fact that authoritative speech, instead of giving rise to further speech (as parliamentary verbalism does), gives rise to acts (this is what military speech does). Authoritative speech does not teach, or inform, or persuade; it commands. One does not argue; one obeys. And that is why the critique of the argument of authority has historically constituted the first principle of free thought.

The revalorization of authoritarian speech acts, which is a constant feature of the literature of the 1930s, thus constitutes in itself a major feature of this literature's opposition to liberalism. To take but one example in a thousand, the rejection of liberal dialogue can be found in Paul Nizan's *The Watchdogs*, where the author writes, with reference to the official philosophers of the Third Republic: "We have no hopes at all of converting them . . . The important thing, however, is not to win them over but to vanquish them."[3] The authority of the verbal weapon proves itself by its unidirectional character: it institutes dissymmetrical exchanges (thus the receiver is never in the position of sender; the second person cannot reply).

The self-designated anticonformist trend that dominated the committed literature of the 1930s and 1940s was launched in 1929 with the roughhewn pamphlets of Emmanuel Berl, *Mort de la pensée bourgeoise* and *Mort de la morale bourgeoise*. In these titles, the word "bourgeois" is synonymous with "liberal." Under the name of bourgeois thought and morality are indicted free thinking, freedom of conscience, free inquiry, the liberal arts, the whole culture that can flourish under the aegis of free time, *otium*, leisure, a culture developing in complete independence and lacking any sense of urgency, a culture unaware of the knife at its throat, oblivious to matters of life and death.

One passage in Berl's pamphlets illustrates with particular clarity the articulation—in itself a rather paradoxical one, since the topic is anticonformity—between this oppositional attitude and the defense of authoritarian values. Liberal society is being torn apart by a double evolution that Berl describes in terms of religious conflict. The bourgeoisie is turning more and more to Protestantism, although it may be unaware that it is doing so—its Protestantism may be unconscious. According to Berl, even if they continue to view themselves as Catholics, members of the bourgeoisie are without exception individuals who feel "more confident of their morality than of the sacraments, more confident of their own conscience than of their spiritual director." Protestantism is thus identified with the religion of free inquiry, a religion without spiritual directors. Intellectuals, on the contrary, find "Catholicism much more attractive than Protestantism";[4] intellectuals and bourgeois are thus evolving in opposite directions. The sectarian labels are not to be taken literally. Still, beyond the question of religious affiliation, this picture traces a line of demarcation that is determined by the issue of direction of conscience. The bourgeoisie rejects it and makes free thinking (subjective autonomy) its intellectual regime, whereas the intellectuals are leaning, if not toward Catholicism itself, at least toward submission to intellectual authority (or intellectual acceptance of authority) of a sort that, in the past, has been embodied by Catholicism.

Thus we are at the opposite pole from the distribution of roles established during the Dreyfus affair. Intellectuals defined themselves in that context by their choice of unlimited exercise of free inquiry and their refusal to cave in before the argument of authority implied by military discipline. Forty years later, it is they who speak of converting to an ethos following the military model. The intellectuals are the ones demanding authority; it is not always clear, moreover, if they are seeking to exercise it rather than to submit to it.

In 1939, ten years after Berl's pamphlets appeared, Jules Monnerot published the last significant postwar survey, in a magazine called *Volontés*, edited by Georges Pelorson. Both the terms of the questionnaire and the responses it elicited showed that Berl's wishes had been widely heard and largely satisfied. Most of those who replied to Monnerot's questions described a modern world abandoned by free thought and given over to modes of thought control that—between psychoanalysis and totalitarian political parties, not to mention advertising—could be compared to medieval theocracy.

Monnerot summed up the responses. Not one spoke out in praise of the parliamentary regime. From this he deduced that, for the French who were "fed up with democracy and contemptuous of fascism," only one avenue was open: that of action, "intellectual" action, of course, "but literally, military also."[5] Fed up with democracy: we are in it, but we want to get out. Contemptuous of fascism: we encourage its advances, but we do not respond to them. The allusion to military action just after the observation that liberalism is in a desperate state is characteristic of the period; it gets those who do not deign to take a step toward fascism off the hook, so that they are not forced to reevaluate their contempt for democracy.

It is important to recall that most of these appeals to authority—Berl's, Monnerot's, and those of the respondents to his 1939 survey—represent themselves, and are viewed by others, as reflecting far-left revolutionary positions. In 1936, for example, the Editions Sociales Internationales, a publishing house controlled by the Communist party, put forth Roger Caillois's journal *Inquisitions*, despite its oddly theocratic title; in the columns of other, more or less stable journals the same Caillois published a series of manifestos in favor of what he called "militant orthodoxy," campaigning for the restoration of forms of authority and hierarchies that were fast fading away if not disappearing altogether.[6] Power is up for grabs—by authority. And Caillois insists: authority belongs only to those who agree to impose constraints without seeking to persuade; it is because he did not understand that definition, Caillois writes (in a 1938 review of Léon Blum's collection of recent political speeches, *L'exercice du pouvoir*), that the Popular Front prime minister has just had to step down. Paulhan's research tends in the same direction; it focuses on the figures of an authoritarian rhetoric, a dynamics of utterance (the power of words, proverbs, the effect of "big words," slogans, and so on) that allow a statement to be effective (to be followed by effects) quite independent of its meaning or the intellectual validity of its content.

The exemplary text of this revalorization of authority was probably the one in which Bataille set forth his program for Contre-Attaque, the far-left group that he established with André Breton, in 1936, during the Popular

Front. In a compelling historical tableau, Bataille denounced the anachronism of revolutionary movements that attempt to overturn liberal regimes by borrowing insurrectional models perfected a century earlier for use against autocratic regimes. "No democratic, stabilized regime," he wrote, "has been overthrown by a classical revolution." From the French Revolution to the Russian Revolution, every revolution has been antiauthoritarian, every one has allowed a liberal regime to take the place of an autocratic regime. The question of authority again serves as touchstone: in autocratic regimes, it was authority—its presence and its weight—that was unbearable; in democracy, the opposite is true. Thus, Bataille writes, democracy "must be fought not as authority but rather as absence of authority." The failure of contemporary revolutionary movements is a logical consequence: the tactics of antiauthoritarian decomposition are not adapted to situations that require authoritarian recomposition. The traditional opposition of an antiauthoritarian left and a militarized right, which has been in place at least since the Dreyfus affair, has lost its relevance. If the French left does not wish to repeat the tragedy of the Italian and German left, it has to agree to submit to the school of authority. Bataille concludes by asking the Popular Front to set up "organizations of coherent and disciplined forces which reconstitute the foundations of the structure of authority within a democracy in the process of decomposition."[7]

The about-face that this appeal to the values of discipline and authority represents for Bataille is striking. Five years earlier, in *Documents*, he was advocating an aesthetics of formlessness whose antiarchitectural inspiration took on all forms of authority as targets; he exalted whatever "has no meaning, no utility, introduces neither hope nor stability, confers no authority." This wording comes from "Le cheval académique," in which Bataille speaks highly of the Gauls, representing them as barbarians "incapable of reducing a burlesque and incoherent agitation . . . to the great guiding ideas that give orderly people an awareness of human authority."[8] Bataille's about-face is related to the shifts in the overall political landscape between 1929 and 1936: in Germany, the antiauthoritarian decomposition of Weimar, successor to the Reich, has just been disciplined by Nazi terror; and in the U.S.S.R., Bolshevik romanticism has yielded to the generalized Soviet work camps.

Contre-Attaque's appeals to authority and discipline are part of an antifascist strategy. Their underlying inspiration nevertheless remains profoundly (and explicitly) antidemocratic. Notwithstanding its antifascist character, the Contre-Attaque strategy implies tactical restoration of what democracy had been instituted to combat. To be effective, the struggle against fascism has to undermine the workings of democracy.

From these propositions it follows (and Bataille himself does not draw these conclusions until after Munich) that war is the only possible weapon—the only real menace—against a liberal regime. According to Bataille, there has never been an antiliberal revolution, and there probably never will be one. To destroy a democracy, it is necessary and perhaps even sufficient to have an army (not necessarily a foreign one), or at least a party organized along military lines. Monnerot's concluding remarks on his survey strike the same note: the revalorization of authority brings immediately to mind the specter of a military regime, the suspension of democratic freedoms.[9]

Days of Hope, Malraux's 1937 novel about the Spanish Civil War, written while that war was going on, correlates point for point with Bataille's program. The novel starts from the postulate that democracies are not defensible—not defensible, at least, in the military sense of the word, but that is also of course the only sense that counts in wartime. "I've seen the democracies come in against pretty well everything—except fascism," one of the novel's characters proclaims.[10] Thus anyone who wants to combat fascism has to begin by setting democracy aside. Bataille wants to transform the Popular Front from a defense organ into a combat unit; he wants to move from antifascist defense to superfascist counterattack. *Days of Hope* describes the same metamorphosis, the transformation of revolution into war. Out of a spontaneous, generous, anarchic insurrection there arises a revolutionary army capable of standing up to the forces of fascism. The secret behind this transformation can be summed up in a word: authority. Manuel, the novel's main character, learns this by undergoing an apprenticeship. After their defeat in Toledo, the distraught Republican troops panic. Manuel, observing their rout, intervenes. Order is restored as soon as his words are heard. Without his knowing how or why, his words have become commands. Malraux's commentary seems to come straight out of Paulhan's studies on the science of proverbs: "He had picked up the language of command, as one picks up a foreign language by echoing what one hears."[11]

But this type of discovery is not available to just anyone. As it happens,

Malraux made his protagonist an artist. (Manuel is a musician who had worked as a sound engineer in studios in Barcelona before Franco's coup d'état.) Underlying the many metamorphoses that punctuate *Days of Hope*, underlying the transformation of revolution into war, the transformation of outrage into an army, we find the transformation of an artist into a leader. Aesthetic distance collapses under the pressure of pragmatic urgency. It is not a matter of putting art at the service of revolution, or even of inventing a revolutionary form of art. It is a matter of interrupting art. If the revolution is to triumph, Manuel has to stop being a musician. Say farewell to music. In wartime, art and culture themselves become counterrevolutionary. In Malraux's writings, military authority is always the authority of an artist who has had the strength to give up his art. In *Days of Hope*, military authority is the reward earned by an artist who has resisted his vocation, who has renounced his work, who has managed to turn away from the world of purposeless aims and conceptless pleasures. Manuel's authority arises directly from the fact that he has bracketed himself, has renounced what he is. On several occasions Malraux has him say, in effect: "I'm through with music."[12] But in order to separate from music, he first had to separate from himself. In terms of the novel's own opposition between being and doing, what he does has to separate him from what he is. The authoritarian voice is always that of an artist who has renounced himself in passing over to action, who has passed from essence to existence. "You must lose your soul," Heinrich tells him. "You've already lost your long hair—and the sound of your voice has changed."[13] Military urgency is thus a form of what Husserl would have again called an *epoch:* it provides the space that is necessary for the production of transcendental consciousness, consciousness with a transcendent ego—that is, as Sartre showed, consciousness detached from its ego, holding the ego at a distance. Hence the right to die. "Every day I'm getting a little less human," Manuel remarks.[14]

From this standpoint, the Manuel of *Days of Hope* is the antithesis of Léon Blum as Caillois depicted him in his 1938 review of two volumes written by the outgoing prime minister, a collection of political speeches, *L'exercice du pouvoir*, and a volume of literary essays, *Nouvelles conversations de Goethe avec Eckermann.*[15] Malraux's protagonist becomes a leader by giving up music. Blum failed, according to Caillois, because the exercise of power changed nothing about the man of taste that he had been before.

The Président du Conseil remained a literary critic, a citizen of the Republic of Letters: liberal, good company, he would never have pulled out his gun when someone talked to him about culture.

The second antiliberal refrain of the 1930s is fraternity. On several occasions in *Days of Hope*, someone invokes the Republican motto. The banner of equality is never raised very high. As for liberty, it is not a good time to talk about that. Fraternity, on the other hand, is a source of unfailing emotion. At the opposite pole from equality, which is dispersive and numerical (Sartre would have called it serial), fraternity is the French, Jacobin name of *Mitsein* (being-with), a magic potion against the anguish of man in his solitude, the Republican promise of belonging to a whole (Sartre would have spoken of a group in fusion). Here the exaltation of fraternity converges with the antiliberalism of the exaltation of authority.

Like authority, moreover, fraternity is a motif that is almost exclusively associated with battle cries and polemics. No framework is more favorable to the experience of being together, of *Mitsein*, than that of armies and military action. The threat of death allows individuals to go beyond themselves, to surpass themselves by communing in an overarching whole, and to give body through that communion to something that exceeds the simple sum of their individualities. Liberalism may allow a person to make his way in life; it does not teach him to lose it. Liberalism is incapable of producing anything worth dying for. Only the risk of death allows an individual to surpass himself, to escape from individualistic decomposition, to sustain himself by experiencing the whole. Gestaltist clichés describe this feeling on the part of the individual that he belongs to a whole that would not exist without him, that he is surpassed by something that exists because of him, the paradoxical feeling of a transcendence dependent on the individual. "There's more nobility in the *ensemble* of my Flight than in almost any of the individuals composing it." But secular existence rules out this sort of surpassing. And since being-together is only another name for being-for-death, this fraternity, according to Malraux, "is only to be found beyond the grave."[16] It is also situated beyond parliamentary oppositions: far-right ideologues like Jean-Pierre Maxence exalt "the ardent unity of a whole people at risk of death" in just the same way.[17]

In reality, in most of these novels, the brotherhood of arms is only a screen behind which the totalitarian shield can be polished. Because its condition of possibility is a militarization of social life that equates with the suspension of liberal legality, the exaltation of the army (and war) under the cover of fraternity is most often just a way of slipping in the totalitarian implications of the military structure itself. We have only to listen to another character from *Days of Hope:* "In the twentieth century," Scali protests, "such a phrase as 'totalitarian civilization' is meaningless. It's as absurd as if one said the army constitutes a totalitarian civilization. And, as for the truth about things in general, the only man who aims at a 'totalitarian reality' is, precisely, the intellectual."[18] But of what benefit are these redefinitions? What does Scali think he is gaining when he says that so-called totalitarian regimes are no more totalitarian than armies? Does he think he is attacking the army or defending totalitarian regimes? And furthermore, why should the army not be called a totalitarian civilization, after all? Why not call totalitarian a regime in which power is in the hands of the army, or else, in the absence of an army, in the hands of a political party structured according to a military model? But the most significant element in Scali's discourse (Scali is an art historian turned Republican fighter) is clearly the way he characterizes the desire for totality, including the military totalization and totalitarian militarization that it implies, as what intellectuals want. It follows that even if the Republican army is fighting fascism, or rather, precisely because it is fighting fascism militarily, the structure of military action allows intellectuals to satisfy, with a clear conscience, a totalitarian desire that constitutes as serious a threat to democracy as the army it is fighting against.

In November 1936, not long before he died, Elie Halévy, the historian of British liberalism and European socialism, gave a talk to the French Philosophical Society on what he called "the era of tyrannies." His thesis is a pessimistic one, as dark as those last days of a life in the late 1930s. It rules out any possible coexistence between war and democracy.

For Halévy, the era of tyrannies began with the First World War. The summer of 1914 marked the end of the liberal era; it inaugurated a generalized state of siege that spread from one end of Europe to the other. From then on, civic life was irreversibly subjected to the model of a wartime regime. Halévy applied his diagnosis to all the totalitarian regimes that grew out of the war, whether of the left or the right. It hardly matters, for example, that unlike fascism, Communism defined itself as a pacifist and antimilitaristic ideology: "The paradox of postwar socialism," he wrote, "is that its recruits often come to it out of hatred and disgust for war, while it offers them a program consisting in the prolongation of the wartime regime in time of peace."[19] Thus Clausewitz's famous dictum has to be turned around: politics is now no more than the continuation of war by other means.

The context of Halévy's work is totally different from that of Bataille's. The parallelism in their logic is all the more remarkable. Both rule out the possibility that revolution, in the classical sense of the term, can threaten a democratic regime. In fact all violence, as soon as it is antiliberal, has to be called war (or tyranny, a synonym for war). The difference between war and revolution depends on the regime under attack. If the regime is authoritarian, we have revolution; if the regime is liberal, we have war.

From which it follows—Halévy writes, "because tyrannical governments cannot continually keep their populations on a war footing without going to war"—that no perspective is more threatening to tyranny than peace. Conversely, for democracy, war is not a threat; it is a condemnation. "If war begins again," Halévy muses (writing two years before Munich), "and if the democracies are forced to adopt totalitarian methods to save themselves from destruction, will there not be a generalization of, a strengthening and spreading of, this form of government?"[20] For Halévy, democracy at war is as contradictory a concept as pacific tyranny.

War thus poses a dilemma for democracy, since for democracies the reward for victory or for defeat is one and the same catastrophe. In the case of defeat, democracy disappears as a result of its failure to militarize. But the price of victory is just a different form of disappearance: in order to defend itself against its external enemies, democracy has to appeal to its internal enemies. It gets ahead of fate and turns itself into a military regime; it establishes a sort of auto-occupation. For French democracy, the French army is scarcely less a threat than the German army. "If war comes," Halévy writes, "the situation of the democracies will be tragic. If they want to wage war effectively, can they remain parliamentary and liberal democracies? It is my view . . . that they cannot."[21] This was also, but for the opposite reasons, Bataille's thesis, and Malraux's.

Julien Benda's name does not appear on the list of audience members who spoke up after Halévy's talk. And yet the book that Benda was writing just as the war broke out, *La grande épreuve des démocraties* (The Great Trial of the Democracies), gives the impression that Benda was in dialogue with the author of *The Era of Tyrannies.* Benda's book, written in France on the eve of the war, appeared in 1942 in French but outside France: it was published by the Maison Française in New York, while Benda was in hiding in Carcassonne. Democracy's great trial includes, among other elements, the fact that it was impossible for Benda to publish *La grande épreuve des démocraties* on French soil.

And yet even despite the context, Benda's arguments are not as pessimistic as Halévy's. It is true that, like Halévy, Benda sees war and democracy as contradictory concepts. But for Halévy this is a fatal, irresistible contradiction from which democracy cannot recover. For Benda, who is more Kantian than ever in this text (*La grande épreuve* is dedicated to Kant), it is a contradiction that democracy must—and can—survive. Thus whereas the crucial date on Halévy's calendar was August 1914, the moment when all of Europe passed definitively over to the regime of a state of emergency, according to Benda's calendar the crucial moment was the 1918 armistice, the farewell to arms, the return to democracy made possible by peace—a democracy that was victorious not only because, on the external front, it had won out against Austro-Hungarian imperialism, but also because, on the home front, it had just canceled the emergency powers vested in the regime.

Let me quote the first few lines of the book: "The great trial for democracies that find themselves having to defend their existence against a military-type State can be put in a word. These regimes find themselves at a preliminary disadvantage owing to the fact that their principles *are adapted to peacetime;* this is natural since peace is a moral value for them, and the state of peace is humanity's normal state; the adversary's dogmas, in contrast, are adapted strictly and uniquely to war, war having been declared the noble form of human life and the natural state for the species. Hence the democracies have to prove on pain of death that in the face of danger they are capable of imposing on their principles the restrictions that the state of war requires, and the determination to save their very existence. That is the nature of the trial."[22]

Benda has a dual target. He is attacking militarism, which values war positively, but he is also attacking pacifism, which misunderstands the relationship between democracy and war. Democracy must oppose war without ruling it out. The borderline between fact and value, between making war and loving war, is the crucial one, more important than the line between war and peace. In other words, war is indeed the opposite of democracy; but if democracy is to survive it must be to assimilate its contrary, must be able to contain what excludes it. Democracy must be able to bracket itself, to suspend itself, to absent itself. Democracy must be capable of war even if war is incapable of democracy.[23]

At the time he was writing *La grande épreuve des démocraties*, Benda was regularly attending meetings of the College of Sociology. Traces of these discussions, to which a long note in his book refers,[24] can be found in the way he deals with war and democracy as dialectical opposites. Indeed, this dialectics is oddly reminiscent of Caillois's theory of the festival and Bataille's theory of transgression. In a talk on the subject at the College, Bataille describes the army as the accursed sector of a democratic society; "within society" it forms "a 'constituted body,' a world closed in on itself, different from the whole." It is only through "pretense," he says, that an army can purport to take on a social role, to be concerned with anything other than its own glory.[25] In Caillois's analyses, the festival is the moment when society suspends its basic rules. Transgression of the rules then becomes obligatory; violation of taboos becomes imperative. Whereas in Benda's view war never ceases to be taboo for democracy, according to Caillois's schema there are circumstances that require violation of this taboo. Similarly, and precisely because there is no such thing as absolute tolerance, because liberalism exists only if there is a threshold of tolerance, liberalism has to make provision for suspending the rules, for making exceptions, for accepting a state in which individual freedoms are withdrawn, civil protections suspended, the private sphere reduced to a minimum. Democracy implies the experience of limits. There are circumstances in which democracy is pushed to the wall.

Totalitarianism begins when politics, reduced to the position of supplicant, allows war to go on in civilian guise, in a reversal of Clausewitz's suggestion that war is a continuation of politics, politics by other means. A totalitarian regime is a regime of civil war. A regime of paramilitary auto-occupation. The difference between the political and the military is erased. War is an *explosante-fixe*, Breton would have said, a stationary explosive: it never ends.

According to Walter Benjamin, fascist ideology couples this reduction of politics to war with a simultaneous reduction of politics to aesthetics.

DESPERANTO

> Around the studios, people were starting to speak an international language that could have been called "Desperanto."
>
> René Lefèvre, *Le film de ma vie*

BENJAMIN

During the summer of 1937, in a letter to Fritz Lieb, Walter Benjamin complains that he is suffering from what I am inclined to call political aphasia.[1] The Spanish Civil War is on his mind (and he mentions it in his letter), but he attributes the atrophy of his faculty of speech to the Moscow trials, which he refers to very discreetly, almost in code, as the "events in Russia." "The destructive effect of events in Russia," he writes, "will inevitably continue to spread. And the bad thing about this is not the facile indignation of the staunch fighters for 'freedom of thought'; what appears to me to be much sadder and much more inevitable at one and the same time is the silence of thinking individuals who, precisely as thinking individuals, would have difficulty in taking themselves for informed individuals. This is the case with me."[2]

This speechlessness is part of a long series of silences mentioned regularly throughout the correspondence. The friendly exchange makes it possible to allude to what sticks in the throat. Virtually all these silences have something to do with the politics of the Popular Front and its twin, antifascism. The speechlessness of the summer of 1937 is a resurgence or a repetition of earlier silences, such as the one that Benjamin and his correspondent—as Benjamin reminds him—had exchanged, as it were, a year before, right after the Popular Front victory, when Paris was celebrating an antifascist Fourteenth of July. "How carefully calculated the displeasure now seems that we dared to utter only in an undertone at that time."[3] We are not far away, chronologically, from Benjamin's essays on the undermining of narrative structures under the influence of the capitalist industrialization of information.[4] We are not far away thematically, either. Speechlessness, an effect of the nontransmissible singularity of experience, does not seem to be a capitalist monopoly. The Popular Front does not improve things in the slightest. This is what Benjamin says, at least to his friends, to those in whom he thinks he can confide.

It would not be forcing the issue to trace the earliest symptoms of these speech problems, in Benjamin's correspondence, back to the moment when antifascism yielded the floor, the right to speak, to intellectuals, the moment when the Popular Front promoted intellectuals along with antifascism, positioning them on the front lines of a struggle that was henceforth to be termed a fight for the defense of culture. We need only think of the letter to Alfred Cohn of July 1935 and the devastating irony with which Benjamin evokes the launching, in Paris, of the International Writers' Congress for the "salvation of culture," as Benjamin says, putting the expression in sarcastic quotation marks, as if to avoid getting his mouth dirty.[5] For even if Benjamin has not broken away from "the culture of redemption," to borrow Leo Bersani's term,[6] he resists "the redemption of culture" with the most caustic skepticism. In what is said, Benjamin is always sensitive to what is not being said, to what is left out. To the discursive rise of antifascism, to the tide of cultural Rousseauism produced by antifascism, he opposes something like what Roland Barthes will refer to much later, in his inaugural lecture at the Collège de France, as the essentially fascist nature of language.

But in Benjamin's 1937 letter, the speechlessness of which he complains probably has to do with a more specific object. Why do the "events in Russia" make him feel especially acutely this speechlessness that has him at bay? One possible explanation is suggested by his relation to the André Gide affair. In 1936 Benjamin had published an article titled "André Gide et ses nouveaux ennemis,"[7] in which he set forth cultural positions very close to those of the Popular Front, especially regarding the use of culture as the weapon of choice in the struggle against fascism. Benjamin wrote the piece right after the July 1935 Congress in which Gide, along with

Malraux, had played a leading role with great seriousness. This conversion of the hedonistic dilettante to Communist humanism, embodied in the hymn to the "new man" sung in *Fruits of the Earth* (1935),[8] brought attacks on Gide from the right-wing ideologues whom Benjamin called "his new enemies."

But unfortunately for the planners, Gide's enemies were renewed as quickly as his "fruits of the earth." In 1936, a few months after Benjamin's article appeared, Gide was seduced into visiting the Soviet Union. What was to have been a consecration turned out to be a cold shower. His enthusiasm did not survive the test of reality. Back in Paris, Gide published his *Return from the U.S.S.R.*,[9] which almost instantly made him the black sheep among the intellectuals of the Popular Front. Albrecht Betz has described the turmoil that the Gide affair produced within the community of German exiles in Paris.[10] It is all the more significant, then, that Benjamin remained silent. That he did not write a piece on "André Gide and his new new enemies: an update on my article of 1935." That he did not at least reexamine the positions he himself had taken two years earlier in the light of the recent dramatic turnabout. The ongoing Moscow trials are not without relevance to Gide's disillusionment. Benjamin is silent.

But why? Is someone forbidding him to speak? It would still be important to know if it is someone inside himself or outside. There is no doubt about it: such an article would not have been easy to write. Still less so to publish. But it is not so much a matter of an interdiction as of an impossibility. Benjamin's speechlessness cannot be reduced to strategic prudence. If he remains silent, it is not because he is following the Party line; it is because he no longer sees the line. Not that he is refraining from saying what he thinks; he does not know what he thinks. What we are seeing here is not the militant's duty to be reserved. We have to go back to the terms of the letter itself: Benjamin is not complaining that he has been forbidden to speak (even though, according to Betz's descriptions of the reactions of the German community, a good deal of pressure would have been exerted if he had tried to speak out). Moreover, the Moscow events have not transformed Benjamin into a conventional liberal, an apostle of free thought or free speech. What he is complaining about is something else entirely. Not that he has been denied the right to speak, but that he is not up to carrying out his duty to speak. Not that he *cannot* say something, but that he *does not know* what to say or to think. If he had to speak, he would not know what to say. The events have become illegible. A thick fog has fallen over the world. Zero visibility.

In his recent history of this century's Communist epos (or tragedy), *Le passé d'une illusion* (The Past of an Illusion), François Furet rightly attributes the seductive power of Marxism to its way of playing on two registers: "The Bolshevik party is charged not only with carrying out the revolution, but also with stating its meaning at each moment."[11] Marxism has brought history out of its infancy, out of its speechlessness; it has given it a sound track. Galileo discovered that the physical world speaks the language of mathematics. Lenin discovered that history speaks the language of dialectical materialism. But there has to be a speaker to broadcast the script. Hence the promotion of intellectuals. Now, with the Moscow trials, all of a sudden the sound track has gone bad. Radio Dialectics is no longer responding. Benjamin's speechlessness is that of the Marxist who is no longer managing to catch the meaning of history on his dial. It is obviously not a matter of tuning in to Radio Moscow and repeating what it says. The problem is that the propaganda of Radio Moscow itself can no longer be deciphered by the Marxist decoders. Even its lies have become meaningless. All this, as we have seen, is happening during the period when Benjamin is analyzing the damage done to narrative art by information. Here, it is disinformation that shuts up the Marxist speaker. The exiled Marxist finds himself in the position of a Job put to the test by the undecipherable absences of his God. Reduced to the Socratism of someone who knows only one thing, which is that he does not know. "The silence of thinking individuals who, precisely as thinking individuals, would have difficulty in taking themselves for informed individuals."[12]

This illegibility on the part of history was bound to increase in the following years, culminating in 1939 with the Nazi-Soviet pact that would lead Benjamin to draft his very somber "Theses on the Philosophy of History."

BATAILLE

It was during those same years, and in relation to the same concerns, that Benjamin and Georges Bataille came into contact. They both shared, perhaps without realizing it, the feeling that the present was indecipherable.[13]

Among the many manifestations of solidarity to which the Spanish Civil War gave rise in the cultural and artistic milieus of the Popular Front in France, one that is often mentioned is Jean-Louis Barrault's staging—one of his very first—of *Numancia*, a tragedy by Cervantes, in the spring of 1937. The sets were by André Masson, and several actors from the October group were in the cast.

Aesthetic considerations aside, the choice of that play has always struck me as a sign, intentional or not, of the low level of optimism that characterized antifascist sentiments. Bataille sums up the plot in his journal *Acéphale:* "The subject of *Numancia* is the inexpiable war pursued by the Roman general Scipio against the rebellious Numantians, who, besieged and exhausted, kill one another rather than surrender." He goes on to denounce the success of the play among antifascist intellectuals as based on a misunderstanding: "It is only an illusion, a cop-out, to like *Numancia* because you see in it an expression of the current struggle."[14]

We still need to know what other reason there is to like it, since quite obviously Bataille likes it. What other reason is there to like it at this moment, in the spring of 1937, when—after the German bombing of Guernica—all of France is living on Spanish time?

In this overly hasty identification Bataille denounces the complacency and compromises of what one might call, in Althusserian language, antifascist ideology, in other words the essentially ideological nature of antifascism, its inherent blindness to its own nature and its stakes (the shadow it casts on itself). In his dramatic fresco inspired by the siege of Numantia, Cervantes shows on one side the Roman legions led by Scipio, on the other the Numantians, who, in a sort of Massada, end up choosing death rather than servitude. An epic, didactic, as it were Brechtian reading of the play would identify Scipio with Franco or with a composite character combining Franco and Mussolini and Hitler, and would lead spectators to conclude that, if Léon Blum does not intervene militarily to support the other side (if the democracies do not commit themselves firmly on the same side as the Soviet Union), today's Spaniards and perhaps tomorrow's Frenchmen will meet the fate of the Numantians.

Bataille resists that reading. Its horizontality, which makes the confrontation a face-off or duel between fascists and antifascists, represses another, more allegorical reading (one that lends itself less readily to the comforting sentimentality of identifications), in which three terms have to come into play in a structure I would call vertical or hierarchical. Representing the confrontation as a duel is too facile—that is, too costly to truth, purchased by too heavy a weight of silence. The Popular Front reading develops a state of guilt, in the French public, for the failure to intervene militarily. What Bataille denounces is almost the opposite: the tragedy of overmilitarization. Whereas Parisian theatergoers identify the antagonists of Cervantes' play with the warring camps on the other side of the Pyrenees, Bataille reframes the Numantians' fate on a broader scale, that of the destiny of European revolutions over the past two decades. What the Numantians were resisting, in this sense, cannot be reduced to the choice of one "camp" over another; it is rather the fact of setting up the "camp" as an exclusive social model, the subjection of society to the camp model (what etymology might lead us to call existential "castration"), in other words the militarization of the world. The subject of Cervantes' tragedy is thus not the opposition between fascists and antifascists, but the depiction of a world over which silence has become generalized, in favor of a terrorist binarization, the symmetrical confrontation between fascism and antifascism. This is the world Marcel Mauss had described in 1936 in his well-known letter to Elie Halévy: the tragedy of Numantia is the tragedy of the stifling homogenization produced by the binarism (as distinguished from dualism) that is constitutive of war formations.[15]

Scipio, Bataille says, is no Arturo Ui. One must not project Franco, Mussolini, or Hitler—leaving their enemies aside—onto the Roman general; one must see him as an allegorical figure of Caesarism in general, one that is valid for fascist and antifascist armies alike. *Numancia* denounces "the comedy which—under the colors of democracy—opposes Soviet Caesarism to German Caesarism."[16] For Bataille, the decisive opposition is the one between revolution and war, between revolutions and armies. The true subject of the play is the catastrophic submission of class warfare to the model of military—that is, national—conflicts; the passage from revolution to war. In this sense, the Numantians' suicide is the allegorical summary of the fate of his generation, the successive tragedies of the German left, the Russian revolution, the Austrian social-democratic movement, each crushed in turn under a military repression. What had been greeted at the beginning of the 1920s as the era of revolutions sold itself out as an era of tyrannies. A generation that, in the aftermath of the First World War, had come together around the rallying cry of revolutionary optimism and internationalist pacifism found itself paralyzed, decimated, eliminated by the radical deprogramming of those two positive, uplifting utopias. Bataille puts a tragic, negative utopia in their place.

"Revolutionary defeatism," invoked by Lenin at the time of the Brest-Litovsk Treaty, has completely changed signs and meaning. For Lenin, it was a matter of using military defeat as a launching pad for the revolution. *Numancia* offers a different version of revolutionary defeatism: the one that identifies defeat with revolution, that makes defeat the revolutionary mode of existence. Revolution is the eternal fate of the defeated, the fate of the eternally defeated. Military defeat, in other words, is not the prelude to a revolution; it is the essential attribute of revolution. The issue of *Acéphale* in which Bataille's piece appeared was published in July 1937. The Guernica massacre, which took place in April of the same year, is not the only one Bataille has in mind. He is also thinking, obviously, of the Communist repression in Barcelona in May 1937, that led to the extermination of the anarchist-leaning P.O.U.M.[17] A revolution that calls itself victorious is, by definition, a revolution betrayed: it is enough to meditate on the cement-sealed insurrection embodied in Lenin's tomb. Revolution and power belong to two mutually exclusive spaces: the idea of revolutionary power is contradictory, to the extent that revolution is the first victim of any seizure of power. This tragic utopianism is emblematic of a generation that history has brought from an epic vision of revolution to a tragic one. In Bataille's Dionysian Christology, revolution is the final incarnation of the crucified one, the last avatar of the dying king.

The article in *Acéphale* continues: "What is great about the tragedy of Numantia is that in it we do not witness just the death of a certain number of men, but the entry into death of the entire city-state: these are not individuals, this is a whole people in its death agony."[18] Suicide, here, is a solution. And when it is collective it magnifies the motif of sacrificial self-mutilation. But it is not the only solution. This is the point where the motif of the secret society arises in Bataille—a motif that earned him frequent accusations of elitism. But it would be more accurate to speak of desperate escapism. Suicide is not the only way to disappear or to make oneself invisible. Another option is to shift to the regime of what I shall call clandestine revolution, the underground, whether it be that of the old mole or that of the church in the catacombs. For Bataille, once the Romantic illusion that led him to envision the Popular Front as a revolution in the street has collapsed, the secret society inherits the mantle of revolutionary exaltation. It represents revolution's last and only mode of existence in the age of its impossibility. Bataille's is a pessimistic utopia, all the more desperate for being the ultimate recourse of an intellectual who has always condemned utopian tendencies.

The message of *Numancia:* the time has come for revolutions to be silenced by the armies that have taken their place, the eradication of the transgressive, insurrectional, left-wing sacred, liberated by the avant-gardes of the 1920s, under the salvos of the firing squads headed by the authoritarian, antisacrificial figures of the right-wing sacred who dominate the 1930s.

MALRAUX

Nineteen-thirty-seven, the year Benjamin wrote his letter to Lieb, the year *Numancia* was staged by Jean-Louis Barrault and reviewed by Bataille, is the year of another, less somber manifestation of the commitment of French antifascist intellectuals on the side of the Spanish Republicans. This is the year Malraux wrote *Days of Hope*, a title that in itself has an optimistic ring. His personal involvement in the Spanish Civil War distanced Malraux from the dead ends in which, in 1933, *Man's Fate* had left the revolution. Bataille had greeted *Man's Fate*, when it came out, as an expression of the passage from epic to tragic revolutionary sensibility. But five years after that tragedy of revolutionary defeat, Malraux returns to the epic mode: *Days of Hope* is the fresco of the revolution in progress, of the transformation of the insurrectional and lyrical apocalypse into a revolutionary army.

This return to epic optimism is not without its costs. Indeed, one has to wonder about the price of hope. *Man's Fate* takes place in China in 1929. And it retraces the destruction, by Chiang Kai-shek's nationalist army, of the Communist insurrection in Shanghai, which had been disavowed by the Komintern. *Days of Hope* is set in Spain during the civil war, and it describes the birth of the popular army that will allow the antifascist forces to win. The 1933 novel associates revolution with defeat; the 1937 novel makes revolution the promise of a victory. Nevertheless, behind that opposition, the two novels share a certain number of narrative constants that shed doubt on the depth of the author's conversion to epic optimism.

In the first case, people *(on, das Man)* died because the Komintern had said "no." In the second case, at least in its key moments, people die because it has said "yes." In other words, there are two ways of condemning a revolution (Bataille would say of transforming the "left" type of the sacred into a "right" type): the first is to repress it (or to allow it to be repressed); the second is to organize it.

During the battle of Madrid, Manuel, one of the novel's main characters, calls a meeting of a war council to try those who fled in the face of the enemy on charges of desertion. The council condemns them to death. As they leave the tribunal, two of them recognize Manuel. In this critical scene (which could be subtitled, *à la* Sartre, "the childhood of a leader"), I would like to single out one particular note. Or rather a silence. Before these faces that are literally clinging to him to plead for their lives, Manuel does not manage to speak. "He could think of nothing to say." Malraux heavily underlines this silence. "Manuel wondered what he could say to them." Until one of the condemned men, giving up, lets him have it: "So that's it? You've no voice now, as far as we're concerned?" As the scene ends, Manuel "realized that he had not spoken a word." What is the status of his silence? It is not that Manuel had chosen to say nothing, to ignore the voices of the victims by keeping silent himself. No, it is only after the fact that he becomes aware of a silence that has taken control of him, as it were, apart from his will, a silence that has befallen him. In the following chapter, Manuel goes so far as to somatize his silence: his voice gives out, so that he can no longer communicate except in writing. "Manuel had lost his voice altogether." That silence, that lost voice, will resonate, so to speak, throughout all the rest of the novel. *Days of Hope* is organized around that absence of voice, for in Manuel's revolutionary development his silence is the symptom of his coming-of-age, an initiatory ordeal ("I'm not going to let myself be deterred by any personal psychological reactions," he affirms).[19]

This scene is a crucial one in several respects. The fact that Manuel is not only something of an intellectual in civilian life but also a technician of sound gives it a highly allegorical value. It dramatizes the fact that antifascism has been launched on the basis of a contract of silence. That its rhetoric is defined less by what it says than by what it does not say. If it pushes the intellectual into the foreground, it gives him speech only so that he can sacrifice his voice.[20]

Not all silences are alike, and it would no doubt be possible to develop a political typology of aphasias loosely modeled on the one Roman Jakobson proposed for neuropathology. In any event, the recurrence of this motif, its importance in quantitative terms (Sartre went so far as to refer to a "literature of silence" paralleling the "republic of silence"),[21] as well as the variety of forms it took during those years, invite speculation as to whether the cohesion of the antifascist Front might not have depended above all on the uncomfortable discipline of "exercises of silence."

Neither Bataille nor Benjamin enjoyed official favor in his day. This is not true for Malraux, whose voice was heard as early as the 1930s on actual political platforms; moreover, he allowed his voice to be stilled when the occasion required it in order to leave the way clear for nonverbal action. This public, historical, objective dimension makes it all the more significant that, in order to describe the artist's metamorphosis into a leader, the passage from affect to action, Malraux was unable to imagine anything other than the extinction of a voice. *Days of Hope*, in this sense, is the opposite of a farewell to arms: rather, it is a farewell to art.

The hero of Hemingway's *For Whom the Bell Tolls* meets a similar fate. Robert Jordan is a novelist who has been led by antifascist solidarity to swap the rhetorician's arsenal for that of the terrorist; he trades in the world of signs and representations for that of action and events. Franco's *pronunciamento* prompts him to leave the United States. However, unlike Manuel, Robert Jordan does not commit himself irreversibly: a novelist outlives the stories he tells. In a counterpoint to his preparations, he allows himself to daydream about the added narrative value he will draw from them.

One may imagine that, for this book to come, Robert Jordan reserves all the "reservations" that revolutionary discipline forbids him to voice. A Marxist in his actions, he keeps his thoughts to himself, restraining himself so that, when the war is over and the novel's time has come, he will be able to say what he thinks about the actions in question. Among Hemingway's most moving stories, we must undoubtedly include those—like "The Snows of Kilimanjaro"—in which a writer, like Moses on the threshold of the promised land, dies just as he was about to write his best book. *For Whom the Bell Tolls* is a novel about a novel that will not be written: death blocks the hero's conversion into a novelist.

However, this death resembles the type of conclusion that defines the novel's form according to René Girard: a farewell to the world that is only the obverse of a narrative takeoff, the launching of a story into a novelistic orbit. "Proust's narrator too dies in *The Past Recaptured* and he too is cured in death. But he comes to life again as novelist. He reappears *in person* in the body of the novel." "The title of hero of a novel must be reserved for the character who triumphs over metaphysical desire in a tragic conclusion and thus becomes *capable of writing the novel.*"[22] Death is the conversion mechanism that ensures that the novelistic utterance will connect with a novelistic enunciation.

But in one respect that seriously compromises the possibility of such a connection, *For Whom the Bell Tolls* differs from the masterpieces Girard offers as exemplary, *The Red and the Black* and *Remembrance of Things Past.* For if it is true that by accepting the death penalty Julien Sorel renounces the world, his renunciation entails no novelistic project. Sorel has never manifested the slightest trace of literary ambition. Conversely, Proust (despite Girard's metaphoric use of the verb) is careful not to have his narrator die (thus in *Remembrance of Things Past* he abandons the third-person narrative voice he had used in *Jean Santeuil*) because that death would imply that the narrator is renouncing not only worldly life but also its novelistic benefits. As for Robert Jordan, he owes something to each of these models: like Marcel, he plans to write a novel, and, like Julien, he dies. Yet by the same token his demise creates a narrative loss. It tolls the death knell of the novel that he was preserving himself to write. And the fact that Hemingway tells Jordan's story only reinforces the feeling of incontrovertible narrative loss: Robert Jordan's death is not a novelistic death. It remains a romantic death. It concludes nothing. It is a dry death, nontestamentary, futureless. It transmits nothing. It burns bridges.

Moreover, it would be unfair to make Robert Jordan's death bear the full responsibility for this abortion. By the time it occurs, Jordan has already committed himself quite decisively to a path on which it is unlikely that he would ever have found the opportunity, the time, or the freedom to write. He has turned his back, irreversibly, on the time of reservations. A Spanish instructor at the University of Missoula, Montana, Robert Jordan took a leave of absence in July 1936 as soon as Franco's coup d'état was announced. Thus he has been fighting for nearly a year—an academic year (the novel's action takes place in the spring of 1937). He has been marked as a "Red" by this escapade; it is doubtful that he will be allowed back into the United States. Where can he go, once the sense of history is back on track in Spain? There is only one way out: Moscow. Moreover, he has been promised some help. "Karkov said after this was over I could go to the Lenin Institute in Moscow if I wanted to. He said I could go to the military academy of the Red Army if I wanted to do that . . . Well, I don't want to be a soldier, he thought. I know that. So that's out. I just want us to win this war."[23] Robert Jordan has burned his bridges behind him. He has passed the point of no return; he has committed himself to a process from which no one, not even a novelist, emerges except as a dead man or a soldier. For one cannot choose the irreversible and at the same time use it as fodder for novels. Despite his initial intentions, Jordan would have been forced into the same farewell to art as Malraux's Manuel. A farewell to the novel. Revolutionary action has led him into a negative literary space, a space where it is doubtful that, to borrow terms Marguerite Duras used in *The War: A Memoir*, he would ever have had the opportunity to see himself writing.[24] Had he made it through, the reservations he had dragged along behind him through all the action, like the fish towed by the fisherman in *The Old Man and the Sea*, would have been torn to shreds by the sharks of the Party. In this sense, his death is almost a happy ending: it frees us from having to imagine Robert Jordan as the people's commissar. Hemingway kills off his protagonist, not as Stendhal did, so as to inherit from him, but on the contrary because he sees the character on the verge of eluding him, because he sees Jordan pulling further and further away from the line of conversion to novelistic truth, and with no hope of return; he sees him as on the verge of becoming, like Sartre's Hugo in *Dirty Hands*, "irrecoverable."

For Whom the Bell Tolls is thus positioned on the threshold of the profoundly anti-Proustian narrative space that Caillois had described, a year earlier, in *Puissances du roman* (Powers of the Novel), when he noted that a growing number of novelists—in the context of the confrontation between fascism and antifascism—were championing the construction of a world in which there would no longer be any room for novels. In this sense, it is perfectly legitimate to apply to Hemingway's novel the paradox by means of which Paul de Man, in one of his best essays, summarizes the ontology of the literary work proposed by Maurice Blanchot: a work that "asserted in fact the impossibility of its own existence."[25]

But there is still another, more technical reason for Robert Jordan's death. Despite the epigraph from John Donne that gives the novel its title, *For Whom the Bell Tolls* is a tragedy of faulty communications. Thus the words that return like a leitmotiv in Jordan's final monologue, his swan song, as it were, take on a quasi-allegorical dimension. "We should have portable short-wave sets, though."[26] When he realizes that the action undertaken by Golz is bound to fail, he sends a messenger to warn headquarters. The messenger begins by getting lost; then, suspected of being a spy, he is prevented from delivering his message by internal rivalries between officers and among the military corps. No one believes him. And so forth. What kills Robert Jordan is a communications gap: messages do not always reach their destinations. The courier from Marathon has often been taken as a model for portraits of the committed writer: according to the legend, the runner breathed his last as he delivered his message.[27] But he was bearing a message of victory. This self-sacrificial version of Hermes is not valid for all dispatches. Happy those who die borne by the winds of history; death does not reduce them to silence. Their sacrifice is covered by insurance; it is automatically converted into a message: the sacrifice of the medium becomes the message. But the same is not true for those who die when history is losing its meaning. There are sacrifices necessary to history, and sacrifices in the wake of which there is no more history.

When he gives Robert Jordan the orders for his mission, Golz gives him some advice at the same time: "Turn off the thinking now, old timer, old comrade. You're a bridge-blower now. Not a thinker."[28] It is not necessary to underline the double bind in which that injunction places Jordan, a professional of the *cogito;* the first bridges it burns are those that would allow the actors and the stage director to communicate, the bridges between local actions and the think tank. *For Whom the Bell Tolls* is constructed like a narrative system without feedback, a program whose curve does not anticipate any trajectory corrections. The action must take place in the absence of any contact with its "narrative headquarters."

For Whom the Bell Tolls is set in a mountainous landscape. Sight lines are poor. The bridge that Jordan is to blow up is at the bottom of a narrow valley. At regular intervals, threatening signs—airplane engines, shells, firearms—can be heard. They are all emitted off screen by sources situated outside the visual field, on the other side of the mountain. "All those lives have their horizons closed beforehand; they would remain sealed even if they did not end tragically," writes Claude-Edmonde Magny, adding: "[Hemingway's] time has no future."[29]

EPILOGUE

A few months after the publication of *Days of Hope*, but also a few days after Nazi troops had entered Vienna, in March 1938, at the Sorbonne, Raymond Aron defended his doctoral thesis in philosophy, *Introduction to the Philosophy of History*. The book that ensued—dedicated to Malraux—has recently been described as destroying in advance "Marxism's claim to endow the historical actor with knowledge of his own action, however little that action may be inspired by the laws of historical materialism."[30] And yet it was one of the paradoxes of those years that, on the level of the aesthetic of the novel, some Marxists exalted the uncertainty principle, the same principle to which Aron subjected the scientific ambitions of historical materialism. The association of an antifascist sensibility with a narrative theory that is profoundly foreign to Marxism served as a platform (simultaneously epistemological, political, and aesthetic) for a front whose major figures were Aron (for history), Nizan (for journalism), and Sartre (for the novel). At the core of its agenda was the exploitation, through a discourse of contemporaneity, of the break in communication with the information center of the subject who was supposed to be in the know.

Hence the promotion of reporting as the exemplary literary genre. In the introduction to his *Chronique de septembre*, Nizan writes its manifesto: a balance sheet of the Munich crisis that he draws up in October and November 1938, under cover of what he calls "a threatening parenthesis."[31] How is one to speak of what has not ended? How can one describe events as they are taking place, how can one describe them in progress, in suspension? What narrative figures are available to a narrator who works in a state of emergency? What are the formal effects of the haste that leads a narrator to tell the story of a war, as Malraux did with the Spanish Civil War, before he knows whether it has been won or lost? Historical truth and novelistic truth are subject here to antithetical enunciative regimes: the crisis of the late 1930s provided the occasion to tell the story of an "informative" and documentary journalistic conversion that was exactly the inverse of the one through which René Girard defines the novel: conversion to the inconclusive, to the not-everything, to the narrative modes of the imperfect.

There is no question but that much of the seductive force of historical materialism stemmed from the radio-guidance service it provided: at every point, even in bad weather, its subscribers could get an update. Could have an overview, and situate themselves in the totality of the process. At every moment, in every place, a Marxist has the possibility of consulting the map or calling on his omniscient narrator. But this is also precisely the reason why someone like Sartre, in his article on Nizan's novel *The Conspiracy*—an article that appeared just a few weeks after the publication of Aron's book, that is, a few weeks after the Munich crisis—casts doubt on the novelistic benefits of such a theoretical cover: "Can a Communist write a novel? I am not convinced."[32] Nizan was a Communist: Sartre's *ad hominem* question cuts both ways, being at once a compliment addressed to Nizan's art and an indirect way of casting doubt on his Communism. The narrative voice needs to be engaged in spaces for which it has no maps. Moreover, Nizan himself often quoted a passage from the conclusion of Dostoevsky's *The Adolescent:* "But then what is there left for a writer who doesn't want to write only historical novels and who is fascinated by the present scene? Well, he'll just have to try to guess and expect to be wrong."[33] "Guess and expect to be wrong": as good a Marxist as he is, and historical materialism notwithstanding, these are the two imperatives of Nizan's narrative aesthetics. Sartre takes them up again almost literally when in *What Is Literature?* he connects the birth of the committed writer to the Munich crisis, which unleashed a desire in novelists to deal with current events, he says, at the same time that it obliged the novelist to abandon the tone of narrative omniscience: "We had to leave doubts, expectations, and the unachieved throughout our works," "to do our job in the face of the incomprehensible and the untenable, to bet, to conjecture without evidence, to undertake in uncertainty and persevere without hope."[34] Using similar terms, Aron had argued that the historian's task is conserving or "restoring to the past the uncertainty of a future"; he has to be alert to maintain "the priority of the future in the historical consciousness."[35] In the same vein, referring to a novel written as the Munich crisis was unfolding, Merleau-Ponty asserted that "the future ceases to be the natural extension of the present."[36] A narration—whether it is historiographic, journalistic, or novelistic—fulfills the requirements of the aesthetics of commitment when the unpredictability that, for better or for worse, defines the event is preserved through its representation.

Aron's thesis is undoubtedly the most substantial testimony in a vast reshuffling of the discourses that, in the wake of the conjoined reading of Marx and Heidegger, are involved in the narrative promotion of the historicity of the present. It is not true that an event becomes historical only by losing its contemporaneity. Before it is the science of the past, history is a dimension of existence. It marks lived experience to the precise extent that what is lived is not transparent. Two definitions of history are competing here, one that includes and one that excludes the present. The clash between them organizes the confrontation of two temporal systems; grammarians will recognize the two verbal modes of the perfect and the imperfect. The perfect? "As for the name *perfect* with which it has been decorated," wrote Nicolas Beauzée in the article devoted to this verbal mode in the *Encyclopédie*, "it is not that the Grammarians saw more perfection in it than in the other tenses; it was only through opposition to the so-called preterite, which was called *imperfect* because something could be detected in it, though in a confused fashion, that was not at all past but present."[37] A past that is not perfectly past is called imperfect—a past from which the present, our present, has not cut itself off.

Between 1937 and 1947 Sartre developed a theory of the novel that is essentially a campaign against narrative forms in the perfect tense. There is undoubtedly some self-criticism in his relentlessness: with the aesthetic of "perfect moments" attributed to Anny, *Nausea* was still attached, at least partially, to belief in the existence of absolute and self-sufficient instants. The article on *The Outsider* (better known in its translation as *The Stranger*) gives this motif its canonical form. Sartre reproaches Camus for borrowing a temporal mode from Hemingway, the "present perfect [*parfait composé*]," which he metaphorizes as a grammatical equivalent of Robert Jordan's terrorist activities: "instead of acting as a bridge between past and future, it [the sentence] is merely a small, isolated, self-sufficient substance." "The sentences in *The Outsider* are islands."[38] Bridges and islands: we are not far from the keywords of *For Whom the Bell Tolls.* Here too, despite its epigraph from Donne, Hemingway's novel is positioned on the side of burned bridges, on the side of refusals to communicate, interruptions, even if it takes this position on the basis not of ignorance of the future but rather of affirmation of the present. The erotic instant and the revolutionary instant meet in the same futureless perfection: "Now is the thing to praise and I am very happy with it. Now, *ahora, maintenant, heute.*"[39] A perfect moment is a present that does not outlive itself, that has no heir, that dies intestate. That Robert Jordan should expire without having written anything of what he has lived is in conformity with the Parmenidean logic of the novel. It is a way of engendering the present by cutting off the bridges to the future. But also by avoiding the risks of the imperfect (guessing, making mistakes). In the absence of feedback, in the face of the silence of the omniscient narrator, Jordan is reduced to silence. But he should have understood that the blackout of the antifascist transmission system was the novel's opportunity.

Hölderlin transformed the experience of the absence of the gods into a poetic resource; in the same way, the first generation of committed narrators worked at making a resource of the collapse of the narrative "big brother." Sartre doubted that one could be a novelist and a Communist at the same time: the inspiration of modern novelists, from storytelling to the information age, comes from their engagement in a contemporary scene whose urgency leaves them unable to take stock. But the great novelists have never been privy to the secrets of the gods. In this connection, the conclusion of Sartre's article on François Mauriac is often cited: "There is no more place for a privileged observer in a real novel than in the world of Einstein . . . M. Mauriac has chosen divine omniscience and omnipotence. But novels are written *by* men and *for* men. In the eyes of God, Who cuts through appearances and goes beyond them, there is no novel, no art, for art thrives on appearances. God is not an artist. Neither is M. Mauriac."[40] The argument, as we have seen, is just as valid for Marxist novelists. Catholics and Communists always know too much; they suffer from omniscience.

The appropriation and subversion of these narrative models, which Jean-François Lyotard calls *grands récits*, major narratives, introduces the agency of current events into the story, that is, the very thing that, in a present, keeps it from being fully present—its *punctum*, its blind spot, what it needs in order to be sufficient unto itself, to be a true present. The impact of the news points the present tense toward the fact that the present is under the sway of the future, that it needs the future to certify it as alive. A present connects with itself only via the future; the future is always what *presents* the present. But what are we to make of that inscription of the future? How can one write novels under the heading of the future?

What Sartre criticizes in the novelists of the past perfect is precisely that they have eliminated the future. They have mutilated time: they have "simply decapitated it. They have deprived it of its future, that is, its dimension of deeds and freedom."[41] The image of decapitation struck a chord. Jean Beaufret picked it up in his presentation of the theses of *Being and Time* in 1945: "To neglect the future is to decapitate time."[42] Claude-Edmonde Magny, as we have seen, used it to describe the blocked horizon of *For Whom the Bell Tolls.* And indeed, the image is a powerful one. Moreover, as the studies collected in the present volume make clear, it is characteristic of the age: the authors who spoke out during the late 1930s were obsessed with the almost infinite possibilities for variation offered by the model of the acephalus (or of acapitalism).

Sartre's image identifies the future with what in Heideggerian language might be called the ecstasy of the head: the future is to time what the head is to the body. It is its *director.* Decapitated time is decerebrated time. When the head is removed, it is the command post, the system of the so-called higher functions, that disappears. But they do not disappear discreetly: a headless body quickly becomes a lifeless body. The ablation of the future makes us lose time, propels us into the absence of time. In the wake of the American novelists' experiments on the narrative command post, the novel lost its sense of chronology. Somewhat pompously, this has been called the "technique of disorder": sound and fury.

But things are not as simple as that. In fact, one may ask to what extent this future that is and must be maintained ahead and as a head—this future that is and must be in advance of the present, this future through which the present outstrips itself, this avant-gardist future—differs from the narrative command post staffed by an omniscient narrator. The metaphor of beheading has profoundly equivocal implications with respect to the declared stakes of Sartre's theory of the novel; moreover, the relation between head and body is not so close-knit as to preclude severance. The neck is a small, fragile isthmus that, for better or for worse, makes the head eminently detachable. But it is also an organ of detachment. In "Les communistes et la paix," Sartre deploys a prodigious dialectical virtuosity to show that, as far as the Communist party is concerned, to assume the head is not the equivalent of cutting oneself off from the body of the masses. But he himself was the one who needed to be convinced first and foremost of this. The intellectuals in his novels, including those who are Communists, like strange lighthouses stand a good head taller than their contemporaries. The same structure of avant-gardist detachment—or cut—of the chief applies to Sartre's "The Childhood of a Leader" and to *Days of Hope.* And that is precisely why these texts speak for the future. The relations between future and present are also structured in the mode of cut, rupture, *décollage.* Thus there is in the very definition of the head something that wants it to be above its body, wants it to dominate the body while standing out, detaching itself. Under these conditions, if the head's role is to cut itself off from the body, how can one distinguish between time that is decapitated and time that is not? How can one tell the difference between aheadness and acephality? How can one know? Does anyone know?

Moreover, did Sartre not extol the Munich crisis precisely for the opposite reason, because it created a narrative situation that forbade the novelist, reduced to the role of reporter, to be even a little bit ahead of his readers? "For him, as for all of us, the future is closed . . . A closed future is still a future." And he ended the essay on Faulkner's *The Sound and the Fury* by quoting *Being and Time:* "Even if human reality has nothing more 'before' it, even if 'its account is closed,' its being is still determined by this 'self-anticipation.' The loss of all hope, for example, does not deprive human reality of its possibilities; it is simply a way of *being* toward these same possibilities."[43] The novel commits itself by turning away from the past and from the "remembrance of things past," the search for lost time: it struggles to inventory the present by the faded light of a future that has let the flame of hope go out.

NOTES

1. MUST LITERATURE BE POSSIBLE?

1. Jean-Paul Sartre, *Nausea*, trans. Lloyd Alexander (New York: New Directions, 1964), p. 39.

2. Sartre, *What Is Literature?* trans. Bernard Frechtman (1949; reprint, Gloucester, Mass.: Peter Smith, 1978), pp. 139–140.

3. Walter Benjamin, "The Storyteller: Reflections on the Works of Nikolai Leskov," in *Illuminations*, trans. Harry Zohn (New York: Schocken Books, 1969), p. 84.

4. Sartre, "Departure and Return," in *Literary and Philosophical Essays*, trans. Annette Michelson (London: Rider, 1955), pp. 132–133.

5. Marguerite Duras, *The War: A Memoir*, trans. Barbara Bray (New York: Pantheon Books, 1986), p. 13.

6. Ibid., p. 3.

7. Oddly enough, this antonym of *ubiquity* (a relative of *Unheimlichkeit*) is an English word. Jacques Lacan claims to have found it in *Roget's Thesaurus:* "Must a letter then, of all objects, be endowed with the property of *nullibiety:* to use a term which the thesaurus known as *Roget* picks up from the semiotic utopia of Bishop Wilkins?"; "Seminar on 'The Purloined Letter,'" trans. Jeffrey Mehlman, in *French Freud: Structural Studies in Psychoanalysis*, ed. Jeffrey Mehlman, *Yale French Studies* 48 (1973): 53.

8. André Malraux, *Days of Wrath*, trans. Haakon M. Chevalier (New York: Random House, 1936), pp. 53–54.

9. Stendhal, *The Life of Henry Brulard*, trans. John Sturrock (London: Penguin, 1995), p. 471.

10. *The Private Diaries of Stendhal*, trans. and ed. Robert Sage (Garden City, N.Y.: Doubleday, 1954), p. 113.

11. Maurice Blanchot, *Faux pas* (Paris: Gallimard, 1943), pp. 10–11.

12. Kafka quoted in Georges Bataille, *Literature and Evil*, trans. Alastair Hamilton (London: Caldar and Boyars, 1973), p. 136.

13. Kafka quoted in Blanchot, *The Space of Literature*, trans. Ann Smock (Lincoln: University of Nebraska Press, 1982), p. 72.

14. Duras, *The War*, p. 4.

15. Sartre, *What Is Literature?* p. 297.

16. Bataille, *Literature and Evil*, p. 85.

17. Blanchot, "Literature and the Right to Death," in *The Work of Fire*, trans. Charlotte Mandell (Stanford: Stanford University Press, 1995), pp. 319, 321.

18. Ibid., p. 316.

19. Bataille, *Literature and Evil*, pp. x, 141.

20. Blanchot, *The Infinite Conversation*, trans. Susan Hanson (Minneapolis: University of Minnesota Press, 1993), p. 182. This schema offers strong analogies with the Jewish kabbalism that Blanchot evokes by citing Gershom G. Scholem's *Major Trends in Jewish Mysticism*, in a footnote to the essay on Kafka in *The Space of Literature:* "There was an ardent desire to break down the Exile by enhancing its torments" (p. 70). On this topic, see Scholem's entire chapter on the heresy of Sabbatai Zevi, according to which apostasy would be the (repugnant) path to redemption. In the conclusion of *Legacies of Anti-Semitism in France* (Minneapolis: University of Minnesota Press, 1983), Jeffrey Mehlman shows to what extent this doctrine of transgressive subversion is enlightening for Walter Benjamin (to whose memory Scholem's book is dedicated).

21. Sartre, *What Is Literature?* p. 65.

22. Blanchot, *The Work of Fire*, p. 301.

23. Pascal Quignard, "Où sont les ombres?" *L'Infini* 30 (Summer 1990): 23.

24. Roger Caillois, *Puissances du roman* (1940), in *Approches de l'imaginaire* (Paris: Gallimard, 1974), p. 231.

25. Caillois, *Approches de l'imaginaire*, p. 152.

26. Ibid., p. 161.

27. Caillois, *Pontius Pilate* (New York: Macmillan, 1963), p. 72.

28. Ibid., p. 111.

29. Ibid., pp. 27, 30.

30. Ibid., p. 76.

31. Ibid., p. 31.

2. DEEDS WITHOUT WORDS

1. The epigraph is from Marcel Proust, *Remembrance of Things Past*, trans. C. K. Scott Moncrieff and Terence Kilmartin (New York: Random House, 1981), vol. 2, p. 542. Another possible epigraph: "The word *under* was underlined by the interior voice, which seemed to put in it a number of meanings"; André Breton, *Communicating Vessels*, trans. Mary Ann Caws and Geoffrey T. Harris (Lincoln: University of Nebraska Press, 1990), p. 100.

2. Jean-Paul Sartre, *The Flies*, trans. Stuart Gilbert, in *No Exit and Three Other Plays* (New York: Vintage Books, 1989), p. 60.

3. In spoken French, possessive adjectives are unstressed. For emphasis, the

possessive can be repeated after the noun in a phrase in which the preposition *à* introduces the corresponding form of the disjunctive (or tonic) pronoun; thus "*my* palace" would be "mon palais à moi." [Translator's note]

4. The passages from *L'être et le néant* are quoted in Sartre, *Existential Psychoanalysis*, trans. Hazel E. Barnes (New York: Philosophical Library, 1953), pp. 117, 130, 144. Cf. Denis Hollier, "The Possessive," in *The Politics of Prose: Essays on Sartre*, trans. Jeffrey Mehlman (Minneapolis: University of Minnesota Press, 1986), p. 151.

5. Sartre, *The Flies*, pp. 90, 59.

6. Ibid., p. 58.

7. Ibid., pp. 59, 88.

8. Ibid., pp. 90, 106, 123.

9. Ibid., p. 91.

10. Hollier, *The Politics of Prose*, pp. 102–106.

11. Sartre, *The Flies*, p. 105.

12. In this regard Orestes resembles Thérèse Desqueyroux, who is trapped by her deed in *The End of the Night* and whose absence of liberty Sartre nevertheless severely condemned; "François Mauriac and Freedom," in *Literary and Philosophical Essays*, trans. Annette Michelson (London: Rider, 1955), pp. 7–23.

13. Sartre, *The Words*, trans. Bernard Frechtman (New York: Braziller, 1964), p. 255.

14. Sartre, *The Flies*, p. 90. On "gently, mortals," the identity of the trace and its effacement, and the phenomenology of skiing in Sartre, see Denis Hollier, "Nizan cinéphobe," in *L'occhio del viaggiatore (Scrittori francese degli anni trenta)*, ed. Sandra Teroni (Florence: Leo S. Olschki, 1986).

15. Sartre, *What Is Literature?* trans. Bernard Frechtman (1949; reprint, Gloucester, Mass.: Peter Smith, 1978), pp. 15, 17.

16. Sartre, *The Psychology of Imagination*, trans. Bernard Frechtman (New York: Citadel Press, 1961).

17. Sartre, *The Flies*, pp. 88, 59.

18. On the conclusion of *The Flies* and the difficulties it presents for the theory of commitment, see Hollier, *The Politics of Prose*, pp. 152–153.

19. Sartre, *The Flies*, p. 123. The first American translation of *Les mains sales* was called *Red Gloves;* see Michel Contat and Michel Rybalka, *The Writings of Jean-Paul Sartre* (Evanston: Northwestern University Press, 1974), vol. 1, pp. 188–189. On a persistent Sartrean jealousy with respect to Lady Macbeth, see Hollier, "A Study of Hands," in *The Politics of Prose*, pp. 118–120.

20. Sartre, *Dirty Hands*, in *No Exit and Three Other Plays*, pp. 219, 247, 235, 236, 234.

21. Ibid., p. 235.

22. Sartre, *No Exit*, ibid., p. 46.

23. Sartre, *Dirty Hands*, pp. 155–156.

24. Sartre, *The Transcendence of the Ego: An Existentialist Theory of Consciousness*, trans. Forrest Williams and Robert Kirkpatrick (New York: Noonday Press, 1962), p. 40. See "Mimesis and Castration," later in this volume.

25. Sartre, *The Transcendence of the Ego*, pp. 53–54.

26. Sartre, *Nausea*, trans. Lloyd Alexander (New York: New Directions, 1964), p. 171.

27. Sartre, *Kean* (Paris: Gallimard, 1954), p. 166. Cf. Frank Hauser's translation, which has Kean say: "I don't really exist" (London: Davis-Poynter, 1972, p. 103).

3. MIMESIS AND CASTRATION 1937

1. Meyer Schapiro, "French Reaction in Exile," *Kenyon Review* 7 (Winter 1945): 29.

2. A substantial account of the College's activities appeared in *Vertical*, a "yearbook" whose only volume was published in 1941 in New York by Georges Duthuit and Eugène Jolas in a press run of only a few hundred copies; André Breton also referred to the College briefly in his 1942 article on Max Ernst in *VVV*. See the latest French edition of *Le Collège de Sociologie* (Paris: Gallimard, 1995).

3. Caillois published two versions of *La communion des forts*. The first appeared in Mexico (Mexico City: Ediciones Quetzal, 1943), the second in France (Marseilles: Le Sagittaire, 1944). Both versions are in French, but the tables of contents do not match: four chapters that appeared in the Mexican volume were cut from the Marseilles edition. Schapiro reviewed the version published in Mexico. According to Caillois, who was still in Buenos Aires when the book came out in France, anticipated attacks by the Vichy censors accounted for the revisions. However, the cuts very probably corresponded to the author's own doubts and satisfied his undeniable desire for self-censorship. After the Liberation, Caillois retrieved two of the four censored essays, "Défense de la République" and "Athènes devant Philippe." The first appears in *Circonstantielles (1940–1945)* (Paris: Gallimard, 1946), the second in *Le rocher de Sisyphe* (Paris: Gallimard, 1946). But the fall of Vichy did not suffice to lift the censorship weighing on "Le vent d'hiver" and "La hiérarchie des êtres." Caillois reissued the first of these texts much later, in *Approches de l'imaginaire* (Paris: Gallimard, 1974). "La hiérarchie des êtres" was never reprinted in the author's lifetime.

4. Schapiro, "French Reaction in Exile," p. 31.

5. In "Résurrection de Corneille," *La nouvelle revue française* 301 (October 1938), Caillois had high praise for Robert Brasillach's *Corneille*. René Bertelé, who reviewed periodicals for *Europe*, expressed concern about Caillois's judgment: "Of course, Caillois, will and self-control are man's most admirable qualities, and Corneille's theater provides striking examples, but I don't like to hear this from M. Brasillach or M. Caraccio"; *Europe* 192 (December 1938): 559.

Another article by Caillois, "L'aridité," published in April 1938 in *Mesures* (and reprinted in both editions of *La communion des forts*), elicited similar comments from Walter Benjamin in a 1938 review in *Zeitschrift für Sozialforschung* (reprinted in *Gesammelten Schriften*, vol. 7 [Frankfurt am Main: Suhrkamp, 1972], p. 549) that he signed J. E. Mabin: "The 'dialectics of voluntary servitude' proposed by Caillois reveals the horror of a deeply buried intellectual landscape in which there lurks a Rastignac who gets involved this time not with the House of Nucingen but with a clique of authoritarian propaganda bosses." Caillois, said Benjamin, provided an example of a "fascist-type praxis."

The positions taken by Caillois at the time were closely scrutinized in Communist periodicals; the party's intellectuals seem to have kept their eyes on this young man whose sensitivity to the worst appeared to predispose him for the best. For example, he received privileged treatment—in contrast to Leiris and Bataille—from Georges Sadoul in his review of the manifesto "Pour un Collège de Sociologie," *Commune* 60 (September–October 1938); see also Pierre Robin's review of *Le mythe et l'homme* in *Commune* 61–62 (November–December): 1669–71.

6. In "Réponse à une enquête de Jacques Bénet," *Cahiers du Sud*, no. 216 (May 1939), Pierre Missac, one of Benjamin's few Parisian friends, accused Caillois of a formalism in which he saw a process of "detachment from the object" that made him "open to fascism." But Missac had to add a last-minute correction at the proofreading stage: "Since this response was written, M. Caillois has made a profession of Communism. So noted. But that changes nothing fundamental in my thesis." On that profession of Communism, see Meyer Schapiro, referring to a note in "La hiérarchie des êtres": "Caillois will even admit the Communists as possible agents of the desired restoration of society, provided they are a secret minority distinct from the masses"; "French Reaction in Exile," p. 33.

7. Roger Caillois, "The Winter Wind," in *The College of Sociology (1937–1939)*, ed. Denis Hollier, trans. Betsy Wing (Minneapolis: University of Minnesota Press, 1988), p. 36.

8. See Caillois, "The Winter Wind," p. 39; "L'aridité," *Mesures* 2 (April 1938): 7–12; "La hiérarchie des êtres," *Les Volontaires* 5, special issue: "Le fascisme contre l'esprit" (April 1939): 318–326.

9. Caillois, "The Winter Wind," p. 41.

10. Caillois, "L'aridité," p. 9. Caillois offered *La nouvelle revue française* a review of Montherlant: "Couldn't we do a chronicle on the subject, called *The Price of Pleasure?*"; letter, November 1938, in *Correspondance Jean Paulhan–Roger Caillois, 1934–1967*, vol. 6 of *Cahiers Jean Paulhan* (Paris: Gallimard, 1991), p. 104.

11. Caillois, *Man and the Sacred* (1939), trans. Meyer Barash (Glencoe, Ill.: Free Press, 1958), p. 89. See also "The Winter Wind," p. 41: "As for power, it is important to treat it as a force of nature against which it is senseless to protest."

12. These lines first appeared in the September 1937 issue of *La nouvelle revue française*, in a review, oddly enough, of two books on chess, including one by Marcel Duchamp, *L'opposition et les cases conjuguées sont réconciliées.* Caillois reprinted the text in *Cases d'un échiquier* (Paris: Gallimard, 1970), p. 45.

13. Pierre Klossowski, "Sade et Fourier," *Topique* 4–5 (October 1970): 89. Cf. Jacques Derrida: "The object is represented as it were [*der Gegenstand gleichsam . . . vorgetelt wird*] obtruding itself for our enjoyment [*als ob es sich zum Genusse aufdränge*]: the disgusting, the vomited is represented in advance as forcing pleasure, and that is why it disgusts, while we strive against it with all our might [*wider den wir doch mit Gewalt streben*]"; "Economimesis," trans. Richard Klein, *Diacritics* 11, no. 2 (Summer 1981): 22. On the manifestations of a "generosity" of the same type in Sartre, see Denis Hollier, *The Politics of Prose: Essays on Sartre*, trans. Jeffrey Mehlman (Minneapolis: University of Minnesota Press, 1986), pp. 149–150; idem, "How Not to Take Pleasure in Talking about Sex," *Enclitic* 7, no. 1–2 (1984).

In a letter to Paulhan dated March 13, 1937, Caillois offered to write a review of Wilhelm Stekel's translation of *La femme frigide* for *La nouvelle revue française.* Stekel's work was essential in shaping Sartre's models of the interpretation of pleasure: in particular, Sartre borrowed from it the description of the strategies of bad faith that make it possible not to identify with the pleasure one is experiencing, that is, to deny that one is experiencing pleasure. The frigid woman is a woman who refuses to let pleasure be imposed on her, who resists a pleasure that someone wants to cause her, who does not want to consent to pleasure, who does not want to take the pleasure she is given.

14. "I was always postponing the infliction of pleasure on her"; Pierre Drieu La Rochelle, *Journal d'un homme trompé* (1934; reprint, Paris: Gallimard, 1978), p. 31.

15. Caillois, "Procès intellectuel de l'art" (1934), in *Approches de l'imaginaire,* p. 41.

16. Cf. "Deeds without Words," earlier in this volume.

17. Cf. the formula Malraux attributes to Alvéar, one of the many voices of *Days of Hope:* "A man devotes to any line of action only a limited part of himself; and the more that line of action sets up to be totalitarian, the smaller is the part of him involved"; trans. Stuart Gilbert and Alistair Macdonald (London: Hamish Hamilton, 1968), p. 277.

18. Caillois, "Récit du délogé," in *Cases d'un échiquier,* p. 309.

19. Ibid., p. 322.

20. Caillois, "Sociologie du clerc," in *Approches de l'imaginaire,* p. 67. This response to Julien Benda's *La trahison des clercs* first appeared in the August 1939 issue of *La nouvelle revue française.* Caillois included it in both editions of *La communion des forts.* For the Bataille-Caillois-Benda exchanges, see the latest edition of *Le Collège de Sociologie* (Paris: Gallimard, 1995), pp. 449, 870–872.

21. Caillois, "Vertiges," in *Instincts et société* (Paris: Gonthier, 1964), p. 47. "Vertiges" appears in both editions of *La communion des forts.*

22. Caillois, "La mante religieuse" and "Mimétisme et psychasthénie légendaire," in *Le mythe et l'homme* (Paris: Gallimard, 1938). An earlier version of the second text is available in English as "Mimicry and Legendary Psychasthenia," trans. John Shepley, *October* 32 (Spring 1985): 17–32.

23. Caillois, *Les démons de midi* (1937; reprint, Paris: Fata Morgana, 1991).

24. Caillois, "Mimicry and Legendary Psychasthenia," p. 17.

25. Caillois, *Le mythe et l'homme,* p. 138. Caillois is referring to Carnot's second principle. (This passage does not appear in the English translation.)

26. Caillois, *La dissymétrie* (1973), in *Cohérences aventureuses* (Paris: Gallimard, 1976), p. 268.

27. Caillois, *Man and the Sacred,* p. 132.

28. Georges Bataille, Roger Caillois, and Michel Leiris, "Declaration of the College of Sociology on the International Crisis," in Hollier, *College,* pp. 46, 45. This declaration, signed by all three, was written by Caillois alone; see Caillois to Paulhan, October 7 and October, 1938; and Paulhan to Caillois, erroneously dated September 6, 1953 (in reality October [14?] 1938, all in *Correspondance Jean Paulhan–Roger Caillois,* pp. 97, 100, and 213–214.

29. In his 1947 afterword to *Manhood* (1939), Leiris uses similar terms to recall his contemporaries on the eve of a new war: they can only watch the collapse of

"that structure of facility which they despaired of trying to invest with not only an authentic fervor but a terrible distinction as well"; trans. Richard Howard (New York: Grossman, 1963), p. 151.

30. Caillois, *Le mythe et l'homme*, p. 131. See "On Equivocation between Literature and Politics," later in this volume.

31. This is a first difference between the two phenomena Caillois compares: whereas the male praying mantis does not survive intercourse, the mimetic insect does not just settle for surviving its psychasthenic crisis but survives because of it.

Another difference follows, one that I can only mention in passing. It has to do with the fact that in the first case, that of the praying mantis, the creature that assimilates and the creature that is assimilated belong to the same species (a species whose genetic patrimony, because it includes the anatomical binarism of sexual difference, requires that each individual be assigned to one or the other of those two categories, that of assimilated or that of assimilator), whereas in the mimetic species, males and females seem to allow themselves to be assimilated in identical fashion by their environment.

This blind spot in Caillois's interpretation may lead us to wonder whether the analogy between castration and mimesis, in other words the disappearance of sexual difference in the passage from castration (the praying mantis) to mimesis (psychasthenia), must not itself be counted among the numerous ruses of mimesis.

32. Caillois, "L'esprit des sectes," in *Instincts et société*, p. 89.

33. "This subject of ghosts," he said, "has been among the torments of my life"; quoted in C. K. Ogden, *Bentham's Theory of Fictions* (London: Kegan Paul, Trench, Trubner, 1932), p. xi.

34. Caillois, "Les secrets trésors," in *Instincts et société*, p. 41. This essay first appeared in *La communion des forts* (both editions).

35. Caillois, "Préambule pour 'L'esprit des sectes'" (1945), in *Instincts et société*, p. 68.

36. From *De l'esprit des lois* to "L'esprit des sectes," Caillois never disavowed his admiration for Montesquieu. Indeed, he was responsible for the Pléiade edition of Montesquieu's *Oeuvres complètes*. The quotation is from book V, chap. 8: *The Spirit of the Laws*, trans. Anne M. Cohler, Basia Carolyn Miller, and Harold Samuel Stone (Cambridge: Cambridge University Press, 1989), pp. 51–52.

4. BATAILLE'S TOMB

1. This essay was written for a meeting organized by Jean-Michel Rey at the Maison de la Culture d'Auxerre to commemorate the twentieth anniversary of Bataille's death. The epigraph is from Bernard Frechtman's translation of *What Is Literature?* (1949; reprint, Gloucester, Mass.: Peter Smith, 1978), p. 258.

2. Georges Bataille, *L'archangélique*, in *Oeuvres complètes*, 12 vols. (Paris: Gallimard, 1971–1988), vol. 3, p. 75.

3. Bataille, "Je sais trop bien . . . ," ibid., vol. 2, pp. 87, 88. See also his contemporary review of *Journey to the End of Night:* Bataille characterizes Céline's novel as "the description of a man's relation to his own death"; *Oeuvres complètes*, vol. 1, p. 320.

4. Bataille, "The Language of Flowers," in *Visions of Excess: Selected Writings, 1927–1939,* trans. and ed. Allan Stoekl (Minneapolis: University of Minnesota Press, 1985), p. 13.

5. Bataille, *Erotism: Death and Sensuality,* trans. Mary Dalwood (San Francisco: City Lights Bookstore, 1986).

6. Maurice Blanchot, *The Infinite Conversation,* trans. Susan Hanson (Minneapolis: University of Minnesota Press, 1993), pp. 188–189.

7. Bataille, "Attraction and Repulsion I: Tropisms, Sexuality, Laughter and Tears," lecture at the College of Sociology, January 22, 1938, in *The College of Sociology (1937–1939),* ed. Denis Hollier, trans. Betsy Wing (Minneapolis: University of Minnesota Press, 1988), pp. 104–105.

8. Ernest Hemingway, *For Whom the Bell Tolls* (New York: Charles Scribner's Sons, 1940), p. 256.

9. Bataille had considered publishing Heine's manuscript in the *Acéphale* collection; see *Oeuvres complètes,* vol. 1, p. 675 nn.

10. See especially Jean Rousset's *Le mythe de Don Juan* (Paris: Armand Colin, 1978). Rousset excludes Casanova and Lovelace figures from his study: "They were wanting in that they had not struggled against death."

11. Bataille, "Nietzsche and Don Juan," in *The Accursed Share: An Essay on General Economy, Volumes II & III,* trans. Robert Hurley (New York: Zone Books, 1991), pp. 404 ff. This section of "Sovereignty" is a reworking of an earlier article, "Nietzsche et Thomas Mann," *Synthèses* 60 (May 1951), reprinted as an appendix to "La souveraineté," in *Oeuvres complètes,* vol. 8, pp. 433–434.

12. Bataille, "Nietzsche et Thomas Mann," pp. 488–489.

13. Ibid., p. 489.

14. Bataille, *Inner Experience,* trans. Leslie Anne Boldt (Albany: State University of New York Press, 1988), p. 76. These pages introduce the section titled "The Blue of Noon," dated August 1934.

15. Bataille, *The Accursed Share,* p. 404.

16. Bataille concludes the Michelet chapter of *Literature and Evil* by quoting a passage from the historian's diary where he explains that, while writing about the bloodiest episodes of the French Revolution, whenever inspiration threatened to fail him, "he . . . would leave his house and go to a public convenience where the stink was stultifying. He would breathe in deeply and then, having 'got as close as possible to the object of his disgust,' return to work" (p. 56).

17. *Les pieds nickelés* was one of the most famous anarchistic comic strips of the prewar popular culture. See Bataille, "Les pieds nickelés," *Documents* 1930, no. 4; reprinted in *Documents,* ed. Jean Jamin (Paris: Jean-Marie Place, Collection "Gradhiva," 1992), vol. 2, p. 215.

18. Bataille, *Story of the Eye,* trans. Joachim Neugroschel (San Francisco: City Lights Books, 1987), pp. 53, 68. See Leo Weinstein, *The Metamorphosis of Don Juan* (Stanford: Stanford University Press, 1959). Chapter 2 provides pertinent details on the life of this "real" Don Juan, who purportedly had himself buried under the porch of the Church of Charity in the city of his birth, and was said to have asked that the following be written on a plaque on his tomb: "Here lie the bones and ashes of the worst man who ever lived."

19. Bataille, "The Sacred Conspiracy," in Stoekl, *Visions of Excess*, p. 181.

20. Jeffrey Mehlman, "Ruse de Rivoli: Politics and Deconstruction," *Modern Language Notes*, October 1976, p. 1065.

21. Bataille, *Blue of Noon*, trans. Harry Mathews (London: Marion Boyars, 1986), pp. 23–24. These aphorisms first appeared in 1943 in the section of *Inner Experience* called "The Blue of Noon." In a brief reference that does not lessen the enigma, *On Nietzsche* situates this scene in Trent (*On Nietzsche*, trans. Bruce Boone [New York: Paragon House, 1992], p. 107). There is no mention of Trent in *Blue of Noon*, which was written around the same time (1934–35) but published much later. A logbook kept by Bataille during the corresponding months was published in Laure (Colette Peignot), *Ecrits, fragments, lettres* (Paris: UGE, 1978), pp. 367–375.

The association of the name Trent (in French *Trente*, a homonym of "thirty") with a macabre lubricity is substantiated by the use Bataille makes of it on two other occasions: when he publishes *Le petit* under the pseudonym Louis Trente (*Oeuvres complètes*, vol. 3, p. 33), and when he is preparing a volume of obscene poems that would bear the title *La tombe de Louis XXX* (*Oeuvres complètes*, vol. 4, p. 151). Printed in 1943, *Le petit* bears as a fake publication date 1934, the year of the events in Trent.

22. Bataille, *Blue of Noon*, p. 42.

23. Ibid., p. 84.

24. What *Blue of Noon* owes to *Man's Fate* is matched only by what *Man's Hope* owes to *Blue of Noon*, which Malraux had read in manuscript when it was submitted for publication at Gallimard. See Kahnweiler's July 9, 1935, letter to Malraux in Isabelle Monod-Fontaine, *Daniel Henry-Kahnweiler* (Paris: Centre Georges Pompidou, 1984), p. 150.

25. Bataille, *Blue of Noon*, p. 146.

26. Ibid., p. 144.

27. Leo Weinstein (*The Metamorphosis of Don Juan*, chap. 11) points out that throughout the Hispanic world José Zorrilla y Moro's *Don Juan Tenorio* is traditionally staged the following day. In keeping with this tradition, John Huston introduced a representation of *Don Juan* in a street scene of his film version of *Under the Volcano:* the events of Malcolm Lowry's novel take place on November 2.

See also Bataille's "Calaveras": "Don Juan also turns up in Mexican village fairs (he is a skeleton)"; *Oeuvres complètes*, vol. 2, p. 409. Written in July 1936 but unpublished in Bataille's lifetime, "Calaveras" is inspired by Sol Lesser's montage of rushes from Eisenstein's *Qué viva Mexico* that selected scenes showing Mexican popular celebrations of the Day of the Dead. See J. Brunius, "Petite tête de mort," *La flèche*, June 12, 1936 (with a still from Eisenstein's film). On the need felt by the left during the Popular Front to compete with fascist festivals, see "On Equivocation between Literature and Politics," later in this volume.

28. Bataille, *The Impossible: A Story of Rats, followed by Dianus and by The Oresteia*, trans. Robert Hurley (San Francisco: City Lights Books, 1991), p. 92.

29. Bataille, *Story of the Eye*, p. 24.

30. Bataille, *Blue of Noon*, p. 42.

31. Laure, *Ecrits*, pp. 369–370. Among the events that are echoed in *Blue of Noon*,

those in Trent are not the only ones to appear on this calendar, whose time span also includes the Day of the Dead that concludes the novel. Bataille was in Trier on November 2, which fell on a Friday: "Errands this morning in Trier then dep[arture] 10:36 Moselle. 12:00 Koblentz l[unch] then coffee 3:35 sailboat Rhine asters and candles. 6:00 Frankfort Romer. dinner Börsenkeller. 5:52 edith leaves for Heidelberg" (p. 375).

32. As always with Bataille, the weather plays a role: in *On Nietzsche*, the elements are mentioned in his reference to "the horrible night in Trent": "a raging storm observed from a room where hell . . . "; *On Nietzsche*, p. 106; and "Sur Nietzsche," in *Oeuvres complètes*, vol. 6, p. 407 nn.

Boris Souvarine refers to these events in the introduction to the reprint edition of *La critique sociale* (Paris: Editions de la Différence, 1983), p. 26: "In 1934, one of our friends whose name hardly matters, an occasional collaborator on the journal *(La critique sociale)*, was leaving, with his wife, for the Tyrol, in the summertime; as they had a car, they took us with them on vacation. In the peaceful mountains where we made a stop, a drama occurred, a flight took place, without warning. Colette had disappeared, eloping with the obliging 'friend' who had transported us to that point. What happened next can scarcely be told, and moreover it has grown somewhat unclear in my memory after nearly a half-century. It is better to remain silent about the incidents that followed, rather than to offer them up as fodder to the scribblers avid for scandal."

33. According to Michel Surya, it was on July 25, the day (in the novel) of the streamers in Vienna, that Colette Peignot left Souvarine to join Bataille; *La mort à l'oeuvre* (Paris: Librairie Séguier, 1987), p. 201. The political portents and sexual provocation aimed at the Commander would thus have been contemporaneous. In the manuscript of *Le coupable*, a note dated April 19, 1943, refers to the Innsbruck episode: "When we entered the house [Bataille's house in Vézelay], coming from Paris, veils of black crepe were drying on the trees in the sunny garden. This lugubrious 'omen' gripped my heart (reminding me of the long black streamers of I., portents of my unhappiness . . .)"; *Oeuvres complètes*, vol. 5, pp. 557–558.

34. Bataille, *Blue of Noon*, pp. 60, 110. In *Man's Fate* Malraux introduces a similar episode in Katov's curriculum vitae: "As a medical student, he had tried to blow up the gates of the Odessa prison" (trans. Haakon M. Chevalier [New York: Modern Library, 1961], pp. 19–20). The prototype is undoubtedly "Steinberg, a revolutionary socialist and commissar of the courts of justice"—as Pradas refers to him in Malraux's *Days of Hope*, trans. Stuart Gilbert and Alistair Macdonald (London: Hamish Hamilton, 1968), p. 173. Izaak Steinberg, Lenin's minister of justice from 1917 to July 1918, had asked for the permanent closing of the Peter and Paul prison.

35. Bataille, *Oeuvres complètes*, vol. 2, p. 435 (note to p. 173).

36. Bataille, "En attendant la grève générale," in *Oeuvres complètes*, ibid., p. 262.

37. Bataille, "Le problème de l'Etat," ibid., vol. 1, p. 334.

38. Bataille, "Le fascisme en France," ibid., vol. 2, pp. 206, 212, 213. The impasse of a political situation in which there is no alternative to fascism (in which the opposition to fascism, whether liberal or Marxist, has been put out of action)

makes Bataille's substitution of *surfascisme*, superfascism, for the traditional "anti-fascism" perfectly logical: fascism cannot be circumvented; it must be overcome. To say that it will not come into being is to play the ostrich. What is required is to go beyond it.

39. Bataille, *The Accursed Share*, p. 261.

40. Bataille, "La souveraineté," in *Oeuvres complètes*, vol. 8, p. 673 nn.

41. Bataille, *The Accursed Share*, p. 332.

42. Ibid., p. 329. For Bataille, "Communism means the end of distinction"; "La souveraineté," p. 658.

43. Bataille, *The Accursed Share*, p. 331.

44. Ibid., p. 434.

45. Bataille, *Literature and Evil*, pp. 125–143. Most of the articles collected in revised form in *Literature and Evil* (*La littérature et le mal*, 1957) had been written before "Sovereignty" (which dates from 1953). The article on Kafka ("Franz Kafka before the Communist Critics") had appeared in *Critique* in October 1950.

46. Bataille, *Oeuvres complètes*, vol. 8, p. 470 (note to p. 271). Cf. *Literature and Evil*, p. 127: "the idea of burning Kafka, even if it was no more than a provocation, had a certain logic for the Communists."

47. Bataille, *Literature and Evil*, p. 141.

48. Ibid., p. 132.

49. Jean Bernier and Georges Bataille, "La vie de famille," in Bataille, *Oeuvres complètes*, vol. 1, p. 388.

50. Bataille, "Le paradoxe de l'utilité absolue," ibid., vol. 2, p. 150.

51. Bataille, "The Solar Anus," in Stoekl, *Visions of Excess*, p. 8.

52. Bataille, "The 'Old Mole' and the Prefix *Sur* in the Words *Surhomme* [Superman] and *Surrealist*," ibid., p. 32.

53. Bataille, "Kinsey, the Underworld, and Work," in *Erotism*, pp. 149–163.

54. Bataille, "Rêve," in *Oeuvres complètes*, vol. 2, p. 9. See the notes from the manuscript of *Guilty* in which Bataille mentions "the descent into the cellar, in connection with that childhood dream so often, so anxiously repeated"; ibid., vol. 5, p. 555.

55. Bataille, *Story of the Eye*, p. 93.

56. Georges Bataille and Raymond Queneau, "The Critique of the Foundations of the Hegelian Dialectic," in Stoekl, *Visions of Excess*, p. 112.

57. Sigmund Freud, "A Child Is Being Beaten: A Contribution to the Study of the Origin of Sexual Perversions," in *The Standard Edition of the Complete Psychological Works of Sigmund Freud*, trans. James Strachey, vol. 17 (London: Hogarth Press, 1955), pp. 198, 189.

58. For a reading of the case of *L'abbé C* in the light of this schema, see Denis Hollier, "Georges Bataille devant la critique communiste," in *Actes du colloque international d'Amsterdam (June 21–22, 1985)*, ed. Jan Versteeg (Amsterdam: Rodopi, 1987), pp. 65–72. For a similarly paradoxical temporality of pleasure in Caillois, see "Mimesis and Castration 1937," earlier in this volume. For other aspects of the mechanism of identification with the aggressor in Bataille, see "On Equivocation between Literature and Politics," later in this volume.

5. UNSATISFIED DESIRE

1. Georges Bataille, *Guilty*, trans. Bruce Boone (Venice, Calif.: Lapis Press, 1961), p. 11. All quotations from this work in the following paragraphs are from this translation.

2. See Bataille, "Discussion sur la guerre," November 21, 1939 (a roundtable with Koyré, Landsberg, Moré, Wahl), in *Digraphe*, December 17, 1978, p. 127: "Today I am determined to show what may be very human—perhaps even the high point of the human spirit—about this apparently unbearable situation. The phenomenon of uncertainty within which we are living may shed light on the nature of things instead of obscuring it; I am determined to show how man may achieve fulfillment by accepting the incompleteness of all things as the element in which he lives, by finding in this incompleteness no longer an orienting subject but a reason for glory."

3. Bataille, "The Sorcerer's Apprentice," in *The College of Sociology (1937–1939)*, ed. Denis Hollier, trans. Betsy Wing (Minneapolis: University of Minnesota Press, 1988), pp. 12–23.

4. This text appears as "Letter to X, Lecturer on Hegel . . .," ibid., pp. 89–93.

5. Ibid., pp. 90, 92.

6. On this poetics of guilt, see "Bataille's Tomb," earlier in this volume.

7. *The Poetry and Prose of William Blake*, ed. David V. Erdbaum (Garden City, N.Y.: Doubleday, 1965), p. 465.

6. ON EQUIVOCATION BETWEEN LITERATURE AND POLITICS

1. Zeev Sternhell, *Neither Right nor Left: Fascist Ideology in France*, trans. David Maisel (Berkeley: University of California Press, 1986), p. 227.

2. René Bertelé, in *The College of Sociology (1937–1939)*, ed. Denis Hollier, trans. Betsy Wing (Minneapolis: University of Minnesota Press, 1988), appendix, pp. 367–368.

3. Michel Surya, *Georges Bataille. La mort à l'oeuvre* (Paris: Librairie Séguier, 1987). Surya uses the College's declaration on the Munich crisis (Hollier, *College*, pp. 43–46) to refute the "accusation of equivocation" leveled by Klossowksi against Bataille: "The clarity of this declaration rules out any form of equivocation." Surya acknowledges some ambiguities, but he asserts that they are only "superficial"; at bottom, Bataille was "one of the most peremptory antifascists as early as 1933" (p. 273). Not a line written by him "justifies the slightest reservation" (p. 250).

This defense, to which I subscribe in part, calls for some clarification. In the first place, concerning the "Declaration": we now know that Bataille did not write it. In a letter to Caillois dated October 10, 1938, he refers to it as "the note you drafted"; Georges Bataille, *Lettres à Roger Caillois (4 août 1935–4 février 1959)*, ed. J.-P. Le Bouler (Paris: Editions Folle Avoine, 1987), p. 90. As for Klossowski, he invoked Walter Benjamin's reservations and his own, especially on the political level, about Bataille's position at the time: "It is undeniable that the deep temptations of fascist cynicism had an influence on his peculiar genius"; quoted in Jean-Maurice Monnoyer, *Le peintre et son démon* (Paris: Flammarion, 1985), p. 187.

At issue here almost certainly is "The Psychological Structure of Fascism," an article Bataille published in 1933 (the date Surya mentions). This text had considerable inspirational value for early antifascist positioning. Still, it is legitimate to ask whether its antifascism stands up to every test. According to Blanchot, Bataille himself ended up sharing Klossowski's reservations: "He turned out to regret the pages he had written on 'The Psychological Structure of Fascism', a piece that might lend itself to more than one reading"; Maurice Blanchot, "Les intellectuels en question," *Le débat* 29 (March 1984): 20. This is just what Benjamin had told Klossowski: Bataille's articles for *La critique sociale* "were working to the advantage of fascism!" (quoted by Giorgio Agamben, "Bataille e il paradosso della sovranità," in *Georges Bataille. Il politico e il sacro*, ed. Jacqueline Risset [Naples: Liguori, 1988], p. 115).

Surya presents Bataille as someone capable of controlling the ambiguities he put into play, while the less powerful minds around him allowed his enterprises to be distorted in ways for which it would be unfair to blame him. Still, for what effects may a sorcerer's apprentice disclaim responsibility?

4. Carlo Ginzburg, "Germanic Mythology and Nazism: Thoughts on an Old Book by Georges Dumézil," in *Clues, Myths, and the Historical Method*, trans. John Tedeschi and Ann C. Tedeschi (Baltimore: Johns Hopkins University Press, 1989), p. 143.

5. Giampiero Moretti and Rocco Ronchi, "L'ermeneutica del mito negli anni trenta. Un dialogo," *Nuovi argumenti* 21 (January–March 1987). See also Carlo Sini, "Bataille o dell'ambiguità," *Rinascita*, April 11, 1987, p. 19. For an overview see Francis Marmande, *Bataille politique* (Lyon: Presses Universitaires de Lyon, 1985).

6. Hollier, *College*, pp. 5, 52.

7. The two final chapters in the French editions since 1987 are "Le fascisme spiritualiste" and "La tentation fasciste." The latter is not included in the English translation.

8. Sternhell, *Neither Right nor Left*, p. 232.

9. Maulnier quoted in ibid., p. 234. On Moeller van den Bruck, see Hans Mayer's presentation at the College, "The Rituals of Political Associations in Germany of the Romantic Period," April 18, 1939; reprinted in Hollier, *College*, pp. 266–267.

The same terrorist logic is developed in Malraux's *Man's Fate*—also published, like Moeller van den Bruck's translation, in 1933—by Ch'en, after he has committed his murder: "Perhaps one thoroughly despises the man one kills. But less than the others . . . [less] than the ones who don't kill"; trans. Haakon M. Chevalier (New York: Modern Library, 1961), p. 64. For other contemporaneous references to the concept of terror, see Blanchot, "Le terrorisme, méthode de salut public", *Combat*, July 1936; and the correspondence between Paulhan and Caillois (and Laurent Jenny's introduction), *Cahiers Jean Paulhan*, vol. 6 (Paris: Gallimard, 1991).

10. Blanchot, "La seule manière d'être Français," *L'Insurgé* 23 (June 16, 1937). And, in an earlier op-ed piece: "Patriotic feelings are mobilized in enterprises directed against the nation"; "Nous les complices de Blum . . . ," *L'Insurgé* 2 (January 20, 1937): 4. See also Jean-Pierre Azéma on the consequences of that same

logic under the occupation: "Jews and Freemasons have been the victims of men who have consciously inverted the order of priorities: those who claimed to be nationalists struggled against a so-called internal enemy rather than against the occupying force"; "Il y a 50 ans, la guerre. 1939–1940. L'année terrible," *Le Monde*, August 26, 1989, p. 2.

11. Jacques Lacan, *De la psychose paranoïaque dans ses rapports avec la personnalité* (Paris: Seuil, 1975), p. 253.

12. In a later formulation Lacan is even more explicit, saying that "the structural effect of identification with the rival can only be conceived of if the way is prepared for it by a primary identification that structures the subject as a rival with himself"; "Aggressivity in Psychoanalysis," in *Ecrits: A Selection*, trans. Alan Sheridan (New York: W. W. Norton, 1977), p. 22. Cf., in *Man's Fate*, the way Kyo interprets Ch'en's terrorism according to this model: "Perhaps he would kill Chiang only to kill himself" (p. 159).

Lacan may well have planned to apply this schema to a political "case": in December 1947 *Critique* (no. 17) announced a forthcoming article by Lacan on "Le cas de Rudolf Hess." Although the article never appeared, the prospect of an *Aimé chez les Nazis* invites speculation: would Lacan have interpreted Hess's epic, his flight to England, and his short-lived betrayal of the Führer as a case of self-punishment paranoia?

On the use of the concept of self-punishment in the psychiatric literature of the 1930s, see Carolyn Dean, "Law and Sacrifice: Bataille, Lacan, and the Critique of the Subject," *Representations* 13 (Winter 1986): 42–62.

13. Benda pursues the debate in *La grande épreuve des démocraties* (New York: Editions de la Maison Française, 1942).

14. Bertrand d'Astorg, "At the College of Sociology," in Hollier, *College*, p. 194.

15. Pierre Missac, "Avec des cartes truquées," *Cahiers du Sud* 216 (May 1939): 424.

16. Roger Caillois, *Man and the Sacred*, trans. Meyer Barash (Glencoe, Ill.: Free Press, 1958), p. 60. One chapter of the book, a lecture delivered at the College in the fall of 1938, is called "The Ambiguity of the Sacred."

17. Bataille, "The Psychological Structure of Fascism," in *Visions of Excess*, trans. and ed. Allan Stoekl (Minneapolis: University of Minnesota Press, 1985), pp. 158–159.

18. Blanchot, "On demande des dissidents," *Combat* 20 (December 1938); reprinted in *Gramma* 5 (1978). Sternhell has a good commentary on this article, *Neither Right nor Left*, p. 223. Jeffrey Mehlman was the first to emphasize the importance of the paralyzed double negation (neither . . . nor) in Blanchot's appeals to terrorism during the 1930s; "Blanchot at *Combat:* Of Literature and Terror," in *Legacies of Antisemitism in France* (Minneapolis: University of Minnesota Press, 1983), pp. 10–11.

19. Friedrich Nietzsche, *The Gay Science*, sec. 125, trans. Walter Kaufmann (New York: Random House, 1974), p. 181; quoted in Bataille, "The Obelisk," in Stoekl, *Visions of Excess*, p. 214.

20. Bataille, "The Sorcerer's Apprentice," in Stoekl, *Visions of Excess*, pp. 223–234.

21. The corpus examined in *Neither Right nor Left* is nevertheless the result of a literary judgment. Sternhell maintains that the 1930s constitute one of "the most sterile periods in French intellectual history," a period in which France "was relatively unproductive and lived chiefly on its cultural heritage" (pp. xiv, 269). It is easy enough to distinguish politics from literature when literature is virtually absent. And yet Malraux wrote all his novels during this period. And what about Céline, Sartre, and Nizan—who would undoubtedly have become one of the major literary figures of the era had he not been killed at Dunkirk in 1940? Not to mention Artaud. And even Aragon, Bernanos, Giono, Giraudoux, Colette . . .

22. Bataille, "The Psychological Structure of Fascism," p. 146.

23. Bataille, "Dans l'histoire comme dans la nature . . . ," in *Oeuvres complètes*, vol. 2 (Paris: Gallimard, 1971), p. 91.

24. Bataille, "The Solar Anus," in Stoekl, *Visions of Excess*, p. 8.

25. Bataille, "Toward Real Revolution," trans. Annette Michelson, *October* 36 (Spring 1986): 37. It is important to recall that this is a left-wing text, inspired by the convergence of the Socialist and Communist parades during the antifascist demonstration in the Cours de Vincennes on February 12, 1934; thus it does not appeal to, nor does it stem in any way from (at least not consciously), any fascist tendencies.

26. Bataille, "Power," in Hollier, *College*, p. 147.

27. The view of sadism implied in these analyses of fascist power is very different from the one found in "The Use Value of D. A. F. de Sade (An Open Letter to My Current Comrades)" (in Stoekl, *Visions of Excess*, pp. 91–102) or in *Erotism.*

28. Bataille, "Power," pp. 133–134. Klossowski, for his part, sees the mutation of images of Christian sovereignty as coming after—well after—the Crucifixion. Positing at the outset that the church is the refutation of the empire, he denounces "the disguising of the empire as a church 'triumphant.'" In other words, there can be no such thing as a church triumphant. However, "Caesar . . . is not yet the Antichrist; it is only after Christ has been revealed to the world, that *Caesar 'with the soul of Christ'* will become the Antichrist." Put yet another way, the "heresy" that transformed the early Christian community into an empire is not achieved until Constantine's *In hoc signo vinces;* Klossowski, "Qui est mon prochain?" *Esprit* 75 (December 1939): 405. This interpretation of church history echoes the attacks on the (Spanish) church triumphant offered, the same year, in Malraux's *Days of Hope.*

Klossowski's essay transposes the heterology of the College into Christian terms: "The 'enemy' corresponds to the more or less concerted ignorance in which I remain with respect to my own potential . . . The soul, heterogeneous in essence, projects outside itself that which in itself belies the homogeneous state that it considers it has reached; henceforth the heterogeneous element will make all the more ravages within the soul inasmuch as its image will have taken shape outside it" (p. 410).

29. Ginzburg, "Germanic Mythology and Nazism," p. 143; cf. Bataille, "Power," p. 135.

30. Bataille, "Power," p. 135. According to Klossowski, Bataille experienced "the temptation of the swastika." Pierre Prévost reports that Bataille regretted

seeing the solar symbol appropriated by the Nazis. Caillois too refers to the mystical (Minoan) background of that symbol. Benjamin was consulted by some Parisian intellectuals on the meaning of the swastika. See Adrienne Monnier, "La swastika," *La nouvelle revue française* 43 (August 1934): 310–311. The assessment of Bataille's political whereabouts in the late 1930s has been considerably enriched by the publication of his correspondence with Pierre Kaan in Georges Bataille, *Contre-Attaques. Gli anni della militanza antifascista. Corrispondenza inedita con Pierre Kaan e Jean Rollin*, ed. Marina Galletti (Rome: Edizione Associate, 1995).

31. G. W. F. Hegel, *The Phenomenology of Spirit*, trans. A. V. Miller (Oxford: Oxford University Press, 1977), vol 1, p. 19. Bataille often quoted these words from the translation Kojève provided in his "L'idée de la mort dans la philosophie de Hegel," in *Introduction à la lecture de Hegel*, ed. Raymond Queneau (Paris: Gallimard, 1947), pp. 540–541. This section is not included in Alan Bloom's edition (*Introduction to the Reading of Hegel, by Alexandre Kojève* [Ithaca: Cornell University Press, 1980]).

32. Ginzburg seems to take this type of macabre meditation (what Bataille calls "the practice of joy before death") and the funereal aesthetic from which it stems as an unambiguous symptom of fascism. But Janine Bourdin points out a series of attempts by the governments of the Third Republic, at the end of the 1930s, to borrow the theatricality that served fascist regimes so well and put it to work for democracy. She cites two instances: in July 1938, for the visit of the English sovereigns, and on November 11 of the same year, for the celebration of the armistice. Neither the left nor the center made any objection to the ceremonial trappings, with their black drapery and mortuary symbols: according to Bourdin, Action Française—manifestly on the extreme right—was virtually alone in expressing disapproval; Janine Bourdin, "Introduction" and "Les anciens combattants et la célébration du 11 novembre 1938," in René Rémond and Janine Bourdin, *La France et les Français en 1938–1939* (Paris: Presses de la Fondation Nationale des Sciences Politiques, 1978), pp. 22, 110. See also Marc Bloch's regrets that "our regime, in spite of all its democratic trappings, has never been able to create for the people of France festivals capable of sounding a note to the ears of all the world. We left it to Hitler to revive the paeans of the Ancient World"; *Strange Defeat: A Statement of Evidence Written in 1940*, trans. Gerard Hopkins (New York: W. W. Norton, 1968), p. 167.

33. When it came out, Dumézil's book was viewed (by Paulhan, Etiemble, and presumably Marc Bloch as well) as a clear condemnation of Nazism's paleo-Germanic references and as a warning against them. Dumézil replied to Ginzburg in "Science et politique. Réponse à Carlo Ginzburg," *Annales (Economies Sociétés Civilisations)* 40 (September–October 1985): 983–989. See also Didier Eribon's substantial response to Ginzburg, *Faut-il brûler Dumézil? Mythologie, science et politique* (Paris: Flammarion, 1992).

34. Dumézil quoted in Ginzburg, "Germanic Mythology and Nazism," p. 129.

35. Bataille, "Nietzsche and the Fascists," in Stoekl, *Visions of Excess*, pp. 189–190. The issue of "artificiality" is at the heart of the distinction between myth and literature that René-Manlius Guastalla develops in his talk at the College. It intersects with the question of the proper name: true myths, which are not the

product of individual will, have no authors and thus do not bear proper names; see "The Birth of Literature," in Hollier, *College*, p. 203.

36. Giving a further twist to the tourniquet of these ambiguities, Henri Dubief, who was close to Bataille at the time, wrote: "The influence of Hitlerian neopaganism is patent at *Acéphale*"; "Témoignage sur Contre-Attaque," *Textures* 6 (1970): 57.

37. Bataille, "Power," p. 132.

38. Ginzburg, "Germanic Mythology and Nazism," p. 126.

39. Hans Mayer recalls that his own talk was scheduled in place of the one Benjamin had been slated to give on Baudelaire. Perhaps ritual associations in German culture were a more burning—and less ambiguous—topic?

Jean-Maurice Monnoyer offers a particularly vivid depiction of the relations between Bataille and Benjamin in his conversations with Klossowski; "L'a-théologie et l'Eglise de la mort de dieu," in *Le peintre et son démon* (Paris: Flammarion, 1985).

40. Jean Paulhan, "Sacred Language," in Hollier, *College*, p. 319.

41. Ibid. For Paulhan's remarks on contemporary political vocabulary, see his 1938 "Lettre aux *Nouveaux Cahiers* sur le pouvoir des mots," reprinted by J.-C. Zylberstein in his edition of *Les fleurs de Tarbes* (Paris: Gallimard, 1973).

42. Giampiero Moretti et Rocco Ronchi, "L'ermenautica," p. 85. See also Denis Hollier, *Against Architecture*, trans. Betsy Wing (Cambridge, Mass.: MIT Press, 1989), pp. 96–98.

43. In "The Use Value of D. A. F. de Sade," Bataille defines the "objects" with which heterology deals precisely as "indefinable," determinable only "through negation . . . there is no way of placing such elements in the immediate objective human domain, in the sense that the pure and simple objectification of their specific character would lead to their incorporation in a homogeneous intellectual system, in other words, to a hypocritical cancellation of the excremental character" (p. 98). See also "The Psychological Structure of Fascism": as a matter of fundamental principle, "science cannot know *heterogeneous* elements as such" (p. 141).

44. Caillois, *Procès intellectuel de l'art* (1936), in *Approches de l'imaginaire* (Paris: Gallimard, 1974), p. 36.

45. Maurice Merleau-Ponty, *Phenomenology of Perception* (1945), trans. Colin Smith (London: Routledge & Kegan Paul, 1962), p. 382.

46. Raymond Aron, *An Introduction to the Philosophy of History: An Essay on the Limits of Historical Objectivity*, trans. George J. Irwin (London: Weidenfeld and Nicolson, 1961), p. 290. See also Aron, *Marxismes imaginaires. D'une sainte famille à l'autre* (Paris: Gallimard, 1970), p. 359: "Every historical work, I had said in one of my earliest books, is *ambiguous* and *inexhaustible*." Hans Mayer refers to Aron's dissertation in his talk at the College (Hollier, *College*, p. 264). On the degree to which Bataille shared such a view, see "Unsatisfied Desire," earlier in this volume.

Cf. Bataille in 1940: "The worlds of history are unfinished worlds. That is what characterizes these worlds *essentially*"; "Discussions sur la guerre," *Digraphe* 17 (December 1978): 129.

47. Bernard Groethuysen, "Une philosophie critique de l'histoire," *La nouvelle revue française* 313 (October 1939): 627.

7. FEAR AND TREMBLING IN THE AGE OF SURREALISM

1. Roger Caillois, *The Necessity of the Mind*, trans. Michael Syrotinski (Venice, Calif.: Lapis Press, 1990), p. 149; idem, *The Writing of Stones*, trans. Barbara Bray (Charlottesville: University of Virginia Press, 1980).

2. Guillaume Apollinaire, "1909," in *Alcools: Poems 1898–1913*, trans. William Meredith (Garden City, N.Y.: Doubleday, 1964), p. 197.

3. Caillois, *The Necessity of the Mind*, p. 61. A line by Alfred Musset, quoted in the chapter on the praying mantis (and in the epigraph to this chapter), stems from the same inspiration. Here the Romantic poet evokes a woman: "She exhausts, she kills, and it only makes her all the more beautiful"; *The Cup and the Lip*, act 4, scene 1, quoted in *The Necessity of the Mind*, p. 82, n. 22.

4. Ibid., p. 68.

5. Caillois, *Le mythe et l'homme* (Paris: Gallimard, 1938), p. 25. In *The Necessity of the Mind*, Caillois speaks of "self-annihilation" (p. 107).

6. Cf. "Deeds without Words" and "Under the Heading of Holofernes," elsewhere in this volume.

7. See "Must Literature Be Possible?" and "Bataille's Tomb," earlier in this volume.

8. Caillois himself—during the Occupation, a time when Frenchmen did not have to play at being Persian to feel foreign in France—had chosen to call *Lettres françaises* the magazine he edited in Buenos Aires. Just as Montesquieu presented his *Persian Letters* (in French) as a book written by Persians from abroad, Caillois's *Lettres françaises* (which were not written in Persian) can be viewed as the organ of a deterritorialized French literature. By extending the opening to alterity toward a questioning of the way in which identity reacquires roots, the transformation of Montesquieu's question "How can one be Persian?" into "How can one be French?" transforms a sociological relativism into a radical historical, linguistic, and literary irredentism.

8. UNDER THE HEADING OF HOLOFERNES

1. Michel Leiris, *Manhood*, trans. Richard Howard (New York: Grossman, 1963). The calligraphy sample in the epigraph is from the Vever Collection at the Smithsonian Institution, 86.0344.

2. Leiris, *Manhood*, pp. 23, 155.

3. Ibid., p. 147.

4. Ibid., pp. 142, 148–149.

5. See Bataille's interpretation of Nazism and desexualized sadism in "On Equivocation between Literature and Politics," earlier in this volume.

6. Leiris, *Manhood*, pp. 51–52, 57, 93. In *La république juive* (Paris: Fayard, 1988), Pierre Birnbaum reproduces an advertisement for *La vieille France* that contrasts Joan of Arc with Judith: "Our heroine is Joan of Arc, the sublime virgin. Theirs is Judith, the bloody trollop."

Maupassant himself evokes Judith in connection with another "patriotic harlot,"

Ball-of-Fat (Boule de Suif), whose name, during the Dreyfus affair, was to become the basis for various anti-Semitic jokes, starting with Boule de Juif.

7. These alternatives do not include the capillary treatment chosen by Leiris, who used to shave his head. This treatment is obviously unsuited to the type of contact that *Manhood* describes between Judith and Holofernes: "fingers and hair mingled in hideous union"; trans. Richard Howard (New York: Grossman, 1963), p. 94.

8. Leiris, *Manhood*, pp. 94–95.

9. Sigmund Freud, "The Taboo of Virginity," in *The Standard Edition of the Complete Psychological Works of Sigmund Freud*, ed. James Strachey, vol. 11 (London: Hogarth Press, 1957), p. 207.

10. The equation of head and genitals entails the equation of decapitation and castration. The same equation presides over André Masson's drawing of the body of Acephalus: the man without a head also lacks a sex, or rather, in place of his genitals he has only the empty skull of the *vanitas.*

11. See Sarah Kofman's excellent essay on Freud's treatment of Hebbel's play, in *Freud and Fiction*, trans. Sarah Wykes (Cambridge: Polity Press, 1991).

12. Leiris makes no reference to Giraudoux, whose *Judith* he probably had not seen or read. Moreover, Leiris had already encountered Cranach's diptych—he had considered using it as an illustration in Bataille's journal *Documents*—when Jouvet put on Giraudoux's play. Oddly, the tragic caryatids of *Manhood* also have their counterparts in Giraudoux's work, where *Judith* appears alongside a *Pour Lucrèce.*

13. *Correspondance Paul Claudel–Darius Milhaud (1912–1953)*, ed. Jacques Petit (Paris: Gallimard, 1961), pp. 192, 196–197. See also Claudel, *Journal (1904–1932)*, ed. François Varillon and Jacques Petit (Paris: Gallimard, 1968), p. 978. Claudel, who was unfamiliar with Hebbel's play (a drama that is not Voltairean in the slightest), was not aware that Giraudoux had invented less than he reproached him for. But Hebbel himself was not the inventor that Freud took him to be. It is mistaken to credit him, as Freud does, with the glory of that premier. For the humanists of the Renaissance, especially the Protestants, Judith had already lost her virginity, even before her meeting with Holofernes (Renaissance painters, too, were the first to represent her naked and to omit the dog, symbol of fidelity, from her iconographic attributes). The biblical version implied a worship of chastity as sacred which these enemies of priestly celibacy had no reason to endorse.

14. Freud, "The Taboo of Virginity," p. 202.

15. Gide is not convinced by this turn of events: "If it is easy to see Judith falling in love with Holofernes, it is impossible on the contrary to understand how she reaches the point of killing him"; November 12, 1931, *Journal 1889–1939* (Paris: Gallimard, 1951), p. 1092. This resistance to Judith's logic might be linked to the aversion Gide expresses in *Corydon* on the tragic dimension of heterosexuality, which, for example, condemns the male praying mantis to offer himself up, in order to satisfy himself, as a holocaust for the survival of the species.

16. Leiris, *Manhood*, p. 219.

17. Or it is imaginary, in the Lacanian sense: "Every imaginary relation comes about via a kind of *you or me* between the subject and the object. That is to say—*If*

it's you, I'm not. If it's me, it's you who isn't"; *The Seminar of Jacques Lacan. Book II: The Ego in Freud's Theory and in the Technique of Psychoanalysis*, trans. Sylvana Tomaselli (New York: W. W. Norton, 1988), p. 169. For a Lacanian reading of Leiris's work, see Jeffrey Mehlman, *A Structural Study of Autobiography* (Ithaca: Cornell University Press, 1974).

18. The fate Judith reserves for Holofernes brings her into the family of praying mantises. It is astonishing, then, that Caillois does not mention the Jewish virgin in his 1934 essay on that devouring insect ("The Praying Mantis," which was written at approximately the same time as *Manhood*, also turns out to be an autobiographical text, as we have realized since the posthumous publication of *The Necessity of the Mind*). See "Mimesis and Castration 1937," earlier in this volume.

It might also be suggested that the *Acéphale* episode was what introduced Bataille to the autobiographical writing of *Inner Experience* and *Guilty*.

19. Louis Marin, *To Destroy Painting* (Chicago: University of Chicago Press, 1995), pp. 133–134. See also Michel Beaujour's excellent remarks on Malraux's *Lazarus*, in *Poetics of the Literary Self-Portrait*, trans. Yara Miles (New York: New York University Press, 1991); Paul de Man, "Autobiography as De-Facement," in *The Rhetoric of Romanticism* (New York: Columbia University Press, 1984), pp. 67–81; Françoise Meltzer, *Salomé and the Dance of Writing* (Chicago: University of Chicago Press, 1987); idem, "1892: Writing and the Dance," in *A New History of French Literature*, ed. Denis Hollier (Cambridge, Mass.: Harvard University Press, 1989), pp. 813–819.

20. Leiris, *Manhood*, pp. 156, 168.

21. Ibid., p. 50.

22. The expression echoes the title of Picasso's 1941 play *Le désir attrapé par la queue*, which was performed in Leiris's apartment during the spring of 1944. [Translator's note]

23. Maurice Blanchot, *The Work of Fire*, trans. Charlotte Mandell (Stanford: Stanford University Press, 1995), pp. 244–255.

24. Leiris, *Aurora*, trans. Anna Warby (London: Atlas Press, 1990), p. 54.

25. The reproduction of the head of Holofernes appears in *Documents* 1930, no. 6; reprinted in *Documents*, ed. Jean Jamin (Paris: Jean-Michel Place, Collection "Gradhiva," 1992), vol. 2, p. 356. It accompanies an article by Dr. Ralph von Koenigswald, "Têtes et crânes (Crânes d'ancêtres et trophées de guerre chez les peuples primitifs)," which is abundantly illustrated by all sorts of severed heads, some authentic ones and some reproductions, but all (with the exception of the head of Holofernes) three-dimensional and originating in primitive societies. The head of Holofernes originates with a Cranach that is not the diptych reproduced as the frontispiece of *Manhood*. It is a detail cut out from *Judith and Holofernes* in which Holofernes' head, severed a second time, as it were, does not really hang down; Judith (having set aside her chief attribute, the sword) is holding the head in both hands, like a chalice, her taut fingers lost in the victim's curls. The selection of this "detail" would confirm, if confirmation were needed, the seminal value for the autobiographical enterprise, not of the Lucrece-Judith diptych, but of Holofernes' severed head.

26. Leiris, *Manhood*, pp. 465, 466.

27. Leiris, "Le 'caput mortuum' ou la femme de l'alchimiste," in *Zébrage* (Paris: Gallimard, 1992), p. 41. First published in *Documents* 1931, no. 8, p. 26; reprint ed., p. 466.

28. Leiris, *Nights as Day, Days as Night*, trans. Richard Sieburth (Hygiene, Colo.: Eridanos Press, 1987), p. 111.

9. POETRY FROM A TO Z

1. After participating in the surrealist movement and the College of Sociology, Michel Leiris devoted the main part of his literary life to the autobiographical enterprise of *La règle du jeu*, published in four volumes: *Biffures* (1948; translated by Lydia Davis as *Scratches* [New York: Paragon House, 1991]), *Fourbis* (1955); *Fibrilles* (1966), and *Frêle bruit* (1976). The fourth and final volume was initially announced by the author under the title of *Fibules*, as his own *Time Recaptured*. But the moment of Proustian conversion did not occur. Once this forty-year endeavor was completed, Leiris collected the poetic outcome of his surrealist youth under the general title *Mots sans mémoire*.

In his autobiography Leiris refers to his wife (Louise Leiris) by either her nickname, Zette, or the initial Z. The present essay explores how much of the mutation of Leiris's writing—from poetic and surrealist to autobiographical and existentialist—can be traced to the entry of Zette, to whom Leiris dedicated *La règle du jeu*, into his life.

2. Leiris, *Fibrilles* (Paris: Gallimard, 1966), p. 58.

3. Ibid.

4. Leiris, *Manhood*, trans. Richard Howard (New York: Grossman, 1963), p. 11.

5. Leiris, *Haut mal*, followed by *Autres lancers* (Paris: Gallimard, 1969), p. 19.

6. Michel de Montaigne, *The Complete Essays of Montaigne*, trans. Donald M. Frame (Stanford: Stanford University Press, 1958), p. 145.

7. Leiris, *Frêle bruit* (Paris: Gallimard, 1976), p. 348.

8. Leiris published his poetic production from the surrealist period under the title *Mots sans mémoire*.

9. Montaigne, *Complete Essays*, pp. 145, 645.

10. Maurice Blanchot, *The Space of Literature*, trans. Ann Smock (Lincoln: University of Nebraska Press, 1982), p. 27.

11. Leiris, *Fibrilles*, p. 246.

12. Leiris, *Manhood*, p. 105.

13. Leiris, *Scratches*, pp. 188, 189.

14. See "Under the Heading of Holofernes," earlier in this volume.

15. Leiris, *Manhood*, pp. 110, 132, 130.

16. Ibid., pp. 130, 121.

17. This response, excerpted from Goethe's *Faust*, appears in the epigraph to the first chapter of *Manhood*, p. 16.

18. Ibid., p. 127.

19. Ibid., p. 135; Leiris, *Fibrilles*, p. 65.

20. Leiris, *Manhood*, p. 136.

21. Leiris, "Le pays de mes rêves," in *Haut mal*, p. 21.

22. Leiris, *Manhood*, pp. 126, 3, 157, 156.

23. Ibid., p. 134.

24. Leiris, *Nights as Day, Days as Night*, trans. Richard Sieburth (Hygiene, Colo.: Eridanos Press, 1987), pp. 82, 111, 160.

25. A note in *Scratches* explains that the abbreviated form comes from the French word *heureusement*, meaning "happily, fortunately, luckily."

26. Leiris, "The Sacred in Everyday Life," in *The College of Sociology (1937–1939)*, ed. Denis Hollier, trans. Betsy Wing (Minneapolis: University of Minnesota Press, 1988), pp. 24–31 (for the published version), 98–102 (for the lecture itself).

27. In Friedrich Hölderlin and Eduard Mörike, *Selected Poems*, trans. Christopher Middleton (Chicago: University of Chicago Press, 1972), p. 35.

28. Leiris, *Haut mal*, p. 204.

29. Leiris, *Fourbis* (Paris: Gallimard, 1955), pp. 234, 27. (This volume has recently been translated as *Scraps*.)

30. Leiris, *Frêle bruit*, p. 366.

31. A very popular type of French riddle (in French, *charade*) is constructed like an oral rebus. A series of crossword-puzzle-type definitions ("my first is . . . ; my second: . . . ," and so on) leads to words or syllables that, added together, produce the lexical unit ("my whole . . . ") that is the key to the riddle.

32. Leiris, *Frêle bruit*, p. 334.

33. Mallarmé, "The Onyx of Her Pure Nails Offered High," in *Stéphane Mallarmé: Selected Poetry and Prose*, trans. Patricia Terry and Maurice Z. Shroder, ed. Mary Ann Caws (New York: New Directions, 1982), p. 49.

10. THE USE VALUE OF THE IMPOSSIBLE

1. Jean Babelon, "Numismatique," in *L'histoire et ses méthodes*, ed. Charles Samaran (Paris: Gallimard, 1961), p. 329. Jean Babelon, who also worked in the Cabinet des Médailles, was a member of the *Documents* editorial board and collaborated on the journal.

2. Apparently, among the Chartists there was still a general consensus around 1929 that Bataille was headed for a fine career in numismatics. In an article in *Documents*, for example, René Grousset refers respectfully to "Mr. G. Bataille's numismatic studies"; "Un cas de régression vers les arts 'barbares': La statuaire du Kafiristan," *Documents* 1930, no. 2, reprint ed., p. 73.

3. Reminiscences concerning *Documents*, in Georges Bataille, *Oeuvres complètes*, vol. 11, ed. Francis Marmande (Paris: Gallimard, 1988), p. 572.

4. In one of the rare references to the journal in the press, a note in *Les nouvelles littéraires* exploits the same innuendos. "In its fourth issue, *Documents* presents some very curious photographic 'documents.'"

5. Bataille, "L'ordre de chevalerie," (1922), in *Oeuvres complètes*, vol. 1, ed. Denis Hollier (Paris: Gallimard, 1970), p. 100. See also Bataille's review (in *Aréthuse*, 1926) of a work on numismatics: "These documents," he wrote, "whose archaeological interest often equals their artistic interest, bring into relief the success of an earlier era in organizing a magnificent circulation network" (ibid., p. 107).

In the same year *Documents* was founded, 1929, Marc Bloch's and Lucien Febvre's *Annales* also saw the light of day. This journal was not at all focused on art; its founders may have known nothing at all about surrealism. In its pages the editors promoted an epistemology of anthropological documents that was not entirely unrelated to the aesthetics of *Documents*. Any text can and must be transformed into a document: "a poem, a painting, a drama," as Lucien Febvre wrote, are "documents for us"; *Combats pour l'histoire* (Paris: Armand Colin, 1953), p. 15.

6. In the first three issues, the heading reads "Doctrines Archéologie Beaux-Arts Ethnographie"; starting with no. 4, it appears as "Archéologie Beaux-Arts Ethnographie Variétés."

7. The only *Documents* collaborator who defended art as such was the prehistorian Henri Martin. Referring to prehistoric sculptures, Martin concluded that they corresponded to an intention that was not merely "cultural or symbolic." The "imperious desire to satisfy a passion: the passion for Art" also had to be taken into account; "L'art solutréen dans la vallée du Roc (Charente)," *Documents* 1929, no. 6, reprint ed., vol. 2, p. 309.

8. Michel Leiris, "Revue des publications. Jean Brunhes, *Races*, documents commentés par Mariel Jean-Brunhes Delamarre [etc.]," *Documents* 1930, no. 6, reprint ed., vol. 2, p. 375.

9. Carl Einstein, "A propos de l'exposition de la Galerie Pigalle," *Documents* 1930, no. 2, p. 104. One can get a sense of the polemical aspect of references to ethnography in connection with primitive art by reading the review of the same exhibition published in *Formes*. It concludes with the following antiethnographic declaration (I leave it up to the reader to add *sic* as desired): "After an exhibit like the one we have just been discussing, no one will be able to categorize Negro art and Oceanic art, those spontaneous expressions of two little-known civilizations, among the ethnographic curiosities"; A. S., *Formes*, 1930.

On the subject of the Galerie Pigalle exhibit, see the contributions of Philippe Peltier ("From Oceania," pp. 99–123) and Jean-Louis Paudrat ("From Africa," pp. 125–175) in the catalogue of the exhibit, *Primitivism in 20th Century Art*, ed. William Rubin (New York: Museum of Modern Art, 1984), vol. 1, pp. 112, 159.

10. The epigraph is from Roland Barthes, *The Pleasure of the Text*, trans. Richard Miller (New York: Hill and Wang, 1975), p. 23.

11. Several of the regular contributors were ethnographers or at least had leanings in that direction: Marcel Griaule, André Schaeffner, Michel Leiris. Among the occasional contributors, the name of Maurice Leenhardt should be noted. Claude Lévi-Strauss should also be mentioned, as the author of the article signed "Georges Monnet" in the special issue in honor of Picasso (his letter to Jean Jamin, July 1986). In 1930, however, Lévi-Strauss was still a long way from being an ethnographer.

12. In this sense, as Jean Jamin has shown convincingly, even in *Documents* the ethnographers and the surrealists never actually had a common enterprise (or, to borrow James Clifford's all-too-seductive expression, there was never any such thing as "surrealist ethnography"). There were merely "encounters with ethnographers," to quote the title of Métraux's article on Bataille, and the ground for these encounters was a certain resistance to mercantile decontextualization. My

aim here is to localize and delimit those encounters. See Jean Jamin, "L'ethnographie mode d'inemploi. De quelques rapports de l'ethnologie avec le malaise dans la civilisation," in *Le mal et la douleur*, ed. Jacques Hainard et Roland Kaehr (Neuchâtel: Musée d'Ethnographie, 1986), pp. 45–79.

13. Karl Marx, *Capital: A Critique of Political Economy*, trans. Ben Fowkes (New York: Vintage Books, 1977), p. 126.

14. Marcel Griaule, "Poterie," *Documents* 1930, no. 4, reprint ed., vol. 2, p. 236. The essential aspect of an object is not its form but its use. And it is rarely possible to deduce the latter from the former: the way an object is used is only exceptionally a consequence of its form. This critique of formalist aestheticism shows up again in Paul Rivet: "Ethnography must not be limited to the strictly morphological study of man-made objects. It must also, and I am even prepared to say that it must especially, study technologies, which last longer than forms and are less easily borrowed"; "L'étude des civilisations matérielles; ethnographie, archéologie, préhistoire," *Documents* 1929, no. 3, reprint ed., vol. 1, p. 132. Moreover, the critique of formalism is not voiced by ethnologists alone. We find it in Carl Einstein as well, according to whom "moralists of pure form preach in favor of the square, filled with drunkenness"; "Tableaux récents de Georges Braque," ibid., no. 6, reprint ed., vol. 1, p. 290.

15. "Next to the exhibit there must be a photograph of the player, of the silent object, its position in the hands of he who suddenly brings it to life, making it multiply"; André Schaeffner, "Musical Instruments in an Ethnographic Museum," trans. Dominic Faccini, *October* 60 (Spring 1992): 37. Georges Duthuit took a similar position in his 1927 article on Coptic fabric in *Cahiers d'art* ("Les tissus coptes"), where he argued against the museographic reification of ceremonial objects; reprinted in Duthuit, *Représentation et présence*, ed. Yves Bonnefoy (Paris: Flammarion, 1974), pp. 161–169.

16. Schaeffner, "Musical Instruments," p. 37. In order to illustrate the extended sense of the word "document" (its extension beyond the written document), *Le trésor de la langue française* quotes a passage from Marcel Griaule's *Méthode de l'ethnographie* (Paris: Presses Universitaires de France, 1957): "In the hands of researchers working in good faith, photography and cinematography provide means for establishing the most independent and impartial documents of the system of ethnological investigation."

17. This reflection on what a museum of use value might look like has something in common with the line of thinking Heidegger in 1935 in connection with Van Gogh's paintings of shoes. It is "the equipmentality of equipment" that "first genuinely arrives at its appearance through the work and only in the work"; "The Origin of the Work of Art," trans. Albert Hofstadter, in Martin Heidegger, *Poetry, Language, Thought* (New York: Harper & Row, 1975), p. 36.

18. Leiris, "Du Musée d'Ethnographie au Musée de l'Homme," *La nouvelle revue française* 299 (August 1938): 344.

19. The epigraph is quoted in Walter Benjamin, "The Work of Art in the Age of Mechanical Reproduction," in *Illuminations*, trans. Harry Zohn (New York: Schocken Books, 1969), p. 249, n. 15.

20. Marcel Proust, *Within a Budding Grove*, in *Remembrance of Things Past*, trans.

C. K. Scott Moncrieff and Terence Kilmartin (New York: Random House, 1981), vol. 1, p. 709.

21. On the origins of the Museum of French Monuments and the project of reintegrating (and even resuscitating) detached fragments within something like a milieu, at the point of transition from a metonymic to a synecdochic presentation of the objects exhibited, see Stephen Bann's chapter on du Sommerard and Alexandre Lenoir, in *The Clothing of Clio: A Study of the Representation of History in Nineteenth-Century Britain and France* (Cambridge: Cambridge University Press, 1984), pp. 85, 91. Bann's analyses amply justify the proximity of these two museums: for the Romantic museum (the Museum of French Monuments), alterity is national and temporal; for the modern museum (the Museum of Ethnography), alterity is exotic and spatial.

22. Benjamin, "The Work of Art," pp. 224, 223.

23. Ibid., p. 224.

24. Leiris, "Civilisation," *Documents* 1929, no. 4, reprint ed., vol. 1, pp. 221–222.

25. Bataille, "L'esprit moderne et le jeu des transpositions," *Documents* 1930, no. 7, reprint ed., vol. 2, p. 490. In a manuscript variant of this article, Bataille opposes "obsession" and "haunting thought" to the "aestheticism of amateurs"; *Oeuvres complètes*, vol. 1, p. 656.

26. This is the period when Bataille is working on "The Use Value of D. A. F. de Sade," in which he denounces (to borrow Jamin's expression) the "instructions for nonuse" by means of which men of letters have paralyzed Sade's work; Sade's use value must not be limited to the bibliophilic enjoyment of amateurs and connaisseurs; *Visions of Excess: Selected Writings, 1927–1939*, trans. and ed. Allan Stoekl (Minneapolis: University of Minnesota Press, 1985), pp. 92–93. See also Bataille, *Blue of Noon*, trans. Harry Mathews (London: Marion Boyars, 1986), p. 69.

27. On the place Heidegger's analyses leave to fetishism, see Jacques Derrida, "Restitutions," in *The Truth in Painting*, trans. Geoff Bennington and Ian McLeod (Chicago: University of Chicago Press, 1978), pp. 291 ff.

28. Bataille, "Van Gogh as Prometheus" (1937), trans. Annette Michelson, *October* 36 (Spring 1986): 60.

29. Georges Henri Rivière, "Le Musée d'ethnographie du Trocadéro," *Documents* 1929, no. 1, reprint ed., vol. 1, p. 58.

30. Rivet, "L'étude des civilisations matérielles," p. 132.

31. Rivière, "Le Musée d'ethnographie du Trocadéro," p. 58. Ethnography and fine arts grow out of distinct institutions. In Rivière's panorama of museographic competencies, we should note their respective attributions: "fine arts and archaeology" belong to the Louvre, "Ethnography" belongs to Trocadéro, and so on. A museum of ethnography, Rivière points out, ought to embrace "primitive and archaic" civilizations "as a whole." For these are societies that constitute wholes; they antedate the separation of functions characteristic of "more evolved societies": this "totalitarianism" (Rivière's word) on the part of primitive societies means that a single institution has to serve simultaneously as "a Museum of Fine Arts, a Museum of Folklore, and a Conservatory of Arts and Crafts."

The surrealists were probably not responsible for the clamor in favor of admitting primitive art into the Louvre. In 1930, after the exhibit at the Galerie Pigalle, Paul

Guillaume expressed his dismay at the cult of the exotic and the savage into which surrealism had allowed the interest in primitive art to degenerate, and he declared that Negro art was ripe for the Louvre.

32. Robert Desnos expresses similar resistance to the site of a different aestheticization, the one from which popular imagery benefits (or suffers): "Popular manifestations flounder the most in these sudden vogues"; "Imagerie moderne," *Documents* 1929, no. 7, reprint ed., vol. 1, p. 377. Bataille strikes the same note: "The truly wretched aesthete, at a loss for objects of admiration, has invented the contemptible 'beauty' of the factory"; "Smokestack" (1929), trans. Annette Michelson, *October* 36 (Spring 1986): 15.

33. Rivet, "L'étude des civilisations matérielles," p. 133.

34. Marcel Griaule, "Un coup de fusil," *Documents* 1930, no. 1, reprint ed., vol. 2, p. 46.

35. Schaeffner, "Musical Instruments," p. 33.

36. James Clifford, "On Ethnographic Surrealism," in *The Predicament of Culture* (Cambridge, Mass.: Harvard University Press, 1988), p. 133. The word "sacrilege" comes from Leiris's article: "Spittle represents the height of sacrilege"; Leiris, "Spittle," in "Critical Dictionary," trans. Dominic Faccini, *October* 30 (Spring 1992): 30.

37. Leiris, "De Bataille l'impossible à l'impossible *Documents*," in *Brisées* (Paris: Mercure de France, 1965), p. 261.

38. Leiris, "Métaphore," *Documents* 1929, no. 3, reprint ed., vol. 1, p. 170.

39. Clifford, "On Ethnographic Surrealism," p. 130.

40. Bataille, "Formless," in Stoekl, *Visions of Excess*, p. 31. On the formless and spitballs in Bataille, see Denis Hollier, *Against Architecture*, trans. Betsy Wing (Cambridge, Mass.: MIT Press, 1989), pp. 98 ff.

41. "*Care of the mouth*. Coughing and spitting technique. Here is a personal observation. A little girl did not know how to spit, and this made every cold she had much worse. I made inquiries. In her father's village, and in her father's family in particular, in Berry, people do not know how to spit. I taught her to do it. I gave her four *sous* per spit. As she was saving up for a bicycle, she learnt to spit. She is the first person in her family who knows how to spit"; Marcel Mauss, "Body Techniques," in *Sociology and Psychology: Essays*, trans. Ben Brewster (London: Routledge & Kegan Paul, 1979), p. 118. This article was written several years after the ones by Griaule and Leiris; it is legitimate to suppose that Mauss, who had taught both Griaule and Leiris and who had contributed to *Documents* himself from time to time, had read their texts.

Clifford does not mention Mauss's reference to spitting. However, he quotes the rather laconic heading that follows: "*Hygiene of natural body functions.* Here I could list numberless facts"; ibid., quoted in Clifford, "On Ethnographic Surrealism," p. 124. Mauss says that he could, but he does not. Out of a sense of decency? Does he not feel, as Clifford puts it, "licensed to shock"?

Lévi-Strauss begins his groundbreaking introduction to Mauss's work with the problems raised by museographic documentation of body techniques (*Introduction to the Work of Marcel Mauss*, trans. Felicity Baker [London: Routledge & Kegan Paul, 1987], pp. 6–9): "We are collectors of the products of human industry," he notes, "but as for the very numerous and varied possibilities of that instrument which is the human body, we are as ignorant as ever" (p. 6). He proposes the establishment of "International Archives of Body Techniques," and he proceeds to provide a short list of the type of thing he has in mind. The first one he mentions involves "the placing of the male's hand in urinating," a gesture that belongs to the "hygiene in the needs of nature" of which Mauss could have listed innumerable examples. The particular example Lévi-Strauss offers is not neutral. It attests once again to the proximity between taboos and use value. It could even be said to represent, on the side of anthropology, the exact negative of what Marcel Duchamp's *Fountain* represents on the side of the avant-garde: once museums of fine art and anthropological museums have succeeded in fusing their celebrations of use value, the unexhibitable position of a male's hand when urinating will finally be able to confront the ready-made urinal. While waiting for this to come about, the two types of museums continue, like china dogs, as far apart as Achilles and his tortoise, to pursue their work of undermining exhibition values.

See also Lévi-Strauss's reflections on the status of anthropological museums in the final chapter of *Structural Anthropology:* their "purpose should be, not merely to collect objects"; today, "men tend to replace objects"; trans. Claire Jacobson and Brooke Grundfest Schoepf (New York: Basic Books, 1963), pp. 376, 377.

42. Leiris, "L'homme et son intérieur," *Documents* 1930, no. 5, reprint ed., vol. 2, p. 261.

43. Bataille, "The Big Toe," in Stoekl, *Visions of Excess,* p. 21.

44. Bataille, "The Deviations of Nature," ibid., p. 55.

45. Bataille, "Figure humaine," *Documents* 1929, no. 4, reprint ed., vol. 1, p. 196.

46. Hans Reichenbach, "Crise de la causalité," *Documents* 1929, no. 2, reprint ed., vol. 1, pp. 105–108.

47. Carl Einstein, "Pablo Picasso. Quelques tableaux de 1928," *Documents* 1929, no. 1, reprint ed., vol. 1, p. 35. Or, with reference to Masson's paintings: "We are tired of biological identity"; Einstein, "André Masson, étude ethnologique," ibid., no. 2, reprint ed., vol. 1, p. 102.

48. Bataille, "X marks the spot," *Documents* 1930, no. 7, reprint ed., vol. 2, p. 437.

49. See "Mimesis and Castration 1937," earlier in this volume.

50. Leiris, *Manhood,* pp. 156, 157.

51. Bataille manifests the same insistence later on, in *The Trial of Gilles de Rais:* "Such scenes are not the work of an author. *They happened*"; trans. Richard Robinson (Los Angeles: Amok, 1991), p. 19.

52. It contains numerous realist professions of faith, such as this one by Leiris: "So as I see it it is completely wrongheaded to forget the fundamentally *realistic* character of Picasso's work"; "Toiles récentes de Picasso," *Documents* 1930, no. 2, reprint ed., vol. 2, p. 62. See also Georges Ribemont-Dessaignes: "I am a realist . . . There are people who talk about What-exists and What-does-not-exist, and who believe only in the latter while denying it any existence . . . These people are merely surrealists." "A painter is always a realist. I don't know a single one who isn't. Too bad for the surrealists: let them give up all truck with painting"; "Giorgio de Chirico," ibid., no. 6, reprint ed., vol. 2, pp. 337, 338. And Desnos, in a review

of *La femme 100 têtes:* "For the poet, there are no hallucinations. There is reality"; "La femme 100 têtes, par Max Ernst," ibid., p. 238.

53. André Breton, *Manifesto of Surrealism* (1924), in *Manifestoes of Surrealism*, trans. Richard Seaver and Helen R. Lane (Ann Arbor: University of Michigan Pess, 1969), p. 5.

54. Roland Barthes, "Les sorties du texte," in *Bataille* (Paris: UGE, 1973), p. 62.

55. And yet the ersatz objects constituted, in Bataille's eyes, by works of art are at the same time insurmountable catachreses: "Nothing truly new can replace them yet," he writes with reference to these irreplaceable replacements; "L'esprit moderne et le jeu des transpositions," *Documents* 1930, no. 8, reprint ed., vol. 2, p. 489.

56. Leiris, "Alberto Giacometti," ibid., 1929, no. 4, reprint ed., vol. 1, p. 209.

57. Emmanuel Berl, *Mort de la morale bourgeoise* (1929; reprint, Paris: Jean-Jacques Pauvert, 1965), p. 174. With the crisis of surrealism as background (and doubtless Suzanne Muzard's comings and goings between Berl and Breton as well), a brief dialogue took place between Berl and Bataille. In "Conformismes freudiens," Berl quotes Bataille in the course of a discussion of what he calls contemporary "fetishism": "The phallus replaces the figleaf, then. Neither more nor less. And to speak the language of Georges Bataille, idealism—a gangrenous excrescence on the fetish—makes of it a *must-be* [*devoir-être*]"; *Formes* 5 (April 1930): 3.

58. Bataille, "Materialism," in Stoekl, *Visions of Excess*, p. 15. Bataille returned to this critique of "ontological materialism" in "Base Materialism and Gnosticism," ibid., p. 45. For the Marxist implications of Bataille's low materialism, see "Bataille's Tomb," earlier in this volume.

59. Berl writes: "Matter is what does not last . . . Materialism therefore rejects all values of permanence, all that clings to duration"; *Mort de la morale bourgeoise*, p. 174.

60. Henry-Charles Puech, "Les 'Prisons' de Jean-Baptiste Piranèse," *Documents* 1930, no. 4, reprint ed., vol. 2, p. 199. Leiris manifests the same nihilism when he enters the fantasy of a wholesale debacle whose "ultimate result, after it had destroyed what was hostile and foreign to itself and then had destroyed itself, would be only that it had wiped out *absolutely everything*"; "Débâcle," *Documents* 1929, no. 7, reprint ed., vol. 1, p. 382.

61. See Denis Hollier, "Bloody Sundays," in *Against Architecture*, pp. ix–xxiii.

11. WHEN EXISTENTIALISM WAS NOT YET A HUMANISM

1. The epigraph is from Laurent Jenny, *La Terreur et les signes* (Paris: Gallimard, 1985), p. 10.

2. Jean Paulhan, *Les fleurs de Tarbes ou la Terreur dans les lettres* (1941), ed. Jean-Claude Zylberstein (Paris: Gallimard, 1973), p. 36.

3. André Breton, *Manifesto of Surrealism* (1924), in *Manifestoes of Surrealism*, trans. Richard Seaver and Helen R. Lane (Ann Arbor: University of Michigan Press, 1969), p. 33.

4. Breton, "Introduction to the Discourse on the Paucity of Reality," trans. Richard Sieburth and Jennifer Gordon, *October* 69 (Summer 1994): 141.

5. Robespierre quoted in Lucien Jaume, *Le discours jacobin et la démocratie* (Paris: Fayard, 1989), p. 197.

6. André Malraux, *Oeuvres complètes*, vol. 1, ed. Pierre Brunet (Paris: Gallimard, 1989), p. xlvii.

7. Paul de Man, *Blindness and Insight* (Minneapolis: University of Minnesota Press, 1983), p. 181. Cf. the French theoretician of twelve-tone composition René Leibowitz's denunciation of "musical psychologism," quoted in Luc Ferry, *Homo Aestheticus: The Invention of Taste in the Democratic Age*, trans. Robert de Loaiza (Chicago: University of Chicago Press, 1993), p. 231.

8. Jean-Paul Sartre, "Intentionality: A Fundamental Idea of Husserl's Phenomenology," *Journal of the British Society for Phenomenology* 1, no. 2 (May 1970): 4–5.

9. Sartre, *The Transcendence of the Ego: An Existentialist Theory of Consciousness*, trans. Forrest Williams and Robert Kirkpatrick (New York: Noonday Press, 1957), pp. 90, 93.

10. Georges Politzer, "Où va la psychologie concrète?" editorial, *Revue de psychologie concrète* (July 1929), in Politzer, *Ecrits*, vol. 2 (Paris: Editions Sociales, 1969), p. 169. See also idem, *Critique of the Foundations of Psychology: The Psychology of Psychoanalysis*, trans. Maurice Apprey (Pittsburgh: Duquesne University Press, 1994). On Politzer, see Elizabeth Roudinesco: "His project of a concrete psychology could not come to fruition since its sole object was to reveal the impasses of psychology itself"; *Jacques Lacan & Co.: A History of Psychoanalysis in France*, trans. Jeffrey Mehlman (Chicago: University of Chicago Press, 1990), p. 65. See also Aragon's review of Jean Renoir's Popular Front film *La Marseillaise.* Aragon congratulates Renoir for the way he highlighted, in his depiction of the French royal family, "the pettiness of family life caught up in the tragic moments of the dawning new world, moments that make the most celebrated psychological novels seem trivial"; *Ce Soir*, February 9, 1938.

11. André Malraux, "L'oeuvre d'art n'est pas une pierre," in *André Malraux*, special issue of *L'Herne*, ed. Michel Cazenave, 1982, p. 286.

12. Malraux, "L'attitude de l'artiste," ibid., p. 292.

13. Antonin Artaud, "Metaphysics and the Mise en Scène," in *The Theater and Its Double*, trans. Mary Caroline Richards (New York: Grove Press, 1958), p. 41.

14. Artaud, "Oriental and Occidental Theatre," ibid., p. 71; cf. Artaud's letter to Jean Paulhan, May 23, 1933, quoted in *Le théâtre et son double* (Paris: Gallimard, 1938), p. 143.

15. Artaud, "On the Balinese Theatre," in *The Theater and Its Double*, p. 58.

16. Garine quotes his father: "He also used to say that you had to be attached to your true self . . . Attached! The little ceremony of binding a living person to a corpse was called . . . 'republican marriage,' wasn't it?"; Malraux, *The Conquerors*, trans. Stephen Becker (New York: Holt, Rinehart and Winston, 1975), p. 150.

17. To the extent that the novel has been linked, almost by definition, to a psychology conceived as the art of reproducing the twists and turns that lead a character from intention to action, or even to a rejection of action, the motif of the gratuitous act, which has obsessed novelists ever since *Les caves du Vatican* (*Lafcadio's Adventures*, trans. Dorothy Bussy [New York: Vintage Books, 1953]), is

a particularly clear symptom of this antipsychological bias: Lafcadio's unmotivated crime and the gunshot Boris fires into his own head are, first and foremost, breaks in continuity with psychological causality.

18. Malraux, "L'oeuvre d'art n'est pas une pierre," p. 288.

19. Malraux, "*L'imposture*, par Georges Bernanos," *La nouvelle revue française* 30 (March 1, 1928): 406.

20. Malraux, "*Contes, historiettes et fabliaux* (Kra); *Dialogue d'un prêtre et d'un moribund* (Standhal et Cie) par le marquis de Sade, introduction de Maurice Heine," *La nouvelle revue française* 30 (June 1, 1928): 854.

21. Malraux, preface to William Faulkner, *Sanctuaire* (Paris: Gallimard, 1933), pp. 9, 8, 11.

22. The same opposition is found in Kierkegaard's meditation on Antigone that Pierre Klossowki presented at the College of Sociology on May 19, 1939: "The action of individuals is not meant to represent the characters but rather . . . the characters are there for the action. This, as we shall easily see, is where modern tragedy moves away from ancient. It is characteristic of the latter that action does not simply proceed from the characters (it is not subjectively reflexive enough for that), although it contains relatively more suffering"; *The College of Sociology (1937–1939)*, ed. Denis Hollier, trans. Betsy Wing (Minneapolis: University of Minnesota Press, 1988), p. 170. For a recent formulation of the same model, see Franco Moretti, "The Comfort of Civilization," trans. Albert Sbragia, *Representations* 12 (Fall 1985): 130: "Unlike what occurs in the short story or in the tragedy, the novelistic episode does not refer back to an objective necessity but to a subjective possibility."

23. Malraux, *Days of Hope*, trans. Stuart Gilbert and Alistair Macdonald (London: Hamish Hamilton, 1968), p. 215; Sartre, "John Dos Passos and '1919,'" in *Literary and Philosophical Essays*, trans. Annette Michelson (London: Rider and Company, 1955), pp. 92, 91.

24. Artaud, "On the Balinese Theatre," p. 58.

25. Sartre, "On *The Sound and the Fury:* Time in the Work of Faulkner," in *Literary and Philosophical Essays*, p. 85.

26. Malraux, "Sur l'héritage culturel," *André Malraux*, p. 294.

27. Albrecht Betz, *Exil et engagement. Les intellectuels allemands et la France (1930–1940)*, trans. Pierre Rusch (Paris: Gallimard, 1991).

28. Philippe Sollers, *Writing and the Experience of Limits*, trans. David Hayman (New York: Columbia University Press, 1983).

29. Bernard Groethuysen, "*Les Conquérants*, par André Malraux," *La nouvelle revue française* 32 (April 1, 1929): 559.

30. Malraux, *Man's Fate*, trans. Haakon M. Chevalier (New York: Modern Library, 1961), pp. 9, 12.

31. Ibid., p. 109. On the symbolic value of the rope that unites mountain climbers, see Antoine de Saint-Exupéry, *Terre des hommes*, in *Oeuvres* (Paris: Gallimard/Pléiade, 1951), p. 252: "The only true comrades are the ones linked together by a single rope." Cf. the English rendering in *Wind, Sand, and Stars*, trans. Lewis Galantière (San Diego: Harcourt Brace Jovanovich, 1967), p. 288: "There is no comradeship except through union in the same high effort."

32. Malraux, *Man's Fate*, p. 10.

33. See Georges Bataille, "La mutilation sacrificielle et l'oreille coupée de Vincent Van Gogh," *Documents* 1930, no. 8, reprint ed., vol. 2, pp. 451–460.

34. Sartre, *The Wall and Other Stories*, trans. Lloyd Alexander (New York: New Directions, 1975), p. 12. Tom, an American with whom Pablo is sharing his cell, says: "I see my corpse: that's not hard, but *I'm* the one who sees it, with *my* eyes" (p. 8). Cf. the same type of lexical oddity in Roger Caillois, *The Necessity of the Mind*, trans. Michael Syrotinsky (Venice, Calif.: Lapis Press, 1990), p. 104: "It is as if I were dead and I were watching over myself." See also the conclusion of "Under the Heading of Holofernes," earlier in this volume.

35. Sartre, *The Transcendence of the Ego*, pp. 105–106.

36. Ibid., pp. 105, 93.

37. In *Speech and Phenomena*, trans. David B. Allison (Evanston: Northwestern University Press, 1973), Derrida uncovers at the heart of Husserlian phenomenology this sort of republican marriage to which the articulation of the psychological and the transcendental leads—like two parallel lines, "one of which is in the world and the other outside the world without being in another world" (p. 14).

38. Sartre, *The Transcendence of the Ego*, p. 36.

39. Paulhan, *Les fleurs de Tarbes*, p. 47.

40. Sartre, *The Transcendence of the Ego*, pp. 53–54.

41. For a similar equivalence between a third person and a nonfirst person, see "Mimetism and Castration 1937," earlier in this volume.

42. Sartre, *The Transcendence of the Ego*, pp. 48–49.

43. See, for example, Maurice Blanchot, *The Work of Fire*, trans. Charlotte Mandell (Stanford: Stanford University Press, 1995), pp. 21, 174, 245 (on Leiris); idem, *The Space of Literature*, trans. Ann Smock (Lincoln: University of Nebraska Press, 1982), p. 27.

44. Emmanuel Levinas, *De l'existence à l'existant* (Paris: Fontaine, 1947), p. 99.

45. Ibid., p. 100.

46. Blanchot, "Literature and the Right to Death," in *The Work of Fire*, pp. 300–344.

47. Sartre, *Nausea*, trans. Lloyd Alexander (New York: New Directions, 1964), pp. 170, 171.

48. Ibid., p. 170.

49. Added by Henry Corbin (Corbin-Petithenry) to his translation of Martin Heidegger, "Qu'est-ce que la métaphysique?" published with an introduction by Alexandre Koyré, *Bifur* 8 (June 1931): 17.

12. A FAREWELL TO ART

1. For Sartre's use of the motif, see "Deeds without Words," earlier in this volume.

2. André Gide, *Lafcadio's Adventures*, trans. Dorothy Bussy (New York: Vintage Books, 1953), pp. 72, 186–188.

3. Paul Nizan, *The Watchdogs: Philosophers and the Established Order*, trans. Paul

Fittingoff (New York: Monthly Review Press, 1971), p. 134. In *Man's Fate*, a statement of the same type is attributed to old Gisors: "Marxism is not a doctrine, it is a *will* . . . You must be Marxists not in order to be right, but in order to conquer without betraying yourselves"; trans. Haakon M. Chevalier (New York: Modern Library, 1961), p. 71.

4. Emmanuel Berl, *Mort de la morale bourgeoise* (1929; reprint, Paris: Jean-Jacques Pauvert, 1965), p. 165.

5. Jules Monnerot, "Inquiry on Spiritual Directors," in *The College of Sociology (1937–1939)*, ed. Denis Hollier, trans. Betsy Wing (Minneapolis: University of Minnesota Press, 1988), p. 68.

6. Roger Caillois, "Pour une orthodoxie militante. Les tâches immédiates de la pensée moderne," *Inquisitions* 1 (June 1936), reprinted as the conclusion of *Le mythe et l'homme* (Paris: Gallimard, 1938).

7. Georges Bataille, "Toward Real Revolution," trans. Annette Michelson, *October* 36 (Spring 1986): 34, 37, 31. Cf. "On Equivocation between Literature and Politics," earlier in this volume.

8. Bataille, "Le cheval académique" (1929), in *Oeuvres complètes*, vol. 1 (Paris: Gallimard, 1971), p. 161. The advocacy of formlessness in *Documents* goes hand in hand with attacks on authority. At the time the Contre-Attaque group was formed, Bataille had in mind less a restoration of form than a conversion of the aesthetics of formlessness into a politics of force, that is, precisely a politics that would not respect forms. The (aesthetically) repulsive pole of formlessness is paired with the (politically) attractive pole of force.

On this return in full force of formlessness, this coming-to-power of what lacks form, cf. André Malraux, *Man's Fate*, trans. Haakon M. Chevalier (New York: Modern Library, 1961), p. 159: "From this human form which Kyo could not even see emanated a blind force which dominated it—the formless matter of which fatality is made."

9. Berl says something similar in *Mort de la pensée bourgeoise* (Paris: Grasset, 1929), p. 189: "The problem, for Malraux, is not one of knowing how an intellectual can adhere to a program, but how an intellectual can become a revolutionary leader."

10. Malraux, *Days of Hope*, trans. Stuart Gilbert and Alistair Macdonald (London: Hamish Hamilton, 1968), p. 100.

11. Ibid., p. 208.

12. Cf. ibid., p. 347: "Music, for instance . . . All that's over, as far as I'm concerned."

13. Ibid., p. 351. For more on that episode, see "Desperanto," later in this volume.

14. Ibid., p. 348. Cf. what Alvear tells Scali: "A man devotes to any line of action only a limited part of himself; and the more that line of action sets up to be 'totalitarian,' the smaller is the part of him involved" (p. 277). This is the doctrine of engagement developed by Sartre in the conclusion of *The Transcendence of the Ego:* the ego is engaged—and engaged without reservation—in the world only to provide the opportunity for a transcendental consciousness to disengage itself—

an absolute reserve—from the burden of its ego. Cf. "Deeds without Words" and "When Existentialism Was Not Yet a Humanism," earlier in this volume.

15. Cited in Bataille, "Power," in Hollier, *College*, pp. 125–126.

16. Malraux, *Days of Hope*, pp. 277, 317.

17. Jean-Pierre Maxence, *Histoire de dix ans (1927–1937)* (Paris: Gallimard, 1939), p. 34.

18. Malraux, *Days of Hope*, p. 337.

19. Elie Halévy, *The Era of Tyrannies*, trans. R. K. Webb (New York: New York University Press, 1986), pp. 266–267.

20. Ibid., p. 282.

21. Ibid., p. 277.

22. Julien Benda, *La grande épreuve des démocraties* (New York: Editions de la Maison Française, 1942).

23. As he does throughout the book, Benda follows Tocqueville here; *Democracy in America*, trans. Henry Reeve, rev. ed. Francis Bowen and Phillips Bradley (New York: Alfred A. Knopf, 1966), vol. 2, part 2, chaps. 23–26.

24. Benda, *La grande épreuve des démocraties*, p. 191; Benda refers to Bataille and Caillois as doctors "hostile to democracy."

25. Caillois, "The Structure and Function of the Army," in Hollier, *College*, pp. 140, 141.

26. Malraux, *The Nation* 144, no. 12 (March 20, 1937): 316.

27. Marinetti quoted in Walter Benjamin, "The Work of Art in the Age of Mechanical Reproductions," in *Illuminations*, trans. Harry Zohn (New York: Schocken Books, 1969), p. 241.

28. Regarding the place assigned to the artist by surrealism, Benjamin wrote that "the interruption of his 'artistic career' has become an essential dimension of his new function"; "Surrealism," in *Reflections: Essays, Aphorisms, Autobiographical Writings*, trans. Edmund Jephcott (New York: Harcourt Brace Jovanovich, 1978), p. 191. Cf. André Breton: "For my part, I am more grateful to Majakowsky for having put the immense talent with which Trotsky credits him at the service of the accomplished Russian revolution than for having, solely for his own benefit, compelled admiration through the striking images of *Le nuage en culotte* [Cloud in Short Pants]"; *Point du jour* (Paris: Gallimard, 1970), p. 81.

13. DESPERANTO

1. The epigraph to this chapter is from René Lefèvre, *Le film de ma vie* (Paris: Gallimard, 1937), p. 215.

2. *The Correspondence of Walter Benjamin*, ed. Gershow Scholem and Theodor W. Adorno, trans. Manfred R. Jacobson and Evelyn M. Jacobson (Chicago: University of Chicago Press, 1994), p. 542.

3. Ibid.

4. See Benjamin, "The Storyteller: Reflections on the Works of Nikolai Leskov," in *Illuminations*, trans. Harry Zohn (New York: Schocken Books, 1969), pp. 83–109.

5. Ibid., p. 493.

6. Leo Bersani, *The Culture of Redemption* (Cambridge, Mass.: Harvard University Press, 1990).

7. Benjamin, "André Gide et ses nouveaux ennemis," in *Oeuvres*, vol. 2: *Poésie et révolution*, ed. and trans. Maurice de Gandillac (Paris: Denoël, 1971).

8. André Gide, *The Fruits of the Earth: Les Nourritures Terrestres and Les Nouvelles Nourritures*, trans. Dorothy Bussy (New York: Alfred A. Knopf, 1949).

9. Gide, *Return from the U.S.S.R.* (1936), trans. Dorothy Bussy (New York: Alfred A. Knopf, 1937).

10. Albrecht Betz, *Exil et engagement. Les intellectuels allemands et la France (1930–1940)*, trans. Pierre Rusch (Paris: Gallimard, 1991), p. 158.

11. François Furet, *Le passé d'une illusion. Essai sur l'idée communiste au XXe siècle* (Paris: Robert Laffont/Calmann-Lévy, 1995), p. 126. With Lenin, Furet says in another passage, "it is at once the science of history and the party" that come to power (p. 123). And also: "What establishes this party's legitimacy is not election by the people, but knowledge of the laws of history . . . The idea of a science of history simultaneously establishes the irreversible character of the October revolution and the necessity of a political oligarchy that will stand guard over that revolution" (ibid.). "With Lenin, as with every Marxist, will receives unhoped-for support from science . . . The party is at once an oligarchy of scientists and of organizers, a meeting of men who change the world through their will even as they obey the laws of history" (p. 174).

12. Letter to Fritz Lieb, July 9, 1937, in *The Correspondence of Walter Benjamin*, ed. Gershom Scholem and Theodor W. Adorno, trans. Manfred R. Jacobson and Evelyn M. Jacobson (Chicago: University of Chicago Press, 1994), p. 542.

13. In an unpublished letter to Michel and Zette Leiris written in September 1938, during the Munich crisis, Bataille begins by speaking of Colette Peignot's illness, then goes on: "I don't know what else to say: what might be said on another subject would not be very cheerful either. I want to hope that you are not reading the newspapers (that exercise has never been more useless): the only serious and well-informed people I have seen say that all the arguments, all the interpretations are absurd, that we can know absolutely nothing as to what may happen. I hope you can enjoy this unpleasant month of September without any worries."

14. Georges Bataille, "Chronique Nietzschéenne," in *Oeuvres complètes*, vol. 1 (Paris: Gallimard, 1971), pp. 485, 488. *Acéphale* was illustrated by André Masson, the set designer for *Numancia*. As a frontispiece for his article, Bataille reproduced Masson's drawing of the *Taureau de Numance* (which was reused after the war as the logo for the Renaud-Barrault company; see the reprint collection of *Acéphale*).

Numancia was performed at the Théâtre Antoine from April 22 to May 6, 1937 (the bombing of Guernica by German warplanes occurred on April 26). In 1965, when Barrault restaged it at the Théâtre de l'Odéon, a special issue of the *Cahiers de la Compagnie Madeleine Renaud–Jean-Louis Barrault* was devoted to the 1937 production. See also Barrault's memoirs, *Memories for Tomorrow*, trans. Jonathan Griffin (New York: Dutton, 1974), p. 89.

15. See "Letter from Marcel Mauss to Elie Halévy," in *The College of Sociology*

(1937–1939), ed. Denis Hollier, trans. Betsy Wing (Minneapolis: University of Minnesota Press, 1988), pp. 347–350.

16. Bataille, "Chronique Nietzschéenne," p. 488. He continues: "Among the various convulsive oppositions of history, the one that is currently tearing apart the entire set of civilized countries, the opposition between fascism and antifascism, appears as the most corrupt."

17. Partido Obrero de Unificación Marxista (Marxist Unification Workers' Party), a dissident Communist party on the extreme left.

18. Bataille, "Chronique Nietzschéenne," p. 488.

19. André Malraux, *Days of Hope*, trans. Stuart Gilbert and Alistair Macdonald (London: Hamish Hamilton, 1968), pp. 332–333, 345, 347. Cf. "When Existentialism Was Not Yet a Humanism," earlier in this volume.

20. Cf. Benjamin, writing to Karl Thieme just after the *Anschluss:* "In the case of Austria, no less than in the case of Spain, the horrible thing seems to me that martyrdom is suffered not in the name of the individual's own cause, but rather in the name of a suggested compromise: . . . revolutionary thought in Spain [is] being compromised by the Machiavellianism of the Russian leadership and the indigenous leadership's worship of Mammon"; *Correspondence of Walter Benjamin*, p. 553.

21. Jean-Paul Sartre, "L'homme ligoté. A propos du journal de Jules Renard" (1945), in *Situations I* (Paris: Gallimard, 1947), p. 294. "La république du silence" is the title Sartre gave to the article in which, in 1944, at the time of the Liberation, he evoked occupied France (this is the first text in the collection titled *Situations II*).

22. René Girard, *Deceit, Desire, and the Novel: Self and Other in Literary Structure*, trans. Yvonne Freccero (Baltimore: Johns Hopkins Press, 1965), pp. 233, 296.

23. Ernest Hemingway, *For Whom the Bell Tolls* (New York: Charles Scribner's Sons, 1940), p. 339.

24. Cf. "Must Literature Be Possible?" earlier in this volume.

25. Paul de Man, "Impersonality in Blanchot," in *Blindness and Insight* (Minneapolis: University of Minnesota Press, 1983), p. 66. De Man's words are even stronger in French: "l'oeuvre n'est que la répétition de son impossibilité d'exister" (the work is nothing but the repetition of the impossibility of its own existence); "La circularité de l'interprétation critique dans l'oeuvre de Maurice Blanchot," *Critique* 229 (June 1966): 550. Blanchot himself writes about a work that, without the circumstantiality of its production, would be "nothing more than the impossibility of writing it"; "Literature and the Right to Death," in *The Gaze of Orpheus*, trans. Lydia Davis (New York: Station Hill, 1981), p. 25.

For Caillois's theory of the novel, see "Must Literature Be Possible?" earlier in this volume, pages 10–14. For the political side of this model, see Raymond Aron: "It is always astonishing that a thinker should appear indulgent to a society which should not tolerate him"; *The Opium of the Intellectuals*, trans. Terence Kilmartin (New York: W. W. Norton, 1962), p. 127.

26. Hemingway, *For Whom the Bell Tolls*, p. 432.

27. "It was said that the courier of Marathon had died an hour before reaching Athens. He had died and was still running; he was running dead, announced the Greek victory dead. This is a fine myth; it shows that the dead still act for a little

while as if they were living. For a little while, a year, ten years, perhaps fifty years; at any rate, a *finite* period; and then they are buried a second time. This is the measure we propose to the writer: as long as his books arouse anger, discomfort, shame, hatred, love, even if he is no more than a shade, he will live. Afterward, the deluge. We stand for an ethics and art of the finite"; Sartre, "Writing for One's Age," in *"What Is Literature?" and Other Essays*, trans. Bernard Frechtman (Cambridge, Mass.: Harvard University Press, 1988), p. 245.

Robert Jordan shares the same instrumental view of one's own death: "your own death seemed of complete unimportance; only a thing to be avoided because it would interfere with the performance of your duty" (*For Whom the Bell Tolls*, p. 235). In the same way, Malraux's Puig, after destroying one of Franco's batteries by driving his car headlong into it, comments on his exploit: "I was scared . . . scared stiff, of not being able to get up to that gun. Living or dead, I *had* to get there" (*Days of Hope*, trans. Stuart Gilbert and Alistair Macdonald [London: Hamish Hamilton, 1968], p. 26). We can also recall that the male praying mantis, too, is dead when it carries out the final steps required for the transmission of its genetic message (cf. Caillois, "La mante religieuse," in *Le mythe et l'homme* [Paris: Gallimard, 1938], p. 85).

28. Hemingway, *For Whom the Bell Tolls*, p. 17.

29. Claude-Edmonde Magny, *The Age of the American Novel: The Film Aesthetic of Fiction between the Two Wars*, trans. Eleanor Hochman (New York: Ungar, 1972), pp. 156, 158.

30. François Furet, "La rencontre d'une idée et d'une vie," *Commentaire*, special issue, "Raymond Aron (1905–1983)," February 1985, p. 54. Perhaps there is no better expression of the position denounced by Furet than one of Maurice Merleau-Ponty's passing remarks in a footnote in *The Phenomenology of Perception* (1945): "There is a way of thinking, in contact with the event, which seeks its concrete structure. A revolution which is really moving with the march of history [*si elle est vraiment dans le sens de l'histoire*] can be thought as well as lived"; trans. Colin Smith (London: Routledge & Kegan Paul, 1962), p. 363. See Denis Hollier, "The Infelicities of the Present Tense," in *The Politics of Prose: Essays on Sartre*, trans. Jeffrey Mehlman (Minneapolis: University of Minnesota Press, 1986), pp. 65 ff. Revolution is a device for giving meaning to history, for making the meaning of history appear, for eliminating static. There is a revolutionary simplification of the world. Revolution reduces the world to the simplicity of a conflict.

31. Paul Nizan, *Chronique de septembre* (1939; reprint, Paris: Gallimard, 1978), p. 15. *Days of Hope* was publicized as a "report novel."

32. Sartre, "*La Conspiration*, par Paul Nizan," *La nouvelle revue française* 54 (November 1, 1938): 844, reprinted in *Situations I*, p. 29.

33. Fyodor Dostoevsky, *The Adolescent*, trans. Andrew R. MacAndrew (Garden City, N.Y.: Doubleday, 1971), p. 585, quoted in French translation by Paul Nizan in *Pour une nouvelle culture*, ed. Susan Suleiman (Paris: Grasset, 1971), p. 143. Nizan uses the quotation from Dostoevsky again in "*Eté 1937*, par Roger Martin du Gard" (1937), ibid., p. 230; and in "Ambition du roman moderne" (1939), in Jean-Jacques Brochier, *Paul Nizan, intellectuel communiste* (Paris: Maspéro, 1970), vol. 1, p. 117.

34. Sartre, *"What Is Literature?" and Other Essays*, pp. 184, 185.

35. Raymond Aron, *Introduction to the Philosophy of History: An Essay on the Limits of Historical Objectivity*, trans. George J. Irwin (London: Weidenfeld and Nicolson, 1961), pp. 179, 311.

36. Maurice Merleau-Ponty, "Metaphysics and the Novel," in *Sense and Non-Sense*, trans. Hubert L. Dreyfus and Patricia Allen Dreyfus (Evanston: Northwestern University Press, 1964), p. 33.

37. Nicolas Beauzée, "Parfait," in *Encyclopédie ou dictionnaire raisonné des arts et métiers* (1765; reprint, Stuttgart: Friedrich Frommann Verlag, 1966), vol. 11, p. 940.

38. Sartre, "Camus' *The Outsider*," in *Literary and Philosophical Essays*, trans. Annette Michelson (London: Rider, 1955), pp. 39, 38.

39. Hemingway, *For Whom the Bell Tolls*, p. 166.

40. Sartre, "François Mauriac and Freedom" (1939), in *Literary and Philosophical Essays*, p. 23.

41. Sartre, "On *The Sound and the Fury:* Time in the Work of Faulkner," ibid., p. 84.

42. Jean Beaufret, "A propos de l'existentialisme," in *Introduction aux philosophies de l'existence* (Paris: Denoël/Gonthier, 1971), p. 36.

43. Sartre, "On *The Sound and the Fury*," p. 87. "Even when it still exists but has nothing more 'before it' and has 'settled [*abgeschlossen*] its account,' its Being is still determined by the 'ahead-of-itself.' Hopelessness, for instance, does not tear Dasein away from its possibilities, but it is only one of its own modes of *Being towards* these possibilities"; Martin Heidegger, *Being and Time*, trans. John Macquarrie and Edward Robinson (New York: Harper & Row, 1962), p. 279.

CREDITS

Most of the essays in this volume have been published elsewhere in somewhat different form. The essays previously published in English are newly translated.

"Deeds without Words": published as "I've Done My Act: An Exercise in Gravity," trans. Beverly Allen, *Representations* 4 (Winter 1983): 88–100. A French version, "Actes sans paroles," appeared in *Les temps modernes* 531–533 (October–December 1990): 803–820.

"Mimesis and Castration 1937": published as "Mimesis and Castration 1937," trans. William Rodarmor, *October* 32 (Spring 1985): 3–15. A French version, "Mimesis et castration 1937," appears in *Roger Caillois, la pensée aventurée*, ed. Laurent Jenny (Paris: Belin, 1992), pp. 71–89.

"Bataille's Tomb": published as "Bataille's Tomb (A Halloween Story)," trans. Richard Miller, *October* 33 (Fall 1985): 92–102.

"On Equivocation between Literature and Politics": published as "On Equivocation (Between Literature and Politics)," trans. Rosalind Krauss, *October* 55 (Winter 1990): 3–22. An Italian version, "Sull'equivoco (tra letteratura e politico," appears as the introduction to *Il Collegio di Sociologia (1937–1939)*, trans. Marina Galletti (Turin: Bollati-Boringhieri, 1991).

"Fear and Trembling in the Age of Surrealism": published as "Fear and Trembling in the Age of Surrealism," afterword to Roger Caillois, *The Necessity of the Mind*, trans. Michael Syrotinski (Venice, Calif.: Lapis Press, 1990), pp. 153–161.

"Under the Heading of Holofernes": published as "A l'en-tête d'Holopherne," *Littérature* 79 (October 1990): 16–28.

"Poetry from A to Z": published as "La poésie jusqu'à Z," *L'ire des vents*, nos. 3–4 (June 1980): 141–154.

"The Use Value of the Impossible": published as "The Use-Value of the Impossible," trans. Liesl Ollman, *October 60* (Spring 1992): 3–24. A French version, "La valeur d'usage de l'impossible," appears as the introduction to the reprint edition of *Documents*, ed. Jean Jamin (Paris: Jean-Michel Place, Collection "Gradhiva," 1992), pp. vii–xxiii.

"A Farewell to Art": published as "A Farewell to the Pen," trans. N. H., *Raritan* 12, no. 1 (Summer 1992): 46–62. A French version, "L'adieu aux plumes," appeared in *La lettre internationale*, no. 27 (Winter 1990–91): 54–57.

INDEX